'ADMIRABLE'
Times Literary Supplement

'In a hundred books the statistics have been sifted, the debits and the credits balanced, the strategy analysed. Yet it seems to have been left to a Frenchman to find the spectator's perspective against which the Significant Moments stand out. It is all compactly marshalled, beautifully written, scrupulously fair' *Evening News*

'A WELCOME ADDITION TO THE LORE OF THAT TERRIBLE YEAR, 1940' *Evening Standard*

Marcel Jullian

The Battle of Britain

July – September 1940

A Panther Book

A Panther Book

First published in Great Britain by Jonathan Cape Limited 1967. Panther edition published 1969.
Printed in England by C. Nicholls & Company Ltd., The Philips Park Press, Manchester, and published by Panther Books, 3 Upper James Street, London, W.1.

Translated from the French by Ann-Yvette and Alan Stewart
for my wife.

Contents

	Preface	13
1	The Battle of Britain Will Never Happen	17
2	The Time of the Cuckoo	30
3	A Study in Blue	42
4	He's Coming	55
5	Men and Ships	65
6	The Day of the Eagle	76
7	The Thirteenth of August	92
8	Black Thursday	104
9	So Few	121
10	A Small Question of Bombs	134
11	Dogfight	145
12	The Worst Week-end	160
13	The Turning Point	172
14	The Gala Opening	187
15	Churchill's Day	205
16	Death of the Sea Lion	220
	Epilogue	243
	Select Bibliography	245
	Index	249

The Battle of Britain

Acknowledgments

Grateful acknowledgments are due to the following for permission to quote extracts from the works named:

Cassell & Co. Ltd. (*The Second World War* by W. S. Churchill); Hutchinson & Co. Ltd. (*Many Mansions* by Air Chief Marshal Lord Dowding, and *Survivor's Story* by Air Marshal Sir Gerald Gibbs); Hodder & Stoughton Ltd. (*Nine Lives* by Air Commodore Alan Deere); Secker & Warburg Ltd. (*The Sky Suspended* by Drew Middleton); Methuen & Co. Ltd. (*The First and the Last* by General Galland); the Literary Executors of the late Richard Hillary, St. Martin's Press Inc., the Macmillan Co. of Canada Ltd., and Macmillan & Co. Ltd., London (*The Last Enemy* by Richard Hillary); and Chatto & Windus Ltd (*Wing Leader* by J. E. Johnson). Also to the Controller of Her Majesty's Stationery Office, for permission to reproduce Air Chief Marshal Sir Hugh Dowding's letter of May 16th, 1940 (Crown copyright).

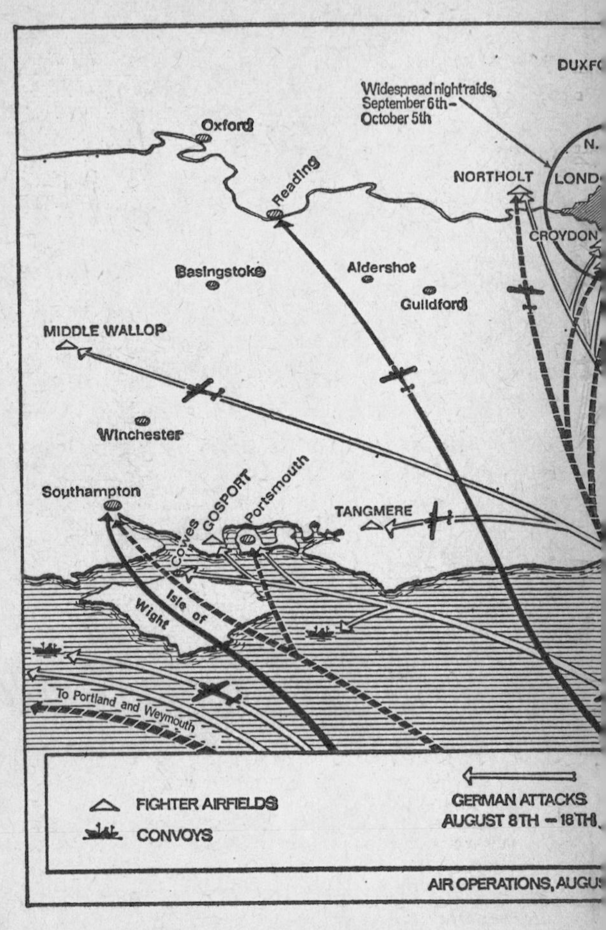
DUXF
Widespread night raids,
September 6th -
October 5th
N.
Oxford
Reading
NORTHOLT
LOND
CROYDON
Basingstoke
Aldershot
Guildford
MIDDLE WALLOP
Winchester
Southampton
Cowes
GOSPORT
Portsmouth
TANGMERE
Isle of
Wight
To Portland and Weymouth
FIGHTER AIRFIELDS
CONVOYS
GERMAN ATTACKS
AUGUST 8TH – 18TH
AIR OPERATIONS, AUGU

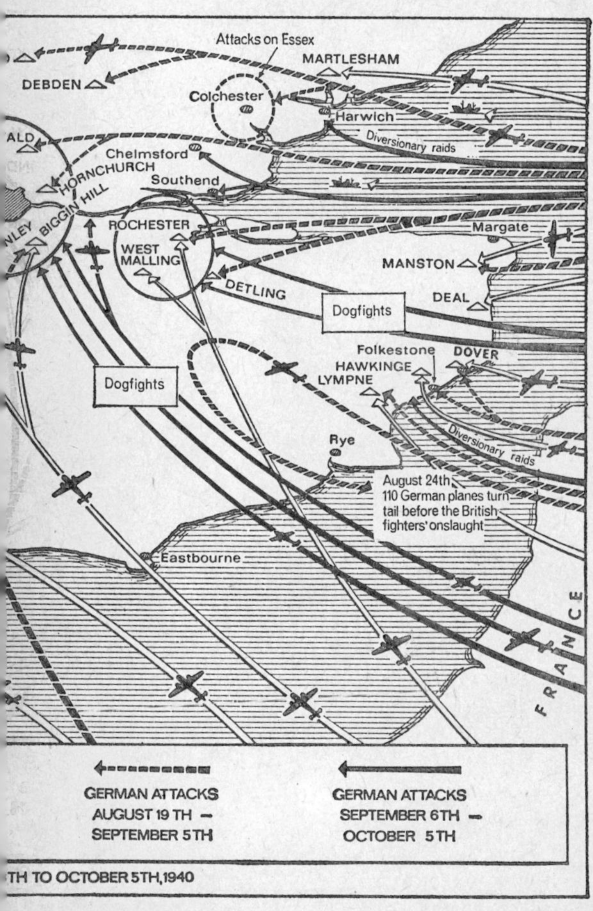

Attacks on Essex
MARTLESHAM
DEBDEN
Colchester
Harwich
Diversionary raids
ALD
Chelmsford
HORNCHURCH
Southend
BIGGIN HILL
NLEY
ROCHESTER
WEST MALLING
Margate
MANSTON
DETLING
DEAL
Dogfights
Folkestone
DOVER
HAWKINGE
LYMPNE
Dogfights
Rye
Diversionary raids
August 24th
110 German planes turn tail before the British fighters' onslaught
Eastbourne
FRANCE
GERMAN ATTACKS AUGUST 19 TH – SEPTEMBER 5TH
GERMAN ATTACKS SEPTEMBER 6TH – OCTOBER 5TH
TH TO OCTOBER 5TH,1940

Preface

I have Colonel Rémy to thank for this book. He suggested that I should write it and it was he who was able to open all doors for me in England. Without his help I should never have undertaken the task. Colonel Rémy is man who is used to working within a network. He established a chain of communication between Paris and London. The links were Colonel Passy, Colonel Guy Westmacott, Air Marshal Sir John Salmond and finally the present Commander-in-Chief of the Royal Air Force, Air Chief Marshal Sir Charles Elworthy. To all of them my deepest gratitude is due.

At Fighter Command, Stanmore, which was the nerve centre of the Battle of Britain and where I was greeted by Air Marshal Sir Douglas Morris, Colonel Williams of the Intelligence Branch entrusted to me his precious personal records which at the time of the battle were secret. Squadron Leader Moorat introduced me to all the different aspects of Bentley Priory. At Hillingdon House, near Uxbridge, Air Commodore Thompson, whilst recounting to me his own memories of the battle, gave me a clearer insight into the problems which confronted 11 Group and 12 Group during the battle. He also introduced me to the Ops Room, preserved today as it then was, from which went out the battle orders to the squadrons which shot down 1,300 of the 1,733 aircraft destroyed during the battle.

For my knowledge of Biggin Hill, the key airfield of the battle, the one which shared the martyrdom of "Manston-in-the-Dust", I am indebted to Air Commodore Deacon Elliott. In a friendly unaffected way he showed me the airfield, the mess – which has remained as it was at the time of the battle – and the famous pilots' chapel. To this he added a rare demonstration of trust in allowing me to use his own day-to-day notes on the battle, which have not so far been published.

In London, I was helped by Air Commodore J. Wallace of the Ministry of Defence, Wing Commander K. Stevens, Mr. L. A. Jackets, chief of the Historical Section of the R.A.F., the unchallenged authority on the battle; and by Mr. Rigby, librarian and archivist of the Imperial War Museum. I wish also to thank the pilots and in particular Air Commodore Deacon Elliott, Air Commodore Alan Deere who dictated at my request certain impressions of the battle which were not recorded in his own book, Wing Commander John Hemingway who searched for and found his log-book for me, Air Commodore S. B. Grant and Group Captains W. A. Toyne and D. P. Kelly.

At the British Embassy in Paris where I went for research and reference, I was met with the greatest goodwill and understanding. This was thanks to Air Commodore A. L. Winskill, the Military Air Attaché, to the Press Councillor Mr. D. A. Logan, and to Miss Winnie M. Towers. I owe my information about Georges Perrin, one of the group of fourteen Frenchmen who took part in the battle, to M. Paul Guilbert. For certain other details about this group I am indebted to M. Marcel Boisot.

I must also thank Colonel Berlin, Military Air Attaché at the Embassy of the Federal German Republic in Paris, who informed me as to the principal German sources, notably the Militärgeschichtliches Forschungsamt at Freiburg and the *Internationale Luftwaffenrevue.*

Finally I must acknowledge freely how much I owe to the authors of works which have already appeared on the subject. First there is Basil Collier's *The Defence of the United Kingdom,* a book regarded in England as the 'Bible' on the Second World War. Then I would select *The Narrow Margin* by Derek Wood and Derek Dempster, *The Sky Suspended* by Drew Middleton, and that excellent *Strike from the Sky* by Alexander McKee. For an understanding of Sir Hugh (now Lord) Dowding, the book *Leader of the Few* by Basil Collier is invaluable, as is the Air Chief Marshal's own work *Many Mansions.* My task has been made easier too by the memoirs of such pilots as Richard Hillary, Johnny Johnson, Alan Deere, Ginger Lacey, etc.

On the German side there is of course *Die Ersten und die Letzten* by Galland, translated in English under the title *The First and the Last.* Another work of great interest is *Angriffshöhe 4 000* by Cajus Bekker. It is in this work that Goering's telegram of August 25th, 1940, is to be found. It is not quoted in any other book so far published on the subject. For the personality of Hermann Goering, I have relied upon the work of Roger Manvell and Heinrich Fraenkel and also upon that of Emmy Goering. They are not at variance with the more general works on the Third Reich and they have contributed details on the personal plane which have been of great value.

The records of newspapers, notably *The Times* and *Signal,* have provided me with countless contemporary impressions of daily life during the three months of the battle.

When I had read all this, the problem arose, what should I do? I had in mind the remark of Air Chief Marshal Sir Hugh Dowding in his report on the battle published in the supplement to the *London Gazette*, September 11th, 1946, 'Any attempt to describe the events of the Battle day by day would make this Despatch unduly long and would prevent the reader from obtaining a comprehensive picture of the events.'

From the heaps of documents, and while they were in process of translation from English and German into French, I had formed some first impressions of the battle. These I incorporated into a series of radio programmes. Then I left for England to find the people who had been involved in the battle and to visit the places from which they had fought. In the north of France I went on the same quest, searching for any traces that might remain of the presence of Goering and his pilots. Wherever I went the eye-witnesses appeared from all sides and the setting, the atmosphere of the battle emerged again out of the past.

It was only then that I sat down to write.

I have tried to reconstruct the battle from a mass of factual evidence, some minute-by-minute accounts of the fighting and from a careful examination of Winston Churchill's three *official* crucial days: August 15th, September 15th and September 27th. Also I have based my reconstruction on three other days, less well known, on whose decisions and mistakes, not combat, the outcome of the Battle of Britain rested. These were May 16th, when Dowding prevented the dispatch of nine squadrons to France; August 24th, when London was bombed in error; and September 3rd, when by a mistaken decision the Germans decided upon the *Zielwechsel,* the change of target.

Have I succeeded? Only the reader can say, but I dream of the day when I shall be told that Air Chief Marshal Lord Dowding has read this book and has recognized, at least in part, *his* battle.

M.J.

1: The Battle of Britain Will Never Happen

For the British, the battle began on July 10th, but for the Germans it did not start until August 8th or even 13th. It is possible, however, that it was won on May 16th.

On that day in a room on the first floor at Bentley Priory in Stanmore, some miles north of London, right at the end of the brown line on the Underground map, Air Chief Marshal Sir Hugh Dowding was getting ready to go down to his office on the ground floor. He put on his blue uniform cap with its two bands of gold braid on the peak surmounted by the badge of the R.A.F. and made a final check on the smartness of his appearance. He was fifty-eight, the chief of Fighter Command, master of the British fighter force. He was also the possessor of a solid reputation for austerity; reportedly severe towards his subordinates, he was known to be merciless to himself. Standing rigidly, buttoned tightly into his uniform, he extended a sensitive hand towards the door knob. At his wrist, as he opened the door, there was a flash of gold, one of his sumptuous collection of cuff-links, each larger and heavier than the next; his sole luxury. Did he, during the four years he lived there and used that door, ever once let his attention stray to the carved wood panel above it? It was a touch of feminine refinement, a souvenir of a former owner of the house, Lady Hamilton, and a present to her from Queen Adelaide, wife of William IV. The Air Chief Marshal descended a flight of stairs and continued along the gilded wooden balcony which runs in a circle looking down into the well of the hall like a gallery of a theatre.

There were many who disliked him and were ready to call him a 'damned obstinate Scot', or, perhaps more hostile still, 'stuffy'. He had the expression of one who is very demanding of other people, a full well-trimmed moustache on an exceptionally thin upper lip. In the best tradition of the old soldier that he was – he had served in India and had flown the string-and-canvas machines of 1914–18 – he carried himself like a young man. He had been a fine polo player and was still an excellent shot and a remarkable skier.

Dowding reached the foot of the stairs. On either side of him a group of three graces dancing supported cream, red-fringed lampshades. Two huge many-paned windows set high in the walls let in the light. A third, lower down, opened on to the lawn and the great dark cedar.

The Air Chief Marshal opened the door of his office below the gallery. It was a sober, simply-furnished room with a great bay window looking out over the Middlesex countryside. But that morning Dowding had no eyes for the landscape before him; it was too calm, too soft. The thoughts behind the dead still-water eyes were far away in France where his 'boys' in the Hurricane squadrons were engaged in an endless indecisive battle. He could almost recite by heart the entries they had made in their log-books since September 1939. They read like an itinerary of northern and eastern France: Maubeuge, Seclin, Saint-Inglevert, Reims, Lille, Douai, Péronne, Le Bourget, etc., but since May there had been some variations. S. A. Hemingway's log-book for example read:

'May 10th. Shot down a Heinkel 111.'

'May 11th. Scored hits on a German aircraft over the lines at Maastricht. It crashed in Belgium.'

The war had begun in earnest with the invasion of Holland and Belgium. The news from the Continent was bad. In ten days two hundred and fifty Hurricanes had been shot down. The Air Chief Marshal could feel his reserves 'running out like the sand in an hour-glass'. Dowding drew up his balance sheet like the fine mathematician he was. He drew it up in ten numbered paragraphs on two typewritten sheets of paper with the reference FC/S 19048 and sent it off to London under the classification SECRET.

'I have the honour to refer to the very serious calls which have recently been made upon the Home Defence Fighter Units in an attempt to stem the German invasion on the Continent.

2. I hope and believe that our Armies may yet be victorious in France and Belgium, but we have to face the possibility that they may be defeated.

3. In this case I presume that there is no-one who will deny that England should fight on, even though the remainder of the Continent of Europe is dominated by the Germans...

5. I would remind the Air Council that the last estimate which they made as to the force necessary to defend this

country was 52 Squadrons, and my strength has now been reduced to the equivalent of 36 Squadrons.'

He goes on to say that the squadrons of Hurricanes remaining in England are seriously depleted and that the more squadrons which are sent to France, the higher will be the wastage and the more insistent the demands for reinforcements. He concludes:

'I believe that, if an adequate fighter force is kept in this country, if the fleet remains in being, and if Home Forces are suitably organised to resist invasion, we should be able to carry on the war single handed for some time, if not indefinitely. But, if the Home Defence Force is drained away in desperate attempts to remedy the situation in France, defeat in France will involve the final, complete and irremediable defeat of this country.'

The letter is signed 'H. C. T. Dowding'.

*

A few days later, the Air Chief Marshal, whose anxiety had been growing because he had not received the assurances he had asked for, requested and obtained permission to expound his thesis in person before the War Cabinet. There is no doubt that this request was granted the more readily because the Prime Minister had expressed a desire to be informed of the views of the various Chiefs of Staff about the military situation of Great Britain if the country should be faced with a 'certain eventuality'.

Since Dowding had sent off his letter, a new name had appeared in the war news: Dunkirk, where the flower of the British army was being forced into the sea. The Air Chief Marshal learnt of the situation with a frown. He sent his 'boys' over, but with orders that they must at all costs return after each mission and land in England. Two squadrons only were kept in reserve. Apart from these two, every single squadron was thrown into the battle.

It was the unanimous opinion of the Chiefs of Staff that Germany 'held almost all the cards'. As they saw it, the problem before them was to know whether the morale of the British population, military and civilian, would be able to outweigh the numerical and material superiority enjoyed by the enemy. To this question, which was put to them by Winston Churchill, their reply was, 'We believe so.'

Dowding left Stanmore for London. In the capital the buildings were surrounded with sandbags, and barrage balloons hung motionless in the calm sky. The pubs were full, but everyone seemed busy, and the inhabitants of London seemed all to be engaged on important work of national defence. Nevertheless there was talk of summer holidays and a general agreement not to go to the seaside – the sound of artillery fire: so disturbing.

The Air Chief Marshal was listened to 'with courtesy and sympathy'. He left with the assurance that not another aeroplane would be sent to the Continent with the exception of the necessary air cover for the final evacuation.

He returned to Stanmore with its cedars, its old panelling, its memories of Lady Hamilton; but June was approaching, and already the daffodils had faded from the lawns.

By the end of May, Great Britain had prepared for the coming struggle. The signposts, milestones and the names of streets, villages and stations had been removed. At night the station platforms were lit only by a feeble under-water light that came from the blue-green lamps illuminating only those parts of the platform immediately beneath them. In the coaches themselves, the compartments had only the weakest of bulbs and the blinds were kept lowered. A fortnight later the government forbade the ringing of church bells, which were to be used in future only as a warning of invasion. An extraordinary calm fell over the English countryside. Instead of coming with the roar of battle, the war took possession of the country quietly. The thousands of church bells were heard no more; unlit by night, silent by day, Great Britain became, like some *terra incognita* on an ancient map of the world, a land without voice or sight.

In France things were happening at breakneck speed. Paris fell on June 14th. Three days later Marshal Pétain's government requested an armistice. The same day a Handley Page aeroplane took off from the airfield of Mérignac near Bordeaux. On board were ten French airmen, among them Sous-lieutenant de la Brière. Their destination was England, where they were to find Sergeant de Mozay who two days earlier had climbed aboard a Royal Air Force machine at Nantes.

On June 18th, the future leader of the Free French launched his appeal: 'I, General de Gaulle, who am at present in London, invite the officers and soldiers of France to place themselves under my command.' It was one of the darkest hours that Great Britain had ever faced, comparable with the days when Napoleon confronted her from the camp at Boulogne, or the days of the Spanish Armada. Winston Churchill, the descendant of Marlborough, had his photograph taken. He sits at a table holding his cigar and wearing a steel helmet. The destiny of the free world lies heavy on his shoulders as he sits, hands on knees, for all the world like a peasant tired after a hard day's work. Beside him on the table lie his discarded walking stick and civilian hat, an eloquent still life of peacetime. A few hours earlier, rising from his place on the benches of the House of Commons, and conscious that in his own person he represented a country of ancient tradition, a country with an enduring monarchy, a powerful Empire, an arrogant command of the sea, he spoke like the captain of a ship who finds himself on a lee shore in a rising gale.

'What General Weygand called the Battle of France is over. I expect that the Battle of Britain is about to begin.'

At Bentley Priory, Dowding was checking over his calculations and drawing up the order of battle for Fighter Command with minute care. Henceforward the Command would consist of four groups equipped with squadrons of Hurricanes, Spitfires, Defiants and Blenheims. There was nothing in the Prime Minister's speech to surprise Dowding. He had seen things clearly a month earlier and he was a man used to expressing unorthodox views. 'Since I was a child', he says, 'I have never accepted ideas purely because they were orthodox, and consequently I have frequently found myself in opposition to generally accepted views. Perhaps, in retrospect, this has not been altogether a bad thing.'

In the House of Commons, where black jacket and stiff collar were still the order of the day, Winston Churchill was winding up his speech:

'Let us therefore brace ourselves to our duties, and so bear ourselves that, if the British Empire and its Commonwealth last for a thousand years, men will still say "this was their finest hour." '

The same day, at Munich, Adolf Hitler met Mussolini, who on June 10th had brought Italy into the war in the wake of

Germany. The Führer was not expressing sanguine hopes of immediate victory but instead showed a certain reserve. To such an extent, indeed, that according to Count Ciano, the Duce was disappointed with the meeting. 'He fears that peace may be near,' writes Mussolini's son-in-law, 'and once again he sees the great dream of his life, glory on the field of battle, slipping away from him.' So strong was this impression that Ciano openly asked his opposite number von Ribbontrop, the German Foreign Minister, the following question:

'Does Germany at this moment prefer peace or war?'

'Peace,' replied Ribbentrop.

This might have been a front put up for the benefit of Germany's ally Italy and, through her, for international public opinion, but a remark of Hitler's to his faithful Goering, head of the Luftwaffe, shows clearly that it was not.

'The war is over, Hermann. I'm going to reach an agreement with England.'

On June 22nd the armistice between France and Germany came into effect. 'That's it,' wrote Jean Giraudoux in Bordeaux, 'it's been announced over the radio; they've signed. The crowd has heard it and is still; still at last. The endless procession round and round in the square below was still flight, a sort of ritual mime of flight. Now they are stopping those people who continue to arrive in their various strange ways; the old man who was pushed all the way from Lisieux in a wheelbarrow, the hunchback who came from Vincennes on a trotting horse, the nuns from Amiens in a hearse . . . For the first time the exodus is halted . . .'

Between June 22nd and the first days of July another twelve pilots managed to escape by air or by sea. Some stole aircraft, old Simouns or Goélands, others borrowed Polish uniforms and slipped aboard a British troopship. Their names were Scitivaux, Guérin, Mouchotte, Fayolle, Labouchère, Bazin, Blaize, Bouquillard, Choran, Lafont, Montbon and Perrin. Together with La Brière and Mozay they formed a small nucleus of French aviators who took part in the Battle of Britain beside the pilots from Britain, Canada, New Zealand, Australia, Belgium, Poland, South Africa, Norway and Czechoslovakia. 'I felt', writes Labouchère, 'that if England was to be beaten, I should at least have saved the honour of France, while if Germany was to lose – well, the Frenchmen who had continued to fight would be able to speak out and to rebuild France.'

Paradoxically it was talk of peace that was in the air. The most fantastic stories were circulating among the embassies. It was said that the King of Sweden was acting as mediator at a meeting of envoys in Stockholm, that the Duke of Alba had had an interview at the Foreign Office in London. The Pope was said to be about to make a decisive intervention. But the most persistent rumour was that through the good offices of Carl Burckhardt and the Swiss Embassy in London, the Duke of Hohenlohe was in contact with the British Ambassador in Berne, Mr. Kelly.

In the German camp, Hitler on several occasions affirmed his belief that a suspension of hostilities was imminent. He declared to von Kleist, who had come to meet him at the airfield at Cambrai: 'The English will take no further part in the war.'

To his Chief of Staff, Halder, he said: 'England's resolve is weakening; believe me.'

Then he gave orders for Berlin to be decked out in flags and for the church bells to be rung in celebration of victory.

In England, on June 28th, Winston Churchill informed his Foreign Secretary, in the most formal manner possible, of his inflexible intention to continue the struggle: 'I hope it will be made clear to the Nuncio that we do not desire to make any inquiries as to terms of peace with Hitler, and that all our agents are strictly forbidden to entertain any such suggestions.'

Deaf and blind to everything except the battle order of Fighter Command, Dowding was busy placing his pieces on the chessboard. At Tangmere he had Squadrons 43, 145 and 601; at Biggin Hill, Squadrons 79 and 32. In conjunction with the Commander-in-Chief of Anti-Aircraft Command, Lieutenant-General Sir Frederick A. Pile, he made the necessary disposition of anti-aircraft batteries, searchlights, barrage balloons and Britain's magic weapon – radar. At night he would go up to his room and lock himself in. Again and again he would take stock of his defences and then open the window to the trees and lawns of the old parkland breathing silently after the heat of the day, peaceful, still inviolate.

Sometimes he would go to a drawer and, taking from it a folder stuffed with newspaper cuttings, leaf through them. He had been compiling this collection for more than twenty years and he was working at it still. The problem of survival after death haunted him. Whenever an article dealt with the subject, he would cut it out and file it. What was life like *on the other side*? How could communication be established with the spirit world? These were the sort of questions that Dowding found so passionately interesting and which he considered in his deceptively cold and scientific manner. One day he said to one of his friends that he had discovered the secret of perpetual motion, and when the other replied that he certainly wasn't the first who thought he had done so, replied in the most serious possible manner, 'True, but I really have!'

Lying asleep among the luxurious appointments of Bentley Priory, the Air Chief Marshal would dream of contact with the world of the dead. In the pubs in London or in messes on the darkened airfields were hundreds of his 'boys' who in a few short weeks would experience it at first hand.

On June 30th, Marshal Goering, who, among his other titles, bore that of Grand Venerer of the Reich, issued in an order of the day instructions for battle.

'Until such time as the enemy air forces have been defeated, the principal objective of the war in the air will be to attack them in all circumstances; by day and by night, in the air and on the ground. This will be done to the exclusion of all other missions.'

Two days later, on July 2nd, Marshal Wilhelm Keitel, in the name of the High Command of the Wehrmacht, announced Hitler's decision. 'A landing in England is possible on condition that the Luftwaffe is able to ensure complete mastery of the air and that certain other necessary conditions are fulfilled in advance.'

In Berlin on the following day, July 3rd, Hitler was walking on flowers. The streets had been strewn with blossom and the Hitler Youth were distributing copies of a victorious pamphlet by the *Gauleiter* of Berlin, Dr Goebbels. When Hitler emerged from the Anhalt station he was greeted by a colossal 'Heil' and the sound rang in his ears all the way to the Chancellery. When he appeared at the balcony in the Wilhelmstrasse, flanked by the Commanders-in-Chief of the three armed forces and von Ribbentrop, the crowd became delirious. A choir of young girls sang: '*Wir fahren gegen Engeland*'. It had all the charm of the German legends, bucolic and martial at the same time:

So give me your hand, your pretty white hand,
For tonight we march against England . . .

It was a beautiful day. The throwing of bouquets had been forbidden – the Führer didn't like it; but once more all the church bells rang out.

Some thirteen hundred miles to the south-west there was a sudden dramatic outburst. The British fleet bombarded the French naval vessels lying in the roads of Mers-el-Kébir after the latter had refused to comply with a British ultimatum calling on them to sail to a neutral port or to join the British fleet. 'This was a hateful decision, the most unnatural and painful in which I have ever been concerned,' wrote Winston Churchill. 'The War Cabinet never hesitated . . . and it resolved that all necessary measures should be taken.'

It was a terrible act which provoked pain and anger in the heart of every Frenchman whether he was in Metropolitan France, in Algeria or in London. But if it was a blow that struck at France directly, it also had its effect upon the Germans. General Rommel wrote to his wife: 'The state of war between France and the British fleet is a fact without precedent.'

For the first time since the evacuation of Dunkirk, the iron dice of war were cast. Not even in the German camp could it be said that 'the Battle of Britain will never happen'.

The preparations for the battle were now taking place. The mayor of the little village of Le Coudray, to the south of Beauvais, observed the arrival of several field-grey vehicles. They stopped in the main street and with a slamming of doors some officers wearing Luftwaffe uniform got out. They asked for the mayor, and M. Laroche introduced himself. During the first days of June most of the inhabitants had left, taking with them in their farm carts or cars everything they could carry. The village was almost completely empty and only one farm in ten was being worked; the others were deserted.

What could the Germans want? Relations between occupiers and occupied were still a new thing. So far they had been restricted to some requisitioning and some enforced bartering which had naturally produced resentment, but the hoardings carried posters showing a soldier of the Wehrmacht holding a child in his arms and offering it a slice of bread and butter. The slogan encouraged the population which had been abandoned by its government to 'have confidence in the German soldier'. M. Laroche stepped forward. One of the officers spoke French. The conversation began.

Two kilometres to the north the same scene was being enacted. Here it was M. Henri Masselin who received a visit. Nor was he the only mayor to do so. Soon it was evident that *something was happening* within a perimeter formed by the villages of La Boissière, Parfondeval, Le Coudray-en-Thelle, Neuville-d'Aumont and Le Déluge. The area lies between two *routes nationales* numbers 1 and 327, leading respectively to Paris and Pontoise. It is a wooded and well-watered area and is intersected by the Paris-Beauvais railway line. What could the Germans want with it?

The first measure they took was to cut the railway between Méru in the south and Saint-Sulpice in the north. A bus shuttle service was provided to carry passengers between the two villages. The reason for cutting the line in this way was that in the forest not far from Le Caudray, the line ran through a tunnel. The Germans now closed the northern end of this tunnel in order to use it to shelter a special train against air attack. In preparation for the arrival of this train, occupation troops started moving into the area. Several farms, the *curé*'s house at Neuville and the *café-tabac* at Le Coudray were requisitioned. Military vehicles began to pour in, barbed wire was put up and civilian movement restricted. Then came the *Feldgendarmes* with their *plat à barbe*[1] and their police dogs. Soon they were followed by lorry-loads of building materials and workmen from Compiègne. By now the summer undergrowth had made the woods impenetrable and the population was forbidden to go into them. In the heart of the

1. Translator's note: *Plat à barbe*: This was a large metal badge hung from a chain round the neck and bearing the inscription 'Feldgendarme' – rather like the labels which hang on sherry decanters.

woods nearly three thousand men were at work night and day.

Their work went on week by week and speculation grew. What was its purpose, for whose benefit? Then one morning the answer was provided. There was an unusual amount of activity; staff cars arrived flying generals' pennants, troops cordoned off the railway between Méru and Le Coudray, bicycle patrols were everywhere. No doubt too the knowledge spread mysteriously between occupier and occupied. That sixth sense, the instinct that enables the prisoner to interpret his jailer's slightest gesture must have operated. They knew, everyone knew – the man who was coming was Reichsmarschall Goering. And then he was there, in the streets of the village. Nobody knew if he had come by road or by his special train, code-named 'Asia'. Each time he came the procedure was the same: there would be a sudden bustle of activity and then he was there.

The train consisted of a pilot train equipped with normal passenger coaches and platform wagons for motor vehicles, followed by the special train itself. It is said that 171 people formed its crew. Goering's own coach, ballasted with lead for a smoother ride, consisted of two bedrooms, a small office and a bathroom. It was followed by a saloon coach with a cinema and by a coach that served as a mobile command post. A fourth coach was fitted out with kitchens and a dining-room. At either end of the train were wagons carrying anti-aircraft batteries. The train was to be seen a lot in that part of France during the Battle of Britain.

Goering seemed releaxed and at ease. Like all extremely fat men he had to work at it. He walked along shirt-sleeved and smiling, surrounded by his staff officers, pausing for a moment to point out a field or a house and then walking on again.

It was very hot and by the roadside the blackberries were turning colour. One of the officers of the Reichsmarschall's suite leant out to pick one . . .

The Reichsmarschall was forty-seven. At the outbreak of war in August 1914 he had been twenty-one, and a subaltern. He had flown first as an observer, then as a pilot, and had twice been wounded in combat. As soon as he had recovered he was appointed to command the Richthofen Squadron whose famous leader had just been killed. Goering used to say that one of the most wonderful days of his life had been when he was awarded the order *Pour le Mérite* to add to his Iron Crosses 1st and 2nd class. We possess a contemporary photograph of him wearing his decorations. It shows a slim-featured man with fair hair and very pale blue eyes; the lips are rather too finely shaped. He is wearing a long beltless tunic with two rows of six buttons. A sabre hangs at his side and at his throat he wears the cross of his order, its ribbon attached to a buttonhole of his tunic. On his breast are pinned two medals and his Iron Cross. His hands are thrust into his pockets and he is slim. Goering slim: incredible idea to those who came to know him as he appeared in photographs at the beginning of the last war – a ridiculous butt for the cartoonists with his pallid obesity, hanging jowls and tunic plastered with a mass of decorations. The early photograph provides a clue to Goering's conduct during the Battle of Britain. He saw himself cast as Siegfried. His was the stature to carry it off; he had the strength, the deep romantic sense, the feeling for beauty and the taste for splendour. His experiences of the first war, in which he had scored twenty-two victories, had led him to believe that the pilot would now replace the cavalryman. Defeat had poured cold water on his hopes. In his last official report he wrote: 'November 11th. Armistice. The squadron returned to Darmstadt in bad weather. Fog.'

Fog. The fog that enveloped Germany enveloped Goering too. From time to time he emerged to speak in public or at reunions of former officers, trying to rekindle some flame from the ashes, showing off his decorations and his wounds. There were some unpleasant stories about him. It was said, for example, that he had challenged the French ace Nungesser to single combat over the Houthulst forest, but had appeared with his whole squadron. The Frenchman had won, however, and Goering had fled. It was said, too, that the former commander of the Richthofen Circus took drugs. This was true, for Goering, a disgusted and neglected ex-hero, had gone to live in Denmark and then in Sweden, but nowhere could he escape the suffering his wounds caused him. He married a Swedish baroness, who divorced her husband to marry him, and whom he loved passionately. Karin became the helpless witness of her husband's agony. One of his wounds – a bullet in the groin which he received when marching beside Hitler at Munich in 1923 – had become infected. 'His whole thigh is a mass of pus. He suffers so much that he bites his pillow and groans the whole time. Even the morphine provides no relief. He is suffering more than ever.' Day by day the grip of drugs grew inexorably greater. By imperceptible steps Siegfried was changing, until at last he had become an obese old woman shut away in a mental hospital at Langbro.

Goering, who subsequently followed Hitler in his 'crusade against the criminals of 1918', withstood the terrible struggles of the climb towards power, endured again insecurity and exile; but when he learnt of the death of Karin, worked-out and epileptic, something broke within him. The hero could find no place now to shelter in the great swollen body. It was then that Goering went beyond all bounds, at times even out-Nazi-ing Hitler. 'Two and two make five if the Führer says so,' he would say. After the triumph of the Nazi Party he became a potentate monster of twenty stones, the victim of his pleasures, vanity and perversion. But beneath the medals and the dress uniforms he guarded the memory of the young, slim, fair-haired man of twenty always ready to die for his country. Emmy Goering, his second wife, relates how after the Feldherrnhalle putsch at Munich, in which he was seriously wounded, Goering flew to Italy with Karin. One evening they went to see the film *Die Niebelungen.* In his efforts to restrain his emotions, Hermann clenched his teeth so violently that he broke two of them. The Siegfried within took a lot of restraining!

And now in this fine victorious summer of 1940, the Reichsmarschall could no longer move without his military doctor, his valet Kropp and his nurse Christa Gormanns. He wanted to handle the controls of a fighter again, but he was too fat to get into the cockpit and, had he been able to do so, his weight was too great for the seat to support him. The modification of an aircraft to make room for his great thighs was seriously considered.

At the beginning of July, Goering appointed Commodore Johannes Fink *Kanalkampfführer,* commander of the Channel battle. He was sent off to Cap Blanc Nez, overlooking the Channel opposite Dover. There he had the target in sight.

The Battle of Britain was about to start.

2: The Time of the Cuckoo

In Surrey it was cuckoo-time. However, on June 21st the fact had to be faced: the birds had gone. Never before had they deserted the nests of their disappointed foster-parents so early, long before their usual migrating season. It was as though they had fled southern England in response to a collective fear.

On July 3rd other birds appeared, flying through the low clouds that hung over the Channel; on their wings they bore black crosses and they dived like hawks on the shipping below. All the squadrons of 11 Group took off in pursuit. Commodore Johannes Fink had announced his arrival at Cap Blanc Nez. Alan Deere of 54 Squadron noted, 'The battle has started.' Sir Hugh Dowding wrote: 'The Battle may be said to have started when the Germans had disposed of the French resistance in the summer of 1940, and turned their attention to this country.'

But even by July 9th, for the mass of the British people nothing much had happened. That day the disappearance of the cuckoos was recorded in *The Times*. It received a short paragraph between letters to the editor and the obituary notices, of which only one in five concerned a death on active service. The news columns, when they made any reference to the war, treated it in a simple anecdotal way. In a letter, H. G. Wells protested against the unjust internment of aliens who had fled from occupied countries. George Bernard Shaw exercised his usual wit on the subject of rationing: 'No more meat, no eggs, it's practically my own vegetarian diet. Does this mean that soon Great Britain will be inhabited by a race of Bernard Shaws? What a wonderful prospect!'

The small-ads columns offered country estates for sale, with park, tennis courts, river; 'ideal for evacuation'. Three hundred English mothers and children had arrived safely at Quebec. Lady Mosley, sister of Nancy Mitford and wife of Sir Oswald, chief of the British Nazis, had been arrested. Somerset Maugham, who had been missing since the fall of Paris, arrived in London in a state of exhaustion. On the sports pages cricket took pride of place as always, particularly as matches were being played between local teams and military units. There was one cloud on the horizon – tea rationing, 2 oz. a week.

Altogether things were not going badly apart from the fact that sometimes, day or night, one was inconvenienced by the sirens. Already in June the government had taken note of the many complaints from people who had been woken up at night to no purpose and had decided that there would no longer be two alerts, one meaning air-raid probable and the other air-raid imminent. The result was not long in coming. On the night of June 26th Cardiff was bombed before warning could be given; but the decision was not altered. It was felt in England that it was possible to be at war whilst at the same time not sacrificing all thoughts of convenience.

'In those days', wrote Drew Middleton, 'you could lie on the cliffs near Dover and watch the British ships come steadily onward from the north.' A long careful examination of the convoy would reveal which of the ships was likely to be picked as target by the *Staffel*, the Stuka dive-bombers. The Stukas would appear flying in three *Ketten* or sections, each consisting of three aircraft in the classic V formation. When they sighted their objective they would slide into one long echelon starboard with the leader on the left and then simultaneously roll and dive on their target, sirens screaming. As soon as the attack was complete they would climb again and, reforming into their original formation, set course for the Continent.

On July 4th, having learnt a lesson from the events of the previous day, Fighter Command decided that henceforth a standing patrol would be flown from one of the forward airfields of each sector. A protective grid was to be established in the Channel skies.

On July 3rd, at Acklington, south of Edinburgh, the pilot Deacon Elliott of 72 Squadron was ordered to fly as No. 3 in Red Section on patrol. He ran to the new Spitfire which had been allocated to him, but it refused to start. He then jumped into his friend Oswald Pigg's machine, P 9444, and took off with the rest of the squadron. Low grey clouds hung over the North Sea and the twelve aircraft were soon in the 'clag', holding tight formation to avoid losing sight of the leader. When they reached 10,000 feet the squadron commander's voice came over the R/T ordering each pilot to turn on his oxygen. Elliott automatically moved his hand to the left where he expected to find the delivery tube. There was nothing there. Elliott supposed that someone had broken the rule that the tube must always be left in the cockpit. There was a shortage of equipment and it had been decided to issue one tube to each aircraft rather than to each pilot. It was certainly very inconvenient, but Elliott felt perfectly well and decided not to make an issue of it. He imagined that the formation would soon be out of the tops of the dark cloud mass they were flying in. At about 20,000 feet he realized that he was still staying in formation but in a rather sloppy fashion, and that he seemed to have slipped out to the left of Red Section. He forced himself to concentrate on the other two Spitfires. Sometimes he could see two, sometimes four. Looking down, he noticed that the stick was flying about all round the cockpit, and then he felt a tremendous weight crushing him down. Suddenly he realized what was happening. His aircraft was in a spiral dive and the centifugal force had him pinned in his seat. Elliott retained enough presence of mind to call out over the R/T in an emotionless voice announcing his predicament. He was well aware that in the next minute or two he might be dead, but this knowledge somehow failed to disturb him. He was at peace with the world and far from being afraid, he had a feeling of intense satisfaction. He said to himself, 'Well, here I go.'

How long this strange sensation of euphoria, like the frogman's rapture of the deep, lasted, he did not know. Suddenly he found himself out of the clouds with rain beating on his windscreen. He came to his senses, saw the sea and took his bearings. He thought he could make out the Lammermuir hills, so he headed towards the coast, passed Coquet Island and from there set course for Acklington.

The Spitfire flew perfectly well wings level, but the moment he tried to apply bank to make it turn, it skidded dangerously. At last he managed to make a landing of sorts at Acklington. He switched off and jumped down to examine the machine. It was as crumpled as a pair of trousers that had been slept in. All the skinning had worked loose and was buckled and bent. The wings, normally attached to the fuselage at right angles, were bent back. The Supermarine engineers who came specially to examine the aircraft were amazed that it flew at all.

Oswald Pigg was furious when he learned that someone had borrowed his beautiful aeroplane and got it into a state where it was only fit to be exhibited as a curiosity in an aeronautical museum. He received a reprimand from the squadron commander for having left the oxygen tube attached to his mask instead of leaving it on the bottle in the aeroplane. Deacon Elliott was so pleased to be alive that he was not too concerned to have his log-book endorsed 'having continued to climb above 15,000 feet knowing that he had no oxygen'.

On July 8th, Flight Lieutenant Desmond MacMullen, with two other Spitfires of 54 Squadron from Rochford, intercepted a formation of Me 110s escorted by Me 109s. There was a very rapid engagement with short bursts of machine-gun fire. Two Spitfires were shot down and the third damaged. The Luftwaffe was showing its teeth.

The next day, Pilot Officer Carey of 43 Squadron, stationed at Tangmere, was flying his Hurricane in No. 3 position in Red Section which had just received orders to intercept an enemy formation over the Isle of Wight. Over the sea, the sky was scattered with small low clouds which would soon be used for a game of Anglo-German hide-and-seek, and six Me 110s were flying in formation at between six and seven thousand feet. When they saw the Hurricanes they changed course for a head-on attack.

Pilot Officer Carey was soon turning with the other aircraft. He pulled back on the stick and applied rudder to carry him up above the Germans who had already opened fire at 900 yards. Three of them were converging on Carey who just had time to see one of the Hurricanes disappearing into a cloud streaming black smoke, and a second turning with a Messerschmitt hanging on his tail. But Carey was determined to cling on to his. He pressed the firing button and in the gunsight he saw the Messerschmitt's tailplane with its two fins and rudders begin to dance about. He managed only a short burst before the German disappeared into a cloud. But the other five were there and had re-formed. Carey could see the wicked-looking red noses, the silver propeller discs, the camouflage paint and the black crosses. He took shelter in a cloud for a short time and then emerged and set off in pursuit of the six Messerschmitts, which had by now resumed their course. When he had closed to about three hundred yards he opened fire again; they all turned back towards him and he was forced once again to dive back into the clouds. When he came out the sky was empty. He returned to Tangmere.

In the Operations Room at Hillingdon a W.A.A.F., looking rather pretty in her blue uniform, squeezed the brass trigger on the handle of her croupier's stick. A little steel spur emerged at the other end and pushed the rectangle that represented Red Section from the pale-green area of the sea towards the white of the English coast. The operation was over.

Commodore Johannes Fink stared down at the sea breaking slowly and majestically below the cliffs of Cap Blanc Nez. Before him, a mere dark line, half hidden in the summer haze, lay the shores of England. They looked so near that he had the impression that he could reach out his hand and touch them. Peter Fleming once said that on a clear day, if you stood on the walls of Dover Castle with a pair of binoculars, you could tell the time by the clock in the belfry at Calais.

Fink had set up his headquarters in a disused bus which he had placed on the sand dunes not far from the monument which commemorates Latham's attempt to fly the Channel. The statue is still there and as the thin grass on the dunes rustles in the wind you half expect that unlucky aviator's scarf to fly away. Under his broad cap, Latham's thin face looks full of care. Fink's looked the same way.

He had the impression of looking into a house from outside. England was there before him, but depending on the weather, which was very uncertain in early July that year, it would appear clearly or fade away and finally disappear again. He was most conscious of its presence when he could not see it but just knew that it was there, hidden by a slanting rain that lashed the grey sea. It was an onerous title that he bore, commander of the battle of the Channel. Fink knew that already people were making fun of him, making a play on words with the double meaning of the word *Kanal* in German – channel or sewer. He knew that he had acquired the nickname *Kanal-arbeiter,* sewer-rat. And what a sewer he had been set to sweep clean! To achieve his task he had seventy-five bombers, sixty Stukas and two hundred fighters. His crews, encouraged by their easy victories in Poland and France, had fallen into bad habits. A pilot can live well in wartime. There is even a tendency to live and to die a little too well. Fink felt it necessary to warn his men against the sweet temptations of champagne and women.

A few miles away, at Wissant, Major General von Döring, another former member of the 'Richthofen Circus', had installed a radio monitoring unit by means of which he was able to intercept the orders sent out by Fighter Command to its squadrons. He was also busy inspecting and improving airfields and had plans for the construction of a radar station, far more rudimentary than its British equivalent, which would permit him to follow the enemy's movements even in bad weather.

At dawn on July 10th a light mist hung over Norwich. At Coltishall, where 66 Squadron was stationed, it was exactly 0440 hours when Sergeant F. N. Robertson took off in his Spitfire No. 3035. Half an hour later, in a patch of clear sky, he spotted a formation of enemy bombers. He attacked immediately and from that moment was oblivious to all around him except for the great 'glasshouse' of the German aeroplane he had picked out as his target. He pressed his firing button and the Spitfire shook as though it had been hit itself. But the bomber dived straight into the sea. Robertson was exultant; pulling hard back on the stick and feeling himself pressed down in his seat he climbed steeply away turning his head to look behind. There were three little black dots, three German airmen splashing around in the water. Robertson made a mental note – twenty miles east of Winterton.

Waves of bombers followed each other during the afternoon. Lieutenant Bechtle, piloting a Dornier 17, discovered a British convoy escorted by six Hurricanes. He broke off and gave the alert. Immediately twenty Dorniers with a fighter cover of thirty Messerschmitt 110s and twenty Messerschmitt 109s flew in to the attack. In England, the observers watched the growing traces on the radar screens and from Bentley Priory the order was given for four squadrons to climb to the assistance of the six Hurricanes from Biggin Hill which were escorting the convoy.

At Ramsgate, A Flight of 56 Squadron was at readiness, its

pilots waiting in a tent beside their aircraft. As soon as the order was received, they were airborne.

It was the baptism of fire for Flying Officer Page. He arrived over the convoy, closed his eyes and hurled himself into the pack of Messerschmitt 110s. The 109s suddenly appeared diving from above to join in the fun. Every time they fired it seemed as though the noses of their machines were being torn apart. Lost in the heart of the mêlée, gritting his teeth, Page pressed his gun button. A 109 passed two or three feet over his cockpit blotting out his view of the sky.

From his Dornier, Bechtle could see the British reinforcements arriving and the battle developing. That was up to the Messerschmitts; he was concerned only with dropping his bombs. It did not stop him having a look round the sky though: 'It was a magnificent dog-fight! From a distance, the aircraft looked like bunches of grapes . . .'

The day's score read: six fighters shot down and one small ship sunk on the British side, against fifteen German aircraft missing. Unfavourable though this result was, the German pilots were in triumphant mood – at last they had brought the British fighters to battle. It was all thanks to Bechtle, and he was duly congratulated. Fink had a table set up in the garden; a vase of carnations, plates of little biscuits and champagne *al fresco*. They stand there in the photograph, a dozen men in grey uniforms, wearing forage caps, their eagle wings pinned at their breasts. Some are wearing the Iron Cross. Together they raise their glasses. Toasts are drunk, mild Virginia cigarettes are smoked. The rain holds off and it's good to be alive. Soon it will be night and there will be a girl to spend it with. For the moment they are happy in each other's company; they have the gestures and familiar phrases that all military comrades share. They are the victorious warriors in a conquered land.

Not far from where this happy group was drinking lay the village of Sangatte with its massive bell-tower standing bluff and square on its great cornerstones. In Arras, farther away to the north, the belfry stood out against the sky, its turrets and onion domes forming a harmonious silhouette of brick and slate under the light of evening rain . . .

On the other side of the Channel, Sergeant Robertson returned from his third sortie of the day, each one made in a different aircraft. He wondered whether his Dornier of the morning sortie had been confirmed. He did not realize that the Battle of Britain had officially begun and that he had been credited with its first victory.

England slept soundly that night, still unaware that the battle had started.

Except for Douglas Bader, the following day was just a day much like any other. For the legless pilot it was the day he hunted a Dornier in the fog and shot it down. When people in England thought about the war, they tried to visualize an enemy invasion. They couldn't bring much conviction to the task. Under the title 'What do I do?', in space presented by the Brewers' Society, *The Times* published the Ministry of Information's recommendations about the action that should be taken if it should be rumoured that the invasion was imminent or had actually taken place. 'What do I do?' – what indeed? 'I remember that this is the moment to act like a soldier. I do *not* get panicky. I *stay put*. I do *not* say: "I must get out of here." I remember that fighting men must have clear roads. I do *not* go on to the road on bicycle, in a car or on foot. Whether I am at work or at home I just *stay put*.'

In similar vein the 'British Silent Column' made the following recommendations to its members: 'If you know anything keep it to yourself and persuade other people to do the same.' It set out seven requirements for membership. Discretition was to become a national institution. 'You will not wear a uniform . . . your only weapons will be your common sense, your ears and your tongue.' Five ways to 'stop other people talking' were set out. It was to be done by intimidation. 'Did you see it yourself?' 'Who told you?' With the threat now thinly disguised, 'If someone is indulging in careless talk, take an old envelope out of your pocket and write down what he says.' The informer's method, now, pure and simple, 'Go to the police, but only as a last resort.'

During the early days of July, the events taking place in their skies did not form the major preoccupation of the British people. The proof of centuries had established the impregnability of their island and in this impregnability they had a deep-rooted belief. Science might change the technique of warfare, but it could not change that. The British drew assurance from their tradition of stability and from this it was but a step, whilst contemplating the enslavement of the Continent, to say to oneself, 'It can't happen here.' Consciously and with pride, Britain took her stand upon the glories of the past.

Hitler, too, seemed to be bogged down in the conventions of a past era. The brown-shirted revolutionary who had made his tanks roll over the harvest fields and through the towns of Europe, who had made a continent feel his grip of steel, was halted now before a gilded barricade guarded by men bearing pikes. What he wanted was to be 'welcomed' into London, there to dictate his conditions. It was as though the upstart player was reluctant to destroy the antique and faded scenery of the stage on which his greatest triumph was to be enacted. It did not escape him that his opponent was relying only upon her proud past and he believed that she would not hesitate to negotiate, would stop at nothing, to preserve it. The road to the palace was guarded by an Elizabethan watch. He could afford to calm his impatient spirit by thinking of the triumph that must soon come. In fact he was wasting precious time. What was needed for victory was a true iconoclast. If Britain could ever have been defeated it was in July. Yet neither Hitler nor Britain herself seemed conscious of the fact.

On July 13th, Halder, the Chief of Staff, accompanied by General von Brauchitsch and Admiral Raeder, went to the Berghof near Salzburg where Hitler had established his eagle's nest. Halder found Hitler 'most upset by Great Britain's persistent refusal to make peace'. The generals suggested various plans of a strategic nature, but their final appreciation was remarkably lacking in vigour: 'For his part, the Führer agrees that invasion should only be considered as a last resort.'

It seems that at this moment Hitler really did wish to hold talks with the British. What can have been his thoughts when, in June, he went to the Invalides, to stand there, jackbooted and victorious, the master of Germany, before the tomb of Napoleon? He must have compared himself with the earlier conqueror. Did he reflect too upon the grand destiny that was never achieved, upon the attempted conquest of England that brought only death in exile? In the calm atmosphere of the Berghof, Britain's stupid rejection of his offers of peace was too irritating a subject for Hitler to pursue at length.

Instead he engaged his Grand Admiral, Raeder, in a lengthy discussion of his plan to build a great city at the head of Trondheim Fjord; the capital of the Germanic race among the ice caves of the frozen North.

July 14th was a great day for the B.B.C. The voice of Winston Churchill, grave, each pause calculated, each silence expressive, was addressing the British people. One of the things that distinguishes a time of peril is that the spoken word suddenly becomes enormously important. Just when each one feels alone, feels isolated and individually threatened in the things that make up his life – his personal relationships, his money, his possessions, his health, his very existence itelf; just then is the time when a voice coming over the radio is able to make him see that he is not alone, but rather is part of a community of millions of men each weak and isolated like himself but together stronger than any one of them could possibly believe.

'Here', said Winston Churchill, 'in this strong City of Refuge which enshrines the title-deeds of human progress and is of deep consequence to Christian civilization; here girt about by the seas and oceans where the Navy reigns; shielded from above by the prowess and devotion of our airmen – we await undismayed the impending assault.'

But some things were obscure and needed clarification. Calm determination, for example; could there be any justification for such an attitude? France had fallen, invaded and overwhelmed within a few days. Did this not give reason for anxiety? Well, no. The structure of France had decayed from within before ever it was attacked from without. Britain, on the other hand, was healthy and strong. Had not Hitler already prepared his devilish plans for the invasion of the British Isles, just as he had for the conquest of every other nation that he had subdued? No doubt he had, but it had been based on the situation that had existed two months earlier when the finest troops of the British army were still on the Continent, within reach of the Wehrmacht's artillery. But now these troops were home. They had escaped from Dunkirk and were now waiting, a strong and seasoned army of a million and a half fully equipped men ready to defend their home soil. Let the invader come. He would have to fight against desperate resistance every inch of the way. The plan would have to be re-thought from top to bottom.

Scarcely had his listeners had time to digest the Prime Minister's words before the B.B.C. brought them their first account of the war. It needed only a microphone and a window overlooking the port of Dover and, as if by a miracle, the Battle of Britain was brought to every fireside in England. The commentator, Charles Gardner, who was reading his script, broke off suddenly to announce the arrival of the Germans.

That was the end of the carefully measured tones of a B.B.C. reporter. From now on he was shouting. Gardner was reacting like any honest man to the terrifying yet wonderful spectacle before him; a spectacle of death. He described what he saw as though he were a sports commentator describing some exciting football match.

'One, two, three, four, five, six, seven ... German dive bombers, Junkers 87s ... there is one going down on its target now ... no, he has missed the ships ... he hasn't hit a single ship ... there are about ten ships in the convoy but he hasn't hit a single one. There you can hear our anti-aircraft going at them now; there are one, two, three, four, five, six ... there are about ten German machines dive-bombing the British convoy which is just out to sea in the Channel. I cannot see anything, no we thought he had got a German one ... then, but now the British fighters are coming up; and here they come, in an absolute steep dive and you can see their bombs actually leave the machines and come into the water. You can hear our own guns going like anything now ... yes, they're being chased home and *how* they're being chased home; there are three Spitfires chasing three Messerschmitts now; oh! boy, look at him going and look how the Messerschmitt ... oh, that is really grand. And there's a Spitfire just behind the first two ... he'll get them! Oh yes ... Oh! boy ... I have never seen anything so good as this; the R.A.F. fighters have really got these boys taped ... no they have chased them right out to sea ... there he goes ...'

The next day, the journalist Conrad Philipps made, with some humour, the suggestion that Charles Gardner should be canonized.

On July 16th Hitler sent the following instruction No. 16 to the German High Command:

'Since, despite its desperate military situation, Great Britain shows no sign of good-will, I have decided that a plan of invasion will be prepared and, if necessary, carried out...'

3: A Study in Blue

On July 16th, 1940, Major Josef Schmid submitted to the Führer his 'Study in Blue' (*Studie Blaue*). It was doubtless this document that, in part at least, decided Hitler to issue his instruction No. 16 – an order of the day.

Schmid, the chief of *Abteilung V*, the department responsible for the Luftwaffe's intelligence service, had for the past year been compiling his study with the help of Generals Milch, Udet and Jeschonnek. It was an unconventional, shapeless piece of work and it dealt not only with the Royal Air Force, its type of aircraft, its strength and support structure, but also with the general organization of the air defence of Great Britain. In collecting his information Schmid had had at his disposal some first-hand material which he owed to General Milch's astuteness and to the naïvety of a London bookseller. Early in 1939, Milch, who two years earlier had made a tour of British airfields and aircraft factories with Udet, was recalling that visit as he glanced through a selection of specialist British magazines and periodicals. He noticed a book that had just appeared which contained a detailed review of Britain's industrial capacity and, noting the title and published price, wrote to a London bookseller on paper bearing the letter-head of the German Air Ministry, ordering a copy. It was, of course, duly received and was paid for out of the funds of *Abteilung V*.

The 'Study in Blue' grew progressively more elaborate as the archives seized by the Wehrmacht during its advance through France became available. On July 16th the report was ready; its full title: 'A Comparative Appreciation of the Striking Power of the Royal Air Force and the Luftwaffe'.

'Beppo' – such was Schmid's nickname – was forced to weigh carefully the significance of everything he included in his report. This sort of appreciation, even if the facts it contains are all entirely accurate, which is rarely the case, has to take account of certain subjective factors, or it will appear false to those for whom it is intended. Before preparing his study, Schmid must have asked himself the question: 'Is it Hitler's intention to invade Great Britain?' Jeschonnek, an officer of Goering's personal staff, commended it to the Reichsmarschall. Its conclusions could therefore be unfavourable neither to the Luftwaffe nor to its Commander-in-Chief. It is easy in later years to pass judgment upon the forecasts of an intelligence officer whose superiors are now, as a result of their defeat, dead or forgotten. At the time they were alive, and their intelligence officer's art consisted of telling them the truth, certainly, but in such a way that from their subjective points of view, it would not appear to be too far out.

To a certain extent it seems that Schmid succeeded. 'With fifty fighter squadrons, each with approximately eighteen aircraft, the R.A.F. possesses 900 first-line fighter aircraft of which 675 (75 per cent) may be considered fully serviceable.' It will be recalled that in his secret letter of May 16th, 1940, Air Chief Marshal Sir Hugh Dowding had quoted fifty-two as the minimum number of squadrons necessary to defend Great Britain. Since then there had been the fighting in France and the evacuation of Dunkirk. By July 1940 the number of serviceable British fighters had fallen to between 500, which was Alan Deere's estimate, and 650, the number that might be available on an ideal day.[1] Schmid's estimate was therefore not very far wrong.

The same could be said of his remarks about the relative performance of the different types of aircraft. 'Beppo' was treading very carefully here: 'Taking into account both their actual combat performance and the fact that they are not yet equipped with cannon, the Hurricane and Spitfire are both inferior to the Messerschmitt 109. The Messerschmitt 110, however, is inferior to the Spitfire if the latter is well piloted.' The chief of *Abteilung V* is here asserting what was in fact an illusory superiority of the Messerschmitt 109 over the Spitfire and it is noticeable that he is concerned to mention that 'they are not yet equipped with cannon'. Having covered himself in this way, it was easier for him to admit the manifest inferiority of the Messerschmitt 110 to the Spitfire.

Throughout his 'Study in Blue' Schmid shows himself to be a skilful politician. In coming down finally in favour of the Luftwaffe, he is careful to stipulate 'so long as large-scale operations are begun early enough to permit of the exploita-

1. It will be seen later than the exact figure was 587.

tion of the relatively favourable meteorological conditions of the months of July to early October.'

It should be remembered that the second half of July had already begun. Schmid's timetable, therefore, gave the Luftwaffe only sixty to seventy-five days in which to gain its victory. In many ways he was mistaken. He believed that Britain was desperately short of aircraft, whilst in fact it was experienced pilots who were lacking most of all. He thought that Fighter Command lacked flexibility and that the squadrons were rigidly tied to their bases, whereas Dowding was careful to switch the squadrons around as necessary to allow the pilots to rest and the aircraft to be repaired. He believed that the higher ranks of the R.A.F. were filled with 'bureaucrats who have lost touch with flying'. The station and group commanders frequently flew on operational sorties. His greatest error was to make no mention of radar in his appreciation. Had he consulted General Martini's *Abteilung III*, the department of radio intelligence, he could scarcely have made such an important omission.

General Martini had already some idea of the importance of radar, or rather, he suspected that the masts with lattice antennae erected along the coast of Britain concealed a radio detection device superior to the *Freya* and *Würzburg* systems available to his own radio intelligence network. He had been concerned with the matter for more than a year and, just about the time when Milch was writing off to the London bookseller, Martini was convincing his colleagues that certain electromagnetic waves that were being emitted from England were worthy of study. On Martini's suggestion the *Graf Zeppelin* was entrusted with the mission of flying over England to detect the points from which they were being transmitted. This expedition took place towards the end of May 1939, but it was not successful. The airship became lost. Its position was plotted by British radar and the controllers at Bentley Priory had the amusing satisfaction of intercepting a message from the Zeppelin to its base reporting its position 'a few miles off the coast of Yorkshire', whilst in fact it was over the city of Hull, having flown up the Humber estuary. Subsequent expeditions of the same type were equally fruitless, but did not change General Martini's opinion. In July 1940 he remained convinced of the potential importance of radar.

Though incomplete and inaccurate, the 'Study in Blue', when it was placed on Hitler's desk, was an unequivocal call to take the offensive. The Führer seems to have given it due weight without adopting all its conclusions.

As is shown clearly by his order of the day, he had by no means abandoned his intention to invade Great Britain. 'A plan of invasion will be prepared and, *if necessary,* carried out.' In truth he was convinced that it would not be necessary. Jodl, one of his regular companions, recalls that Hitler told him in confidence on May 20th:

'England can have peace whenever she wishes.'

This should be seen in the light of the remark he made in June which so surprised Mussolini:

'After all, the British Empire is a force to be reckoned with in the world.'

Hitler's heir apparent, Rudolf Hess, the man whose eyes, burning yet vacant, stared out from beneath thick dark brows, could not forget what the Führer had said after France fell:

'We shall come to a profound mutual understanding with Great Britain. I have been determined upon this since the beginning of my political career.'

Hess turned this over and over in his mind until at last, in May 1941, he could stand it no more. He went to the Messerschmitt factory and demanded to be given a fighter fully fuelled. He then took off and landed in Great Britain in a field, convinced that even at the eleventh hour, he could make his Führer's dream reality.

But by now Hitler had had second thoughts. Churchill annoyed him; Chamberlain had not been so bad. He took comfort from the thought that he could afford to spare England as long as he could eliminate its more objectionable features: the bombastic utterances of the descendant of the Marlborough line, and the plutocratic lords of the City together with their accomplices drawn from the ranks of international Jewry. He would place the Duke of Windsor, the true King, back on the throne. Churchill would be replaced by Lloyd George. Only then could Great Britain take her place, an appointed place, but a respectable one, in the Europe of the New Order.

But by the evening of July 16th, Major Schmid must have

felt that the inspiration of his work dated November 22nd, 1939, and entitled 'Proposition for the Conduct of the War in the Air', was at last to be translated into action. It had contained the prophetic phrase, 'The war cannot be brought to a successful conclusion until we have conquered Great Britain.'

Hitler's order of the day had now been given and was making its way along the straight furrows of the military communication system. The Führer himself had turned to wider fields and was fully occupied with the preparation of the speech he had decided to make three days later before the assembled Reichstag. He longed to speak directly to his opponents. He would declare his desire for an honourable peace, but at the same time he would show them that if his magnanimity had certain limits, the power of his arms had none. He felt the phrases taking shape on his lips. On July 19th he would throw them in Winston Churchill's face in one great broadside of invective.

On the other side, British Intelligence too was making serious mistakes. One which is frequently quoted concerns a mistranslation of a passage in one of Hitler's speeches. This led a specialist in secret weapons to make frantic researches into a weapon that would render its victims 'blind and deaf', whereas what Hitler had said was that he would 'strike his enemies dumb with stupefaction'. It was not until the opinion of a modern language tutor had been expressed that the passage was correctly translated and the research discontinued. The Messerschmitt 109 is the subject of two more depressing anecdotes. After the war had started, the British were fortunate enough to get hold of the device which enabled the German pilots to dive their aircraft at will without the risk that their motors would cut from fuel starvation. This component was thought at first to be of no interest, and when at last attention was turned to it, the device had been lost. In the same way, the pilots' handling notes for the Messerschmitt 109, which had been photocopied in some haste lest the 'borrowing' of the original should be discovered, were subsequently mislaid. There is a printed card which in a way symbolizes the British sense of humour when faced with a serious job. Today it hangs in the office of the Intelligence Branch of Fighter Command at Bentley Priory. It reads: 'My job is so secret that I don't know what I'm doing.' Clearly this card was not printed in 1940.

With the arrival of Squadron Leaders Williams and Knights Whittome, things changed. From that moment people started to wake up, and nothing was neglected that could provide any information about the enemy forces or about ways of overcoming them. Wing Commander Bill Coope, who had been British Military Attaché in Berlin when war was declared, was called upon, as were other officers whose work had brought them into contact with their German opposite numbers. In the summer of 1940 Bill Coope gave up flying, much to his regret, to devote himself entirely to intelligence work. He was an expert in the jargon of the Luftwaffe and among German pilots would have passed as one of the family. When the available information had been collected and sifted, there emerged an account of the German forces so accurate (ninety per cent is the agreed figure) that during the battle no type of aircraft was shot down and no squadron markings identified that had not been predicted by British Intelligence.

Air Chief Marshal Sir Hugh Dowding sat in his office at Stanmore. It was mid-July and around him lay the peaceful countryside. All the facts were before him as he set out his pieces on the board ready for the *Kriegspiel* to begin. He knew that he was confronted by three *Luftflotten*. *Luftflotte III* was commanded from Paris by General Sperrle, *Luftflotte II* from Brussels by General Kesselring, and in Norway there was *Luftflotte V* under General Stumpff. The first two were far more important than the third. Kesselring had been in command of the attack on Poland and Sperrle in Spain. They were regarded as the two most dangerous of the Luftwaffe generals. Between them they now had 2,600 aircraft, whilst in Norway Stumpff had 190. Thus, against his 650 machines, Dowding saw nearly 3,000 aircraft drawn up on the other side.

The figures are, as always, approximate and depend upon what documents are consulted. Some give total figures, others state the number of aircraft that can be considered fully serviceable and battle-worthy. In any event, Dowding was aware that he was up against an enemy force that outnumbered his own by four or five to one.

As to the relative merits of the different types of aircraft, it is an unquestionable fact that the Hurricane, with which two-thirds of the squadrons were equipped, was inferior to the German fighters. Schmid's report is confirmed by the statement of two Luftwaffe pilots, Galland and Steinhof. Galland found the Hurricanes 'very pleasant to shoot down' and Steinhof said, 'We were always delighted to meet them.' By contrast, a Spitfire when well handled was the equal of the Messerschmitt 109. Galland and Steinhof on the German side and Jeffrey Quill, the Spitfire test pilot, are agreed on this: 'One had to push the Spitfire to its limits, of course, to cope with the Messerschmitts, but at altitude there was little to choose between us and they treated us with respect.'

Where the pilots were concerned, only the battle would tell which side was to prove superior. The Condor Legion with its star, Galland, got their hand in during the Spanish Civil War and had had the campaigns of Poland, Holland, Belgium and France to complete and perfect their combat technique. On the British side there were the pilots who had fought in France and who were now home again, bringing with them the precious experience they had had of dog-fighting. In theory they would be excellent teachers for those who had not yet received their baptism of fire, but in practice this was not easy to achieve. Most of the pilots who had fought in France were deeply attached to their squadron loyalties. They wanted to maintain the sense of companionship and squadron spirit that had been built up in those few weeks. The idea of being posted as instructors to some other squadron did not appeal, especially as what they most wanted to do was to take their revenge on the Hun, immediately and among their own friends. The other pilots nicknamed them 'the cowboys'. They must have seemed a bit sure of themselves and engagingly wild.

Dowding organized his slender force into four groups: No. 10 Group commanded by Air Vice-Marshal Sir Christopher Joseph Quintin Brand, with headquarters at Box in Wiltshire; No. 11 Group under Air Vice-Marshal Sir Keith Rodney Park, with headquarters at Uxbridge in Middlesex; No. 12 Group under Air Vice-Marshal Sir Trafford Leigh-Mallory, with headquarters at Watnall in Nottinghamshire; and No. 13 Group under Air Vice-Marshal R. E. Saul, with headquarters at Newcastle-upon-Tyne. No. 10 Group had four squadrons, No. 11 Group, which was to bear the brunt of the enemy attack, twenty-three, whilst Nos 12 and 13 Groups each had thirteen squadrons. There were thus fifty-four squadrons, to which might be added a further four non-operational squadrons, bringing the total to fifty-eight. 'The number of aircraft on the line for each squadron', wrote Dowding, 'was sixteen, of which twelve were at any one time available for action. The other four aircraft were usually undergoing maintenance or modification. In addition each squadron had a reserve of from three to five aircraft.' As twenty-six was the number of pilots required by each squadron, it can be seen that in July 1940, Fighter Command should have had a strength of 1,508 pilots. In fact it had only 1,253, of which 58 were naval pilots who had been lent to the Royal Air Force in June. It was this shortage of pilots that worried Dowding, far more than the disproportionate aircraft odds against which he was fighting.

From Britain's point of view the battle that was about to take place was to be a defensive siege operation. Fighter Command therefore had to establish a fighter umbrella over the island and this had to be reinforced with a defence network of anti-aircraft artillery, searchlights, balloons and radar plotting stations. 'Radar' is an abbreviation of the phrase 'radio detection and ranging', the most sensational technical discovery of the early part of the war. There is no doubt that Sir Robert Watson-Watt, who invented it and applied it to the defence of Great Britain, deserves to be regarded as one of the victors of the battle. Radar gave eyes to the blind. Behind their castle walls, through their castle walls, the besieged garrison had only to look at its luminous screens to *see* its enemies moving forward to the attack. The principal of radar is simple. It relies upon the properties of electromagnetic waves of extremely high frequency; these travel at the speed of light and in straight lines. When they encounter a solid object, they are reflected back without delay and at the same speed. The application of this principle is readily understood. If the enemy formation is used as the solid object, its position, speed and size will be shown on the radar screen.

It had been a long day for Dowding. His eyes were bloodshot from long nights without sleep as he lay awake counting and recounting his squadrons and trying to estimate the odds against his 'boys'. He climbed up the carved staircase of Bentley Priory. Below, in the circular room that was the pride of the house, he had had a scaffolding structure erected to form a balcony. On this balcony, surrounded by telephones, sat the fighter controllers looking down on the great table where the W.A.A.F.s pushed counters across the grid lines with their croupiers' sticks. In front of them was the board on which was displayed the state of readiness of each squadron. In the room there was a sense of alertness and anticipation, of hope. A huge invisible spider's web had been spread out over Great Britain. Now was the time of waiting to see if the enemy would come out of the night to enmesh himself in it. As he pushed open the door of his room Dowding ticked off another day that had come to its end. Each day meant four and a half new aircraft delivered from the factories. Lord Beaverbrook had by now taken over and had produced an amazing change in the country's aircraft production. Seventeen new aircraft were now being produced every four days.

The hour-glass had been turned again. Each Hurricane, each Spitfire that was shot down was one grain of sand that had run out, but every Spitfire delivered from the factories helped to fill up the hour-glass again. As long as the replacements outnumbered the losses everything remained possible – so long as there were still pilots.

*

The pilots were coming in from all sides. The Commonwealth pilots added an exotic touch to the squadrons whilst remaining typically British, but the others, who came from the occupied countries, were more difficult to accommodate. To begin with it was necessary to treat them with some suspicion and to subject them to a series of irritating interrogations to ensure that no enemy agent managed to pass himself off as one of their number. Then there was the question of training and new aircraft. The training methods and aircraft that they had known in Poland, Belgium, Czechoslovakia or France were very different from what they were to find in England. To give but one example, some of them were used to pushing the throttle forward to apply full power, others pulled it back. Once it had been established that they were allies, these pilots, a wild lot, were sent off to train at airfields like St. Athan. To begin with they were amazed and delighted. René Mouchotte wrote: 'English comfort is not an empty expression. Quietness and conformity. It's as though we were living in a beehive or a monastery.' But very soon impatience followed. There were complaints about the delay in being posted to operational squadrons. July was very wet and as the rain fell softly on the lawns outside the mess, the pilots began to wonder whether the battle wouldn't have been won before they had a chance to take part.

During the middle of July, the events of the 10th were to happen again and again. The Germans would patrol the Channel or fly up the Thames Estuary. There they would encounter the British fighters that had been alerted in time, thanks to radar, and there would follow some fierce fighting engagements. The Stukas meanwhile would dive screaming on their targets, the convoys.

There were already some lessons to be drawn from these early engagements. It soon became clear that the Luftwaffe was handicapped by the distance of its bases from the scene of the battle. When their pilots had to bale out, they fell either on British soil or in British territorial waters and were usually captured. The British pilots who suffered the same inconvenience were picked up, given medical treatment if necessary and were usually back in action the following day and sometimes even the same afternoon.

On the other hand it was very difficult for the British to bring their squadrons into action quickly enough. On average it took the German fighters six minutes to cross the Straits of Dover. A Spitfire needed thirteen minutes to climb to 20,000 feet and it took a Hurricane squadron sixteen minutes. Even if the British fighters happened to be already airborne and at combat altitude, it took four minutes from the time the most conscientious radar operator could identify an enemy formation on his screen at the time when a corresponding counter could be moved into place on the plotting board. In those four minutes, the enemy was three-quarters of the way across the Channel.

The officer in command of the group had therefore to decide quickly what action to take. He had to be right first time.

He was in the position of a *Kriegspiel* player who knows the position of the enemy at a given moment, but who has only a very approximate idea of his strength. He would call up the leader of the nearest airborne patrol and an R/T conversation like this would follow:

'Hello Blue Leader, bandits fifteen plus, angels one eight, two zero miles south-west Southampton, vector north-north-east.'

'Roger.'

This would mean that an enemy formation, estimated at more than fifteen aircraft, was flying at 18,000 feet twenty miles south-west of Southampton and was heading north-north-east. The controller and the section leader would identify themselves with their code names and the conversation would end. On the plotting table a white counter with a red F would be moved towards a yellow piece bearing a black H, as the fighters turned and flew off to intercept the enemy formation.

The minutes that followed were anxious ones for the group commander. There were so many mistakes he could have made. Possibly he had called up too many patrols and left undefended some sector where at any moment another attack might take place. On the other hand, he might have sent too small a force into an unequal combat. Again, the sections he had sent into action might already have been in the air for some time and their pilots run short of fuel at a crucial moment during the engagement. As the days went by, the delays in communications were reduced and at both ends of the system men found that their judgment and powers of decision were improving. The errors were gradually being eliminated. But in mid-July they were still feeling their way.

The theories about the relative merits of the different types of aircraft were now being put to the test, and the results confirmed what had been thought. The Messerschmitt 110 was no match for the Spitfire or even for the Hurricane. On the other hand the Messerschmitt 109 was proving to be a very tough opponent. Between July 11th and 17th the R.A.F. lost eighteen aircraft against forty-four enemy aircraft destroyed. It was only skirmishing as yet, but even so the British fighters had shown that despite their inferiority in numbers, they were a force to be reckoned with. On July 11th General

Stapf had reported to Halder: 'We shall need two weeks to a month to smash the enemy's air force.' That his was a sanguine view of the situation had already been demonstrated.

On the evening of July 17th the radio building in Berlin was packed with journalists drawn from the many different countries, among them William Schirer, who was then German correspondent for several American papers. They were all listening to the B.B.C., impatient to hear Britain's reaction to the announcement of the impending invasion. In the tired, drawn faces around him, Schirer saw the blank expression of disorientation and disappointment. The B.B.C. was making a joke of the whole affair and ridiculing the German pretensions. The journalists parted at dawn and made their way back to their hotels. For a moment there had seemed to be some hope that peace might come, but now it was farther away than ever.

Two days later, on July 19th, Hitler spoke before the Reichstag:

'At this hour I feel it is my duty to appeal once more, in good faith, for reason and wise counsel on the part of Great Britain as of all other countries. I consider that my position allows me to make this appeal, since I do not speak as a defeated man begging favours, but as the victor speaking in the name of reason. I can really see no reason why this war should continue.'

The members of the Reichstag applauded, but Hitler would have given all their applause for one sign that England had taken note of what he had said; that would have been precious indeed! As though realizing that the whole population of the British Isles had closed their eyes and ears to him, Hitler went into the attack, the personal attack, upon the man with whom he had now come face to face; the old lion with the slack disdainful mouth, the florid, whisky-toping, cigar-smoking Englishman who was to be his opponent in the great battle that was now brewing. And he now delivered his attack on Churchill in person:

'Mr. Churchill ought, for once, to believe me when I say that a great empire will be destroyed – an empire which it was never my intention to destroy or harm.

'It gives me pain when I realize that I am the man who

has been picked out by destiny to deliver the final blow to the edifice that these men have already shaken . . .'

On that day, July 19th, Hitler wanted to forget the war. He took a number of spectacular measures to show that he regarded it as finished and that if it were prolonged, against all good sense, the responsibility would rest with his opponents and not with him. Public dancing was allowed again, on Wednesdays and Saturdays. To those close to him he declared that a page of history had been turned. Rommel thereupon wrote to his wife, 'In my opinion, the war will be over in a fortnight.' Taking auguries from the heavens to support the official optimism, the general went on, 'Beautiful weather; if anything too much sun.' To celebrate this wonderful day Hitler held a public investiture to reward the victors of the *Blitzkrieg*. Goering was bedecked with a host of new decorations and titles, among them that of Reichsmarschall. Twelve generals were promoted field-marshal. Could there be a clearer way of showing that he thought of the war as a thing of the past? Schacht, Hitler's minister of finance, records that when Hitler stepped down from his train to pass along the line of his ministers, he was beaming. He shook each of them by the hand and then stopped before Schacht and with a triumphant smile said, 'Well, Schacht, what have you got to say now?'

When the British heard of Hitler's threats and ceremonial in Berlin, they thought back one hundred and thirty-six years. Napoleon too had handed out field-marshals' batons and spoken of universal peace. They thought back too to find a slogan with which to meet the threatened invasion. It had been used when Napoleon was making his preparations and they used it again:

'He's coming.'

4: He's Coming

On July 20th the weather was gloomy and the forecast predicted local thunderstorms with bright intervals and cloudy conditions over the Pas de Calais. The newsvendors in the streets of London went about their task with a little more animation than usual. *The Times* had an article about Hitler's threats to Great Britain.

Churchill wondered whether to issue a reply to Hitler in the form of a motion of the House of Commons and in the House of Lords, but when Chamberlain and Attlee were consulted they judged that this would be to accord too great an importance to a matter about which everyone was in any case agreed.

In the meantime the government was trying to prepare the British people, who persisted in regarding the war as a sort of cricket match. Gas masks had been distributed, but every day hundreds were left in the tube or on buses and trains and were returned to the lost property offices. G. B. Shaw refused to wear his on the grounds that he would have to shave off his beard. In a letter to a London paper a woman wrote in all seriousness explaining how she divided her husband's beard into two equal tresses, lifted them away from his mouth on both sides, held them in place with hair grips and was then able to fit his mask. The cinemas were showing *Gone with the Wind* and the pubs were full. It really was about time people woke up.

A radio and press campaign was launched with the Home Office setting the tone: 'If Great Britain is invaded you will receive detailed instructions in good time.' The B.B.C. launched an economy campaign: 'Buy carefully ... Spend wisely at Harrods ... fatten up pigs ... keep rabbits ... rear goats ...' There was also more general advice: 'Do everything you can to bring victory ... be watchful during the night ... do not speak carelessly.' Drivers were told that if they must abandon their cars because of an enemy invasion they must 'make a hole in their petrol tank with a nail at the lowest possible level'.

'He's coming' ... 'He's on his way': such expressions began to be heard everywhere. 'He' became the name applied not only to Hitler but, by extension to his general staff, his army, anything that was German. Mrs. Knoyes, a Dover landlady, told a journalist that she didn't care whether he came or he didn't come so long as he didn't come when she was serving lunch. The manager of the Esplanade Hotel, Mr. Tilbrooke, said that he had no intention of putting up his prices even though his rooms looked on to the sea front and would allow his guests to watch the fighting from their bedrooms. The chairman of the Kent Civil Defence Committee was summoned urgently to a farm where it was thought that a German parachutist had landed. What he found was an old lady in tears who had called for help because her tortoise had fallen into a vat of apple sauce.

But all the time the danger was there. By now there were bombs falling and the fields were littered with the wreckage of German aircraft. Torn parachutes and twisted metal were put on exhibition. The landmarks of the city disappeared behind sand-bags. On their blackboards the newsvendors marked the day's score in chalk, German aircraft shot down on the left, British losses on the right. For the late night editions they added the words 'after extra time', like a football result. All available men joined the Home Guard. Old men, the proud veterans of colonial campaigns, practised their arms drill with wooden rifles by the side of schoolboys of seventeen. There was a sixty-three-year-old Zulu, and a former sergeant-major of the Black Watch who at the age of eighty-eight was undisputed patriarch of the service. However, the recruitment of the Home Guard was not completed without recrimination. One ex-officer who had won the Victoria Cross in the First World War was refused when it was discovered that his parents were non-naturalized Russians. This provoked a question in the House of Commons.

An appeal was made for arms by the Commander-in-Chief, Home Forces: 'Do not despise your shotguns. We have more than a million charges of buckshot that could kill a leopard at two hundred yards.'

Arms flooded in from all sides. The King set an example by donating his whole collection of shotguns. Each ex-India Army officer contributed a sabre. People who had travelled the world came to the Home Guard posts with assagais, machetes and clubs. Golfers even sacrificed their golf clubs. An archery club near Uxbridge suddenly found its membership growing when it announced that it was offering training in shooting holes in German airmen's parachutes. Housewives brought packets of pepper 'to throw in the Germans' eyes'.

Lord Beaverbrook invited people to empty their kitchen cupboards. Aluminium was suddenly worth its weight in gold. 'Give me your saucepans, your frying pans, your shoe-trees, your coat hangers, your kettles, the accessories of your vacuum cleaners,' asked the Minister. 'I will make Spitfires, Hurricanes, Blenheims and Wellingtons from them.' The Royal Air Force, which until yesterday had been the 'Cinderella Service', was now given first call on industrial production.

A silent revolution was taking place unperceived in British society. The British, fiercely individualistic people, had to sacrifice certain of their national traits in order to survive. In a sense they did not sacrifice them, but rather modified them or pretended to have forgotten that they existed. Whether consciously or not the British people clung to their natural character as though they sensed that when the blows began to fall they would need something to hold on to; that something might even be their faults. Only later were they to realize that in those summer weeks of 1940 when their whole national existence was threatened, their society had undergone a social and political transformation.

Barrage balloons stood guard around the larger towns like herds of elephants that had simultaneously learnt the secret of levitation. As many as 1,500 were grouped together and floated at an altitude of 5,000 feet to hinder the dive-bombers. Their cables presented such a problem to the attackers that Hanna Reitsch, the German woman test pilot, was given the task of developing a device that would enable aircraft to cut them. She was very seriously injured in the course of experiments and received the Iron Cross. The Londoners soon found nicknames for the great goat-skins floating over their city. The most bloated and crumpled one was called Hermann, after Hermann Goering; the W.A.A.F.s called one of theirs 'Romeo', because they couldn't take their eyes off him all day. Already a new expression had slipped into the vocabulary to describe trouble approaching. People now said: 'When the balloon goes up'.

Churchill was everywhere; visiting training depots, observation posts, voluntary recruitment centres. In Lincolnshire, whilst he was reviewing a parade of a Guards unit that had returned from Dunkirk, a guardsman was punished for talking on parade. Churchill inquired what he had said, but the colonel, embarrassed, tried to evade the question. Churchill insisted.

'Very well, sir. He said, "He's a real fighter, the old bastard!"'

Churchill journeyed back to London. On his desk, beside the two schoolboy inkwells, one for red ink and one for blue, he found a piece of wood, and a selection of pins with either cylindrical or round heads. Some were turquoise, others yellow, green or red. They were destined for the Defence Map Room and would serve to mark the hot spots, places where men were fighting and dying.

On July 20th the Air Ministry communiqué mentioned attacks on convoys and single ships near Dover and minelaying activity. 'Activity in the Dover area has grown to such a point', added the announcer, 'that people are beginning to refer to it as "Hell's Corner".'

That afternoon the weather was exceptionally fine and the pilots of 501 Squadron at Middle Wallop were sun-bathing on the grass beside their dispersal huts. Among them was a Yorkshire man with freckles and a mop of flaming hair, his forage cap rather askew, called James Lacey, but always known as 'Ginger'. It was tea-time when the order suddenly came to scramble. The pilots ran to their Hurricanes and took off to defend a convoy off Jersey. The Dorset countryside slipped by beneath their wings and they flew out across the Portland peninsula in a neat formation. Now the waters of the Channel lay below, blue and sparkling. Almost at once, and much sooner than their instructions had led them to believe, they saw the convoy, about halfway between the Channel Islands and the British coast. The pilots of 501 could see the Stukas, Junkers 87s, diving on to their targets, the grey ships that looked like little toys that had been placed in the water. The escort of Messerschmitt 109s was coming down fast from above; a real hornet's nest.

Then came the leader's 'Tally-ho', the sighting cry borrowed from the hunting field and now used by the leaders to rally their pilots for the kill. At a range of two hundred yards Lacey noticed a 109 turning towards him. He huddled down in his cockpit. It was a moment when it was comforting to feel oneself a part of the fuselage, but there was also the disquieting thought that the fuel tanks were inadequately armoured. One's reflexes tightened up in readiness. The 109 was upon him and Lacey broke as hard as he could, pulling away to the side. The German's fire missed by fifty yards. My turn now, thought Lacey. I must get into position to fire at the next pass. Both aircraft were turning tightly as Lacey tried to get the German in his sights. He had a smaller turning radius and could stay on the inside of the turn, but still the German was trying to out-turn him to get in another shot. Lacey pulled tighter still. Now! He fired, and just behind the cockpit the camouflaged fuselage started to rip away. The German turned tail and dived away towards the sea, looking like a bull that had suffered badly from the pic. 'Ginger' Lacey pushed his throttle through the gate and dived after the German, clinging to his tail, his finger pressed on the gun button. He held the burst for a few glorious seconds and saw his bullets literally chop the 109's engine in pieces. Finally he broke off and climbed back up again. Looking down over the trailing edge of his wing he could follow the fall of the grey-and-blue machine with its black crosses outlined in white as it dropped away growing smaller and smaller. He thought what a nice neat plop it would make as it plunged straight into the sea some thousands of feet below.

'People of Britain,' the German radio repeated *ad infinitum*, 'we are on our way. Pack up your belongings so that when we arrive you will just have to pick them up and go . . . We are coming . . .'

The Berlin papers proclaimed that for Britain it was the beginning of the end. The *Nachtausgabe* saw the continuation of the war as a crime committed by Churchill against the British people. The crudest progapands was being broadcast. British hospitals were reported to be packed with patients suffering from ethyl alcohol poisoning, having sought refuge from their terror in drink. The Jews of London were supposed to have their hair turning grey and their noses straightening out at the thought of the coming invasion. Else Wendel was to write:

'Here in Germany everything was fine. Great Britain had wanted the war and had been rewarded with Dunkirk. We all waited impatiently for the invasion, many of us were astonished that it had not taken place already. At that time we had very little hate for the British. Rather we were dismayed at the thought of the dreadful fate they were to suffer. We felt that Great Britain would make a valuable ally when she had been beaten and cured of her pride.'

In high official circles the belief in peace persisted. The daily report of the naval staff stated, 'It appears that there are a certain number of important people in England who wish to know what terms might be offered in an armistice.' Count Ciano, after an interview with Hitler, noted in his diary: 'I believe his desire for peace to be sincere.' In fact it was, for when, late in the evening of the day of his speech to the Reichstag, the reactions from London were known to be unfavourable, Hitler's famous 'patience' was still not exhausted. He informed an official of the Ministry of Foreign Affairs that he had decided to postpone the invasion once again.

But already there were murmurings among some senior officers. Marshal von Manstein wrote later: 'The temporary weakness of the enemy should have been exploited at once.' General Student, lying wounded in a hospital bed in Rotterdam, was seething with rage that he was not able to go to Berlin to argue the case for an immediate attack. 'Now', he wrote, 'is the time to act, before the British have managed to perfect their defence.'

But Hitler was the sole master who could decide on peace or war, and Hitler's eyes were on Sweden, whose King was going to offer to mediate with the British.

July 21st dawned fine. Fighter Command flew 571 sorties, losing six aircraft against seven destroyed. Around the Operations Room plotting table the W.A.A.F.s were moving the pieces representing the squadrons as they flew into battle over the Channel. Now there was direct R/T contact between the pilots and the Operations Room and so, with the voices from the sky, war and death were admitted to the closed room itself. The voices invaded the room, echoing from wall to wall: shouted orders, curses, gasps of terror. Suddenly the girls in the Air Force blue tunics saw their giant roulette game in a new and terrible human light. The voices were swearing and shouting. Until now the girls had merely been moving counters about; now they could hear men dying. The senior officers became worried. In the air the boys were at grips with death; what they were living was rage and terror. They were not worrying about what they were saying. It was suggested that the girls should be replaced. They refused. The counters continued to slide across the table. '*Faites vos jeux.*' '*Rien ne va plus.*' Each time there was a minimum stake, a man's life. The noise of the voices went on.

A young pilot's voice came over the radio. He was trying to control the tremulous note of fear; to remain dignified. It was his first sortie and he was calling his leader. His aircraft was in flames and the cockpit canopy had been jammed by a shell splinter. He was diving towards the sea and wanted to know what he should do. A brief exchange of question and answer showed that there was nothing to be done. The radio went silent. The young pilot was gone.

On July 21st Hitler called a meeting of his Commanders-in-Chief to study the prospects for the invasion. Von Brauchitsch would not guarantee the success of the operation unless the Navy could undertake to transport forty divisions across the Channel and to get them there without serious loss. The Navy would accept the responsibility of transporting ten. The Führer then turned to Halder:

'It's suicide!' was Halder's response.

Goering remained resolutely optimistic.

'Give me just five days of good weather . . .'

The discussion went on at length and turned to divisions, shipping, tonnage of bombs available. Plans were even made for the administration of a conquered Britain. The pound would be worth nine marks and 60 pfennigs. All English males between the ages of seventeen and forty-five would be deported to the Continent. A specimen of the notice, printed in both languages, that was to be posted on requisitioned buildings, was passed round. Hitler's thoughts seemed to be elsewhere. When he did open his mouth it was to say,

'We are up against a well-prepared and fiercely resolute enemy.'

And again:

'The invasion of Great Britain is a particularly audacious

undertaking. Even if the sea distance is short, we are not dealing with a river crossing, but with the open sea controlled by the enemy.'

Finally the day was fixed for September 11th and the operation received the code-name *Seelöwe,* sea lion.

Galland writes: 'The dice were thus cast. In July 1940 the 2nd and 3rd Air Fleets took up their positions along the Channel coast. My unit, the 3rd wing of the 26th Fighter Group, was stationed at a well camouflaged airfield near Guines. The 26th Fighter Group was part of the 2nd Air Corps which itself formed part of Marshal Kesselring's 2nd Air Fleet.' The grey uniforms of the Luftwaffe were to be seen everywhere. The pale-eyed officers with their coloured flashes and long raincoats that reached down to their calves were soon a familiar sight in Brussels, Ghent, Boulogne, Compiègne, Caen, Deauville, Saint-Denis, Villacoublay and even in the Ritz in Paris.

To the south of Beauvais the work was going ahead fast. The road from Coudray to Parfondeval was cut and a road block installed. The whole area had by now been fenced off by barbed wire and was patrolled day and night by soldiers with police dogs. The tobacco shop had been requisitioned and was being used to house the camp tailor and bootmaker. Beyond was forbidden territory. Each morning an aircraft landed on the strip that had been prepared at Champ-L'Évêque. It brought in the dispatches and then left, sometimes taking the commanding officer to Paris or to some other destination. The German grip on the countryside tightened with no opposition. M. Masselin, the mayor of Neuville, brought in his beetroot harvest. He stored three cartloads in a barn that in theory the Germans had requisitioned but which in fact they had never used. The following day a German officer got to hear of it. He was not at all pleased. Apparently his name was Schuschner; at least that was how the French read his signature as Camp Commandant on each *Ausweis*, or 'pass', that was issued. He always went around with a mastiff and set out to inspire fear. He claimed to have been a prisoner in France during the First World War and to have suffered extreme ill-treatment. He said that the French had smashed his fingers to try to make him talk. When his car arrived the barrier would rise as if by magic and the guards would spring forward to light his cigarette. He went about with an interpreter named Wagner who was said to have worked in a bank in France right up till September 1939.

Slowly information began to filter through. From the stores that went in every week it was possible to have some idea of the number of people living in the forest. There must have been about four thousand of them and the work was still going on. It was to go on all winter. Casual contacts between the occupiers and the occupied furnished other details. It was learnt that a station with a long wooden platform had been built just before the blocked tunnel near where a road passed under the railway. They had built tennis courts, surrounded with wire netting, there too. Frenchmen, at first in small numbers, were now being employed in the camp. They were well paid and each received an *Ausweis* which allowed him to pass the barrier twice each day. From these workmen it was learnt that inside the gate the Commandant's office lay on the right and that just beyond it were some cells which had been built to receive the civilians who were caught by the patrols wandering near the barbed-wire fences. Farther on, work had started on the construction of a giant *Blockhaus* which months later was to become known as the Goering *Blockhaus*. It had thirty-seven steps leading down to the subterranean offices. Details were now piling up. Frequently people who had been kept in the cells for two or three days for entering the camp without authorization, or for bartering with a German soldier, came out with fantastic reports of what they had seen. These reports, when put together with a little imagination, eventually provided a fairly accurate picture of the lay-out of the camp.

The picture formed showed that what had been constructed was a great military administrative centre grouped around the central bunker. There were fifty-two permanent barrack buildings, workshops, garages, an electrical power station, seven munitions dumps, a large restaurant, showers, two swimming pools, a fire station and, near the tunnel that was to shelter the Reichsmarschall's special train, a petrol storage area equipped with deeply buried tanks. A force of sixty men was employed on maintaining the camouflage, which was changed four times a year with the change of seasons. The camp, with its bunker, all its buildings, the tunnel, the miles of newly metalled road, the landing strip, melted into the landscape. In the countryside around the people watched. And of course they traded. Five litres of aviation petrol were worth half a pound of butter. From time to time there would be a stir and commotion. Staff cars with motor-cycle and side-car escorts would rush like wind through the village streets. Or sometimes the railway would be lined with soldiers. It meant one thing: Goering was not far away. One day he was observed walking in the streets of Le Coudray in civilian clothes. Among the crowd of officers was a second Goering in uniform: his double. There were so many extraordinary things to be seen! Could it have been Hitler himself who had been spotted, riding across the forest paths of the camp on a white horse?

In Berlin Major Schmid was listening to the radio. He heard the announcer describe Britain's reaction to the Führer's words as 'a tissue of insults, insolence and arrogance'. Schmid knew that the hour had come when his 'Study in Blue' was to be orchestrated into a sonata for bomb, machine-gun and cannon.

Schmid's feeling was confirmed on July 22nd when Lord Halifax, His Majesty's Secretary of State for Foreign Affairs, delivered a measured and judicial speech which he concluded with these words: 'We shall not cease fighting until freedom for ourselves and others is secure.'

5: Men and Ships

A light mist covered the Pas de Calais on July 23rd and from time to time a little fine rain would fall, soaking the cottage roofs and flowering creepers and the soft lawns. The convoys had, for the most part, been diverted from the Straits of Dover to avoid the incessant attacks of the bombers with their fighter escorts. Now they sailed through the North Channel into the Irish Sea and thus reached Britain by the service entrance, the Bristol Channel.

After dark, 'Ginger' Lacey, the red-headed pilot of 501 Squadron, took off from Middle Wallop for a night patrol. Flying in the darkness he felt as though the 'Ops Room' was holding his hand. A strange sightless relationship was developing between the pilots and the ground controllers. They were getting to know each other; there were ways in which they could recognize who was speaking. They became involved in each other's existence. Only when the fighting actually began did they cease to talk to each other. On the ground the controller would await the issue of the duel. In a few moments he would hear the pilot's shout of victory or else hear him cursing over a chance missed. Only if he heard nothing would he know that their dialogue had ceased for ever. The voices in the night were sometimes indiscreet. It was dark and one was alone; it led to the sort of confidences that would not be passed over a pint of beer at the bar.

In this way, two pilots, congratulating each other on their victory one night, realized that they had attacked the same aeroplane. The ground controller overheard.

Lacey saw the Heinkel 111 burst out of the darkness as it was caught in a searchlight's beam. From head on it looked like a great mosquito. Its great glazed nose and the motors set close in to the fuselage, as well as the single fin and rudder, distinguished it from the Messerschmitt 110. With a top speed of 250 miles per hour and a rate of climb between one-third and a quarter that of the Hurricane, it was an easy prey. It had five machine-guns, but the hand-operated turrets did not make for rapid firing. Lacey smiled at the thought of how he would play with the Heinkel, driving its pilot mad trying to escape his manoeuvres. He opened his throttle.

All at once some of the searchlights left the Heinkel, and caught him in their beams. Lacey realized that he must give the signal of the day, a coded light signal that changed every twenty-four hours and which the British pilots must send to the searchlight crews by using their downward identification lights. Lacey tried to remember what the signal was, found it and tapped it out on his light button. He was still watching his great mosquito and was just about ready to fire. He saw the Heinkel, give a signal too, a red followed by a green, and then, with terrifying suddenness, before him there was nothing but darkness. All the searchlights had left the Heinkel and were now focused on him. Ten seconds passed and then the anti-aircraft guns opened up *on him*. They were making things extremely hot and as one shell-burst, nearer than the rest, shook his Hurricane, Lacey, furious at having lost his prey and having changed roles from hunter to quarry, kicked his aircraft into a spin and went tumbling down to escape the blinding circle of light in which he was trapped. The searchlights waved forlornly about the sky trying to find him again and Lacey, diving towards the ground, turned and fled for Middle Wallop like a fox running for its earth. He landed and leapt out of his Hurricane. There was only one thing he wanted to do now and that was to get his hands on one of those stupid searchlight operators or gunners. His fingers were itching. As soon as he was back on solid earth he glanced at his watch to note the time of the incident and then all at once he understood. It was after midnight. It was tomorrow and the signal had changed. What he had sent had been the signal valid for yesterday. The searchlight operators had doubtless suspected a trick and had therefore clung to him while the Heinkel, whether by luck or some well-informed espionage system, had given the correct signal of the day for a British bomber and had been allowed to escape. Boiling inwardly, Lacey went into the dispersal hut. He was still thinking of the great dark mosquito going about its work of death with impunity.

A few hours later on the morning of July 24th, a German formation appeared through a gap in the clouds over the mouth of the Thames. The alert was given and 54 Squadron took off from Rochford to intercept. The leader of Red Section was Alan Deere, a big fair-haired fellow built like a lumber-jack with a broad nose and square chin, and wearing a polka-dot silk scarf. Dowding said of him: 'Perhaps his was one of those rugged characters which never *would* crack this side of death.' At 20,000 feet the Spitfires met the first wave of bombers and were just going into the attack when the second wave appeared:

'The enemy formation,' wrote Alan Deere, 'the largest I had seen up to that time, consisted of about 18 Dorniers protected by a considerable number of escort fighters weaving and criss-crossing above and behind the bombers.'

The leader of Red Section radioed to the 'Ops Room' for reinforcements and then flung himself into the mêlée and action became very heated as the aircraft fought in and out of the clouds. No. 54 Squadron split in two sections and both were immediately absorbed into the centre of the great wheeling dogfight.

Galland, who had arrived at the French coast the evening before, took part in the fun. It was his first sortie in the Battle of Britain: 'Together with Staff Flight,' he writes, 'I selected one formation as our prey, and we made a surprise attack from a favourably higher altitude.'

Aircraft were now falling out of the sky on all sides. A British pilot, Colin Gray, shot down a Messerschmitt 109. Then he heard someone calling to him for help and he dived into a cloud just as a fireman rushes into the smoke of a burning building to rescue someone inside. But there he found no Spitfire in trouble. What he did find was a 109 flying peacefully round in the cloud. Gray was so surprised that he pressed his gun button without even thinking about the deflection. It shouldn't have worked, but it did, and Gray shot down his second German for the day. Galland tucked himself in behind the last aircraft on the left wing of the British formation, 'and during a right-handed turn, I managed to get in a long burst ... the Spitfire went down almost vertically.' Galland followed him down and saw the canopy fly off and the pilot jump. He watched the Spitfire until it crashed, and then looked back just in time to see the pilot, whose parachute had not opened, plummet into the sea.

'When we returned,' writes Galland, 'we looked at each other thoughtfully. We were no longer in doubt that the R.A.F. would prove a most formidable opponent.'

When he landed back at Rochford, Alan Deere was informed by the pilot who had flown as number two to his friend Johnny Allen, that Allen had been shot down in the first attack. He had been hit by a 109 and had tried to reach Manston, but his aircraft was burning and finally his engine caught fire and he had crashed on the outskirts of Foreness. Another two or three miles and he would have been safe. He had shot down eight enemy aircraft.

By an ironic twist of fate when Deere got back to Rochford he received an apology for the fact that it had not been possible to send in reinforcements sooner. He was assured, however, that there was now a full squadron over the convoy where the action had just taken place.

The day's score read eight Germans shot down for the loss of three British.

The rain had set in again.

That night when taking leave of his listeners, the B.B.C. announcer Frank Phillips gave his normal 'Good night everybody ...' and then he added a short phrase that drew the attention of many who were listening. He said: '... and good luck.'

Then there was silence.

At Karinhall, which was named after his first wife, Hermann Goering received a curious visitor: Dr. Albert Plesman, the chairman of the Dutch airline K.L.M.

While the fighting over the Thames estuary from which Galland was to draw his first important lesson for the conduct of the battle, was taking place, it was peace that was being spoken of at Karinhall. Plesman already knew Goering, whose nephew he had employed as a pilot. It was at his request that the interview was taking place. He offered his services as mediator between the German and British governments. He had a peace plan all worked out. He took it out of his pocket and showed it to Goering.

The Reichsmarschall must have smiled as he recalled another visit he had received a month earlier from General Milch, the Inspector-general of the Luftwaffe. At that time Goering had been staying in Belgium where he had installed his headquarters. Milch arrived in his personal aircraft from Dunkirk where he had flown over the beach-head. He had made up his mind. The British army as it embarked had left behind almost all its tanks, artillery and transport. Now was the time to make hay while the sun shone, so as to deny the enemy the time to regroup. Goering had found the idea 'absurd'.

Now he was disposed to listen to this Dutchman who spoke of ending the war. He promised to report the conversation to the Führer when he came back from Berchtesgaden.

Siegfried installed in his castle was tasting the delicious flavour of power.

In England a man was arrested and sentenced to seven years for demonstrating his sympathy for the Axis powers in a particularly vandalistic way. He had smashed nine public telephone booths in order to render them useless for when they might be needed to telephone the Civil Defence forces during an enemy raid. A few days earlier it was a schoolteacher who had been advancing defeatist theories to his pupils who went to jail.

'During the midsummer weeks in 1940', wrote Galland, 'the 2nd and 3rd Air Fleets were concentrated on the Channel coast ... Establishing our aircraft in these positions brought to an end the first phase of the Battle of Britain on July 24th, 1940. Up to then the action of the Luftwaffe had been directed against the Navy and merchant shipping.'

On July 25th there was mist over the Pas de Calais and a light north-westerly wind off the sea. In his converted bus at Cap Blank Nez, Fink learned of a convoy assembling off Southend. The *Kanalkampfführer* now had a radar plotting system at his disposal and, although it was less developed than the British radar, it did permit him to call up his forces in time. The rules of the game were still simple enough: the British would attempt to run a convoy through the Straits of Dover and they would be spotted by the Germans who would send out the Stukas. The leader of the British escort fighters or a radar operator would see the Stukas and the British would send out reinforcements. Then the battle would begin.

On that morning the first piece in the game of *Kriegspiel* was called C.W.8. It was a convoy of twenty-one merchant ships escorted by two armed trawlers. Once he knew that it was off Southend, Fink had only to look up his tide table to know at what time it would attempt the passage of the Straits of Dover. It would be about the middle of the afternoon.

As the convoy came into the straits the mist cleared away. Now Fink had a grandstand view. He sent out three formations of Stukas escorted by 109s. Galland was there. Previous engagements had taught him that 'Junkers 87s attracted Spitfires as honey attracts flies'. He realized that 'the Stuka is practically defenceless as soon as it breaks formation and dives on its own'. He was determined not to let the British fighters use them for target practice.

The alert was received at Bentley Priory and one of the flights of 54 Squadron was ordered to intercept the enemy. The leader of this formation of five Spitfires was 'Wonky' Way. Despite the odds, he did not hesitate for a second before calling 'Tally-ho'.

Colin Gray, his number two, saw him fly straight in among the mass of German fighters, which closed in around him. Gray lost sight of him.

The Stukas had not yet started their diving attacks. Galland hurled himself at the Spitfires, sending one down to break up in the water just off the harbour wall at Dover.

Below, among the ships, it was like a scene from the *Inferno*. Now the Stukas were dropping their bombs and climbing up again, leaving behind them great fountains of spray. Black smoke was rising over the dark-blue water as some of the ships rolled on their sides like dying fish. The gunners on the ships clung on to their triggers, swinging their turrets and turning a deaf ear to the sound of bullets crashing into their armour plate or howling about their ears as they ricocheted away. One of them blew a Stuka to pieces as it dived at his ship but immediately there was another spitting death in its place.

From the chalk cliffs on both sides of the Channel spectators followed the course of the furious action. It seemed that the sea was boiling and the sky was on fire. The exploding bombs, great jets of steam, the roar of motors and the howl of sirens punctuated by the piercing rattle of machine-gun fire could have been a scene from some magnificent Wagnerian opera.

Alan Deere arrived with his flight overhead the convoy. In his earphones he heard a shout from one of the pilots of the first flight, George Gribble.

'Watch out, Blue One, 109s coming in from above – hundreds of them.'

George's voice sounded terribly excited. Other orders crackled out:

'Break . . . break . . .'

This time the voice was Colin Gray's. Who was he shouting to? Then new orders.

Deere called the control centre and asked for permission to mix it. This was refused and he was ordered to remain at altitude. He felt like someone stuck in bed in hospital with some trivial illness while important things are happening. There were more disjointed cries on the radio. Deere thought he heard 'Wonky' get his Stuka. But had he got it right? What was the matter with George? He was screaming 'Break, Wonky, break!' George sounded as though he was having a nervous breakdown. He was sobbing. Deere gritted his teeth. He cursed the controller. He would have given ten years of his life to drop down a few thousand feet and see what was what. However, he must restrain himself. He would be needed later and for the moment he must think of himself as a pawn; that's all he was. But a pawn is blind and deaf; unlike him.

'Damn and blast this bloody war, they've got Wonky.'

It was George's voice cursing and sobbing. It burst into his earphones as if his friend was sitting beside him.

Deere alone in his cockpit, way up above the battle, closed his eyes for a second. A pawn! He must remember, just a pawn.

Galland, on the other hand, was having a marvellous time. He was still at the stage where his heart was in the fighting. 'I attacked another Hurricane but he made a half roll and got away from me. In the space of about fifteen minutes I saw four fighters dive into the sea and one pilot descending by parachute.'

According to Colin Gray the Hurricanes arrived too late when everything was over. 'They came over to me to make sure I wasn't a 109.'

Below in the convoy all was chaos. The water was covered with wreckage. Of the twenty-one ships that had left Southend, eleven had been hit. Of these, five had sunk and the other six were disabled. Two destroyers, the *Brilliant* and the *Boreas*, left Dover harbour and were seen steaming through the oil patches and past the wrecks at full speed. They steered straight across the Channel and fired broadsides at Fink's command post. Stupefied, the Commodore watched the shells falling round his converted bus.

'They've got a bloody cheek!'

Fink ordered the Stukas to attack the destroyers for their temerity. They dived again and again on the two destroyers which had now turned and were heading back, zigzagging towards Dover. Both were hit and one had to be towed in.

Above, the Hurricanes, seeing the Messerschmitts disappear, tore into the Stukas. 'A fine old dance,' said Page. 'A Ju 87 followed by a Hurricane, then another Ju 87 on the tail of the Hurricane, and then another Hurricane on his tail . . .' Page himself was chasing one of the Stukas that was spraying him with machine-gun fire. Page fired back and the German caught fire, belching out masses of black smoke, but continuing to fly. Finally it dived into the sea. All that came to the surface was one wheel and a small patch of burning oil. The combat seemed to be over at last.

On both sides of the Channel the day's balance sheet was being drawn up. The Germans had lost sixteen aircraft, the British seven. But, as Alan Deere pointed out, 54 Squadron had lost three pilots killed in three days; one per day. Of the seventeen pilots who made up the squadron after Dunkirk, there remained only five. All the others were dead or unable to fight because of their injuries. Where were replacements to be found?

*

Between July 25th and 31st the Royal Air Force flew 3,629 sorties. It shot down forty-eight enemy aircraft for a loss of twenty-one.

In Berlin optimism remained the rule among the military chiefs with the exception of Halder. At a meeting of the O.K.W. General Jodl declared: 'The German soldier can expect to encounter only a feeble resistance from the British army which has not had time to profit from the lessons the war has taught it.' But Hitler remained evasive about the date of the invasion. He spoke sometimes of mounting it on September 15th after a week of uninterrupted aerial bombardment, and again he talked of postponing it until May 1941. Could it be that Operation Sea Lion was destined never to get off the ground? Or was it that Hitler was awaiting some reply from Sweden? In any case Plesman's plan had not yet been submitted to the British. Lord Halifax was not to hear of it until the end of August, at which time he rejected it. Goering had asked Hitler for *carte blanche* to 'attack the British fighter aircraft and their pilots, the aircraft factories, ports, industrial centres, petrol installations and the whole of the Channel sector.'

The French pilots, gathered at St. Athan, were authorized to fly the aircraft in which they had escaped from France on condition that they bore British markings and had their undersurfaces painted yellow.[1] Two Potez, three Dewoitines, four Caudrons and one Farman thereupon changed nationality. Perrin, one of the French pilots, recorded his experiences when he was posted to a squadron at North Weald. 'The Squadron Commander wasn't the sort of chap to waste time on formalities. I hadn't been in the place five minutes before I was swept off in a car full of the boys, to a pub about five miles away, the only one still open. "I thought we'd both like a bit of peace," said the boss.' René Mouchotte noted in his diary: 'This morning the papers said, "All military personnel declared rebels, who have joined a foreign army to continue fighting, will be sentenced to death if they have not returned to France by August 15th." '

In France the weather was fine and it was becoming warmer than it had been recently. A grey Luftwaffe car drew up in front of Marshal Kesselring's forward headquarters at Cap Gris Nez. A pilot got out. He was wearing high boots and his cap was set at a slight angle. Beneath his thick black moustache he was chewing on a cigar. It was Galland and he was in a hurry. The Marshal was waiting to decorate him with the Knight's Cross.

As Kesselring was performing the ceremony some fighters passed overhead. The Marshal turned to Galland:

'What are those aircraft?'

'Spitfires, sir.'

'Good God! They haven't wasted any time in coming to congratulate you.'

1. Translator's note: Yellow was the colour that distinguished aircraft used for training purposes. The order had no discriminatory significance.

On August 1st Hitler issued his order of the day No. 17:

'I have decided that war against Great Britain will be pursued and intensified by sea and by air with the object of bringing about the country's final defeat.'

At last he was striking a decisive note.

'1. The Luftwaffe must deploy its full strength in order to destroy the British air force as soon as possible.

2. When command of the air has been achieved, even on a local or temporary basis, the air attack will be directed against the ports and special attention will be given to food depots, particularly those which serve London.

3. Attacks upon shipping, whether naval or merchant, will be accorded a priority secondary only to the efforts directed against the destruction of the enemy's power in the air.'

The destruction of the Royal Air Force was given a clear priority over all other objectives. The order even went on to prescribe how it should be achieved: 'First the aircraft, then their ground support organization and fuel supplies. Afterwards the aircraft industry, including the factories producing anti-aircraft weapons.' As to attacks upon shipping, the order went on to state that these should be conducted only when 'particularly suitable targets present themselves or when it is necessary to use enemy ships as targets for the training of Luftwaffe aircrew'.

That Hitler had not given up the idea of Operation Sea Lion was shown by his fourth paragraph which laid down that 'the fighter force must be held in readiness to support this operation'. In paragraph 5 he reserved the right to order 'bomber attacks in reply to the enemy's terror raids'. In his concluding paragraph, number 6, he specified the date on which 'the intensification of the war in the air might begin'. This date was August 5th, 1940, but it was left to the general staff of the Luftwaffe to determine the precise date, 'bearing in mind the state of preparedness and the meteorological situation.'

The night of August 1st–2nd was fine; a real bomber's night.

The German aircraft came, but on a strangely peaceful mission, without their bombs. Over Hampshire and Somerset they dropped packets of pamphlets entitled 'The last Appeal to Reason'. They contained a translation of Hitler's speech to the Reichstag.

In the morning the green and yellow leaflets were discovered. They passed from hand to hand, were talked about and finally auctioned in aid of the Red Cross. It was on the following day, wrote Peter Fleming, that 'various attempts to hawk the olive-branch round neutral capitals culminated on August 3rd in a well-meant offer by the King of Sweden to act as mediator. To this, and to the other tentatives which had preceded it, the British declined to pay the slightest attention.'

It was on August 2nd, in pursuance of the order of the day No. 17, that Goering charged the Luftwaffe with the task of destroying the R.A.F.

That evening the steamer *Highlander* returned proudly to port. It had shot down two Heinkel 111s. The wreckage of one was lodged in its bridge.

It's easy once you think of it. If you don't want to get flies in your jam, keep the jampot in the cupboard. After C.W.8 no more convoys entered the Channel. Hence no more Stukas, no more interceptions, no more losses of pilots.

Fink sent out his aircraft to patrol the Channel. It was empty. In early August the Air Ministry communiqués were often very uninformative. The weather was cloudy and misty and the R.A.F. had had its orders from Dowding. It was staying on the ground. The Air Chief Marshal had beaten the hour-glass. By August 3rd he had 708 aircraft and 1,434 pilots, as against 587 aircraft and 1,253 pilots on June 30th. Time was working in his favour.

The same day, a German submarine was surreptitiously approaching the coast of Ireland. On board it carried two chiefs of the I.R.A., that collection of blindly obstinate and courageous men who had sworn to continue the fight against England. One of them was John Russell, the other Frank Ryan. They had scoured the camps of British prisoners in Germany and had found a few Irishmen who were willing to help them in their unsavoury task. Now, as they slid along below the surface of the sea, they knew that in two hours they would be home on the soil of Old Ireland. Their task was simple: to make contacts and stir up hate against the British and to guarantee the independence of Ireland when the war should be over. To do that and to wait. How long? Russell had wanted to know. He was told that the invasion was imminent.

'When shall I be informed?'

'At the last moment.'

'How?'

'A bunch of red roses will be placed in the window of one of the rooms in the living quarters of the German Legation in Dublin.'

Frank Ryan succumbed to a heart attack during the voyage, whether from emotion or from fear of the risk is not known. In any event the submarine turned back. There were never to be any red roses at the window in Dublin.

Other things, too, were happening on August 3rd. German bombs were falling on England. One of them knocked out a post of the Observer Corps. In Essex the wheat crop was set on fire.

On August 4th and 6th the communiqués referred to 'light activity'. On the 7th General Sander announced over the German radio that the launching of air attacks against Great Britain was imminent. In London people were getting accustomed to the brief lull in the fighting. At the first sign of sunshine everybody made for the parks or for the river. Men in shirtsleeves, women in flowered dresses rubbed shoulders with soldiers in khaki who spoke all the languages of Europe. It was pleasant to stretch out on the grass eating ice-creams or to play bowls under the protection of the barrage balloons.

Lord Beaverbrook expressed his gratitude for the amazing response to his appeal. He was staggering under the weight of the saucepans and frying pans that had been contributed. He even received from Jamaica a consignment of snakes, though it was not clear what connection these had with building Spitfires. Darryl Zanuck sent two thousand pounds to buy an ambulance. The large tailoring firm, Moss Bros., was offering Royal Air Force officers' uniforms ready to wear or made to measure in 36 to 40 hours. American civil pilots had been engaged by the Ministry of Aircraft Production and were on their way. They were to be used to ferry new aircraft from the factories to the airfields and to bring back machines that needed repairs. Goering certainly wouldn't have been impressed by this arrangement. He was accustomed to sneer at the Americans who, he said, were only good at one thing – making razor blades.

His Majesty had decided to strike out the name of Mussolini from the Order of the Bath and that of King Umberto from the Order of the Garter. The King of Italy's Knight's banner went into cold storage at Windsor Castle, where it joined the banner of the Kaiser which had been in the same situation since the First World War.

Although they didn't want to say as much, for fear of putting their natural pride to the test, the British people felt that the Americans would have been well advised to take a more active part in the events that were going on. In particular they felt that Roosevelt could have been better employed than in spending a holiday on his yacht on the Potomac fishing for eels. General de Gaulle, in his memoirs, recalls seeing Churchill just about this time, holding his fists towards the sky as he cried:

'So they won't come!'

This astonished de Gaulle and he replied:

'Are you in such a hurry to see your towns smashed to bits?' To which he received the reply:

'You see, the bombing of Oxford, Coventry, Canterbury will cause such a wave of indignation in the U.S. that they'll come into the war.'

It was decided to take the pot of jam out of the cupboard during the night of August 7th. Another convoy, code-named C.W.9, was made ready. It was to follow the course of its tragic predecessor C.W.8, 'the suicide squad', through the Channel. At night the flies should be sleeping. What was not realized was that the German radar could see in the dark.

It was now the turn of Major Schmid to take the stage. Usually he was inconspicuous, standing behind Goering, his right hand clasping the third button on his tunic. He was said to be an ambitious officer and a social climber. The air-crews disliked him because he was not a pilot. On August 7th he sent out a circular to the three *Luftflotten* that were drawn up against Great Britain. It concerned the British system of controlling the fighters from the ground. 'From the fact that the British fighters are controlled by radio from the ground,' he wrote, 'it will be seen that they are dependent upon their respective airfields and thus have a restricted mobility.' He advanced the idea of massive attacks upon specific points. This should ensure that the attackers always had a great numerical superiority since the British could not take the risk of dispersing their forces, and would have to be prepared to defend their whole country without knowing which points the Germans intended to attack.

On August 8th the following order of the day was read aloud to every member of the Royal Air Force:

'The Battle of Britain is about to begin. Members of the Royal Air Force, the fate of generations lies in your hands.'

At dawn on August 8th high-speed German surface craft went after C.W.9 like a pack of hounds with a stag at bay.

The thirty-one ships of the convoy scattered and in the confusion two collided. Three were sunk by the attackers.

In his look-out at Cap Blanc Nez, Fink was rubbing his hands. His work was going well. He had been told to sweep the Channel clean and he was doing so. Yet he realized that he controlled only a restricted area and that only by day. The weather cleared and he sent in his aircraft. Galland with his 27th fighter group was escorting the Stukas.

On the British side it was the Hurricanes of 145 Squadron from Westhampnett who were involved. They immediately found themselves confronted with an amazingly large force of Stukas. As one of their pilots put it, 'There were so many of them that it would have been possible to shoot down two with one burst.' But the 109s were there. Some of them had slid in among the Stukas. They would dive with the Junkers 87s, throttling back so as not to overtake them, and then just when the Hurricanes were ready to attack as the Stukas pulled out of their dive, the 109s would be there waiting. This is what Werner Andres did. He attached himself to a formation of Stukas not far from the Isle of Wight. He briefed his number two to act as 'weaver' guarding the rear of the formation. This role was normally given to a new pilot serving his apprenticeship in a squadron. The Germans nicknamed him *Katchmarek,* a word borrowed from Polish meaning 'old family retainer'. When he had dived with the Stukas like a hare keeping pace with the tortoises, Andres looked round for his *Katchmarek.* He was not there, but in his place was an English fighter. There was one burst of machine-gun fire and Werner Andres found himself floating in the Channel in his 'Mae West' while the noise of the battle went on overhead as he waited for the rescue vessel to come and pick him up.

Fink's men had been ordered not to return to base until they had sunk the whole convoy. They were pressing their attack home fiercely.

'The enemy fighters,' writes Squadron Leader Peel of 145 Squadron, 'which were painted silver, were half rolling, diving and zooming in climbing turns. I fired two five-second bursts at one and saw it dive into the sea. Then I followed another up in a zoom and got him as he stalled.'

The balance sheet of the engagement was as follows: on

the sea, four ships sunk and six damaged; in the air, thirty-one German aircraft destroyed against nineteen British aircraft lost. On both sides of the Channel exaggerated claims were made. The Royal Air Force announced that it had destroyed twenty-four enemy bombers and thirty-six fighters, while the Germans claimed to have shot down forty-nine British machines. But the actual number of aircraft destroyed, a total of fifty, made this the most bloody action since the start of the Battle of Britain. Winston Churchill sent his congratulations to the pilots.

'Ginger' Lacey of 501 Squadron watched Sergeants Howarth and Wilkinson landing together. They collided and both aircraft were destroyed, but neither pilot was hurt. The accident took place in poor visibility. In fact the weather over Kent and East Sussex was terrible.

At Le Coudray, Parfondeval, Neuville, La Boissière, Le Déluge there was a coming and going of grey staff cars. Patrols were active. Goering had returned. He was waiting in his special train for the commanders of all the Luftwaffe units engaged in the battle. Anti-aircraft batteries guarded the camouflaged train and near by there was the open tunnel, ready to receive it and its occupants.

The Reichsmarschall was in a bad mood. He complained that the full force of the Luftwaffe, as he had it down on paper, was not being deployed. More and more frequently he had to leave the meeting to receive attention from his doctor or nurse. When he returned and spread his enormous hands over his papers, the officers around him noticed six diamonds on his right hand and on his left an emerald an inch square. He cursed the weather which still wouldn't turn fine; he cursed the meteorological service, *Abteilung V*, everyone in sight. Finally he was brought back to good humour by accounts of the successes of his Luftwaffe. 'I alone was responsible,' he was to say at Nuremberg, 'for I was at once the Commander-in-Chief of the Luftwaffe and the Air Minister. I was responsible for the creation of the Luftwaffe, for its equipment and for its fighting spirit.'

Goering fixed on August 10th as the day for launching the aerial attack on Great Britain. It was christened *Adlertag*, 'Eagle Day'. Every day orders would be sent out from the *Oberkommando der Luftwaffe* to the commanders of the three *Luftflotten*, Kesselring, Sperrle and Stumpff, giving them their targets for the day.

The Germans now had 3,358 aircraft, of which 2,250 were fully serviceable, drawn up between Cherbourg and Norway; that is to say, 75 per cent of their total aerial strength.[1] Johannes Fink was called to Kesselring's headquarters where he learnt that the battle was now to begin in earnest. He wrote: 'Until now we have scarcely flown over the British Isles at all. Even in the most favourable conditions we have been prohibited from attacking ground targets, for Hitler has been hoping for a peaceful solution. This time, however, we met to discuss how best to attack the R.A.F. and, more particularly, its airfields.'

These airfields were carefully hidden away. René Mouchotte writes in his *Carnets*:

'Little Odiham is the most ravishing specimen of the English countryside. Therefore, so as not to conflict with such a scene by constructing a military camp, a kind of village has been built in which each house represents mess, canteen, shop, postal section, etc. The village has its streets, squares, lawns and tennis courts. The aerodrome is admirably camouflaged. Artificial hedges and thickets break it up and disguise it to such an extent that at 300 metres up it is hard to distinguish it from the rest of the country. I have seen English aerodromes on which the hangars, for better concealment, were entirely covered with turf.'

At Bentley Priory, Air Chief Marshal Sir Hugh Dowding realized that the hour had struck. H. H. Arnold wrote, 'On August 8th the commanders of the British fighter force set themselves to save the nation. By the end of September it was saved.'

In his bedroom on the second floor, Dowding had his favourite books at hand: *Raymond* by Sir Oliver Lodge and *The Eternal Question* by Allen Clarke. But they lay untouched; it was his 'boys' he was thinking of. Between June 10th and August 10th they had shot down 277 German

1. Group Captain Gerald Bowman has pointed out that up till this time 'Goering had used about 5 to 10 per cent of his Luftwaffe in attacks on our airfields near the coast, on shipping and docks, on general reconnaissance of our inland airfields . . .'

aircraft and lost 96 of their own machines, but how long, wondered Dowding, could they continue to fight against odds of five to one? Winston Churchill sometimes took Dowding to task for asking too many favours of his 'chicks'. It is true that he asked for them to have bullet-proof windscreens.

'I do not see why the gangsters of Chicago should be able to have bullet-proof glass when our pilots cannot.'

'Showers and thunderstorms with some clear intervals.' Such were the unpromising weather conditions on August 10th. Goering postponed *Adlertag*.

The following day, with clear skies, Fink's men were in the air by 7 a.m. and so were Dowding's. To have patrols airborne and at altitude was the key to the rapid intervention tactics that Fighter Command adopted. No. 74 Squadron, led by Squadron Leader Malan, the South African pilot who had already acquired a great reputation for his skill and authority, was operating that day from its forward airfield, Manston. It was soon brought into action in which one of its aircraft was shot down. The pilot managed to escape and was picked out of the sea.

Two hours later the Germans were going back again attacking Dover, especially its barrage balloons. 'It always puzzled me', wrote Alan Deere, 'why the Huns bothered to shoot down these balloons, unless it was to clear the way for dive-bombing attacks on the harbour by Junkers 87s. Even then it didn't make sense; these aircraft could pull out at a height which would enable them to clear the balloons, and yet bomb effectively.' In fact the Germans had a reason for their attack: it was a diversion. Their real objective was Portland, and in making repeated sorties against Dover they hoped, as Schmid had suggested in his circular, to draw the British patrols and leave the Portland area, some hundred and sixty miles to the west, clear. It was there that their principal effort was to be directed.

At 11.30 a.m., Yellow Section of 85 Squadron from Martlesham, led by Flight Lieutenant Peter Townsend, came upon a Dornier 17 over a line of ships, the convoy 'Booty'. The convoy was a few miles off Clacton. Townsend already had the appearance of a romantic hero – the slightly bored look, the studiously blasé smile. He looked older than he was: a man among boys. Now he was engaged in juggling with the

Dornier. He made his first attack from three hundred yards astern, but the bomber disappeared into a cloud. When it came out again Townsend got in two more bursts and set the right-hand engine on fire. The German went into cloud again. The sky was getting cloudier as the day went on and it was only at the last minute that Yellow Section caught sight of the twenty Messerschmitt 109s that had been escorting the bomber and were now rushing in to the attack. The fight started. One 109 was shot down and another damaged. No. 74 also took part in the engagement, its third of the morning.

No. 54 Squadron, too, was in battle for the third time. Alan Deere added another to his score and the squadron, although it lost two pilots and had three Spitfires damaged, brought its total of confirmed victories to twenty.

It was from the radar station at Ventnor in the Isle of Wight that the first warning came of a large enemy formation heading towards Weymouth. From Bentley Priory the call went out, and on the plotting table the discs marked with an 'F' for 'fighter' started to move towards Portland Bill. Seven squadrons – 145, 238, 152, 601, 213, 609 and 287 – took off to meet a hundred German bombers escorted by 109s and 110s. Some of them had a long way to go, but this was not always a disadvantage. Squadron leader Thompson remarked that the closer you were the less time had you to gain altitude before being attacked.

Over Portland the battle was joined. The fighters became engaged with their enemy counterparts as the Stukas and Heinkels pressed home their attack on the docks, petrol dumps, barracks and gasometers. At the same time the convoy 'Booty' was suffering further severe attacks. Two of its ships were sunk.

At 1356 hours 74 Squadron was once more called upon. It fought an inconclusive engagement near Margate.

In the day's fighting thirty-eight German aircraft had been shot down as against British losses of thirty-two. It had been a very close thing and a very costly day for 11 Group whose squadrons had suffered most of the losses.

That evening there was a surprise in store for the pilots of 54 Squadron as they flew up the Thames towards their home base, Hornchurch. The Windmill Girls had been invited to give a show at the camp. There could be nothing more relaxing for tired nerves than the sight of girls dressed in as little as possible – assuming, of course, that they were of the right age and appearance. That, 54 Squadron would soon know. George Gribble took it all very calmly and Deere decided that his thoughts must still be with the little W.A.A.F. he had left behind at Catterick. Colin Gray said to him,

'Well, you needn't go, all the more for us to choose from.'

George retorted:

'My dear Colin, when I cease to be interested in the spectacle of partly clad females, and from what I hear luscious ones, you can ask to have me transferred to bombers because then I really will be a "dead-beat".'

There was no doubt about it, the girls were pretty. They stayed on after the show. They did more, they promised to come again.

No. 54 Squadron had that day scored its twentieth victory in the air. Its victories on the ground were not officially recorded.

On August 12th, the opening of the grouse season, twenty-seven correspondents wrote to *The Times* remarking that the cuckoo song had never been so fine as it had that year. Evidently they had returned.

*

In his special train Goering was keeping a watch on the Azores High, darling of the meteorologists. If it spread, fine weather would settle on the Channel and the wretched early summer would give place to bright sunlight. The Reichsmarschall looked frequently at his wrist-watch with its blinding encrustation of emeralds, as he waited for the sun that was to shine on his victory.

A dispersal is a shelter built for an aircraft near the runway. Near this shelter would be placed a hut or a tent, also called a dispersal. Each squadron had its own dispersal even when three or four squadrons shared the same airfield, as was the case at Hornchurch where 54, 65, 74 and 41 Squadrons, all equipped with Spitfires, were based. It was in the dispersal that the most precious raw material of the whole battle, the pilots, were to be found. It was logical that if they were dispersed there was less risk.

The dispersal was a far cry from the squadron bar that the literature of the First World War had made famous. They had only one thing in common: pictures of undressed girls. In the first war these were drawings from *risqué* magazines; in the second they were pin-up photographs. Apart from these and a few other souvenirs of more pleasant hours – reminders perhaps of a ball or of some short-lived affair – the atmosphere was strictly warlike. There were models of enemy aircraft suspended on wires from the ceiling, parachutes, flying helmets, log-books, gloves. Three things were jointly sovereign in the dispersal: playing cards which were good friends, the tea-kettle which was neutral and the telephone which was the enemy.

On August 12th the 'boys' of 54 Squadron were in dispersal at their forward airfield, Manston, when the telephone rang. 'Its very note', wrote Alan Deere, 'was abnormal and the unexpectedness with which it rang had the immediate effect of producing an awful sick feeling in the pit of one's tummy. A pin could have been heard to drop as, with cards poised and eyes turned expectantly towards the orderly as he reached for the receiver, we strained to hear the message from the now faintly urgent voice which came over the wire.'

'Hornet squadron scramble.'

Cards went flying, the door was flung open and everyone rushed for his aeroplane. Money was left lying on the table. The survivors would settle up afterwards.

Once more they met the enemy over Dover, a place that was living up to its sinister nickname 'Hell's Corner'.

This time it was thirty Dorniers escorted by more than one hundred Messerschmitt 109s with their evil-looking shark noses. In brilliant sunshine their windscreens gleamed and it looked as though they had already opened fire. As the proverb said, 'Beware the Hun in the sun'.

Tally-ho!

By now the different squadrons had evolved their own subtle methods of combat. Modern air fighting required a standard form of tactics, but it did also permit variations at section level. There were a few rare pilots, the real killers, who were particularly skilful aerobatic experts. They would fight their battles solo, their eyes glued to the gunsight, gloved hands resting on the stick, ready to fire at the most fleeting chance that offered. Their judgment of deflection was instantaneous and they rarely missed. Other pilots, also very gifted, would play the part of a decoy. They would draw the enemy fighters after them, somehow being able to lure them on in a frantic tail chase to where other fighters would be waiting to pounce; yet all the time staying just out of harm's way.

Deere wrote: 'The fight was over in a matter of minutes and the sky was clear of aircraft.' The Messerschmitts had broken off the engagement and vanished. Deere had chased one to the outskirts of Deal when he heard the controller's voice. 'All Hornet aircraft to land at home base. I repeat, home base.'

Deere was puzzled. What could have got into them to send the squadron back to Hornchurch when there was so much work to do over Kent? Far more sensible to land at Manston to refuel and rearm. He was not puzzled for long. Manston lay just to his right as he set course for Hornchurch. Deere looked down and saw the smoke rising. The airfield from which he had taken off a few minutes before was now a lunar desert, pock-marked with bomb craters. The Germans had passed that way.

'Ginger' Lacey was also airborne that day, on patrol with 501 Squadron between the squadron's new base, Gravesend, and Hawkinge. He heard the voice of the controller at Biggin Hill. 'Vector zero eight zero. Thirty Bandits approaching the Thames estuary.'

With the simple code word 'Buster', the squadron commander called for full power and the Hurricanes rushed towards the enemy. It was a strange feeling, rather wonderful, to have the sky to yourself for a little while, knowing all the time that a few minutes on the course you were steering would see you at grips with the enemy, going hammer and tongs. Everything was very calm and quiet. Occasionally a leader's voice would be heard shouting at a pilot who had dropped out of position. Then things started to happen fast.

'Bastards at three o'clock!' And there were the Stukas diving on a destroyer as it zigzagged about trying to avoid their tactics. There also, as always, were the Messerschmitts up above. The British pilots ignored them. They knew that if they were quick, they could have a few brief moments alone with the Stukas before the Messerschmitts could join in and the demented dance began. Lacey settled himself comfortably in his cockpit, his right boot tucked well into the toe strap of his rudder pedal whilst his left foot tapped its usual nervous rhythm on the cockpit flooring. He pressed his gun button, aiming at a Stuka from above and to the left. A kick on the rudder and he skidded sharply across to the right. A second burst, of three seconds this time, and the Stuka dived into the sea in a great column of water and spray. Lacey was already looking for his next target. No. 65 Squadron managed somehow or other to land at Manston where they were soon joined by 54 Squadron, returning from their sixth patrol of the day. There they found the station personnel and the boys of 600 Squadron dazed. It was rumoured that Hawkinge and Lympne had both been badly hit. At Hawkinge two hangars were reported destroyed as well as workshops and stores damaged, and four aircraft knocked out in addition to the losses in dead and wounded. The aerodrome at Lympne was unfit for use. At Manston, 65 Squadron's Spitfires had taken off as the German bombs were falling round them. A haze of fine chalk dust was hanging in suspension over the field and settling out in a film over everything: the shattered buildings, the aircraft and the men. Ghostlike animated plaster statues walked about and exchanged words, their mouths full of a whitish slime. Manston had found its symbol – chalk.

Portsmouth, too, was the target of a heavy attack by fifteen Stukas escorted by the 53rd Messerschmitt Squadron based on Guernsey and commanded by Leutnant Erich Bodendiek. He wrote: 'We were able to watch a fine firework display. As there was no reason for us to dive with the Stukas we amused ourselves with the balloons. Over the coast we met the fighters as usual. It's such a regular thing to find them right on our route that we have begun to wonder if there isn't a direct line between Guernsey and England, and somebody who telephones to warn them every time we take off.'

Unquestionably August 12th was a gala performance. Galland came out with the 3rd wing of the 26th Fighter Group. He fired at a Hurricane and then followed it like a winged pheasant until it ditched on its belly not far from Margate.

The noise of aircraft was everywhere. It filled the sky. The R.A.F. flew 758 sorties and the Luftwaffe 440; both figures were the highest since the start of the battle. Two convoys were harassed in the Thames estuary and several villages were bombed.

*

But that was not all. The same day, the Germans set themselves a new target. Fink had grown tired of staring through his binoculars at those radio masts. They stood there like sentries on the battlements watching his every move. He ordered his fighters to destroy them. The task was entrusted to Captain Walter Rubensdorffer commanding No. 210 experimental unit, the only one of its kind in the Luftwaffe. He sent Oberleutnant Otto Hintze to attack the station at Dover with Messerschmitt 109s, and himself led twelve Messerschmitt 110s in an attack a little farther to the west. Slightly before 11 o'clock Rubensdorffer was in sight of Eastbourne and could clearly distinguish the masts of the radar station at Pevensey. Oberleutnant Martin Lutz attacked it with five-hundred kilogramme bombs and the station went off the air.

Five minutes later Oberleutnant Rössinger launched his attack on the station at Rye, where his two-hundred-and-fifty and five-hundred kilogramme bombs did considerable damage. Oberleutnant Hintze was meanwhile trying to destroy the masts at Dover. Two were hit, but he couldn't knock the cursed things down. In all the stations the W.A.A.F.s went on with their work. They were to be seen moving the counters towards the very stations in which they were working. They left off only when the first bombs had fallen. Of the six stations attacked, only one was knocked out: that at Ventnor in the Isle of Wight. The station at Rye was severely damaged but was working again three hours after the raid. During the afternoon all the other stations came back into operation.

Reading the pilots' reports on the evening of August 12th, General Wolfgang Martini could conclude that his *bête noire*, the enemy radar system (actually the Germans did not yet use the term 'radar'; they referred to the system as *Funkmess*),[1] had been destroyed. This error was to prove expensive as the battle proceeded. With aerodromes too, the Luftwaffe general staff tended to confuse attack with destruction. A stroke of a chinagraph pencil completed the destruction of an airfield which the pilots reported they had devastated. Draw-

1. Translator's note: Neither did the British. The system was known as R.D.F. = Radio Direction Finding. In 1941 it was first referred to publicly as 'radiolocation'. The American term 'radar' was adopted in 1943.

ing up an account of the operations from August 12th to 17th Beppo Schmid asserted that of forty-four airfields attacked, eleven had been definitely destroyed. Of these, six were not Fighter Command airfields. In reality Manston alone was forced to suspend operations for any length of time.

On the evening of August 12th the German radio announced that seventy-one British aircraft had been shot down including 'the whole of No. 65 Squadron from Manston'. This soon became part of the German fighter pilots' folklore. Whenever they met 65 Squadron again they would report with tongue in cheek that they had once more encountered the famous Manston squadron and once more completely destroyed it. The true figures were much lower. The R.A.F. had shot down thirty-two aircraft and had lost twenty-two.

But from the scattered fighting of August 12th several significant facts emerged. The first was the destruction of a Heinkel 59 seaplane, the St. Bernard dog of the Channel. Escorted by Messerschmitt 109s, this aircraft, which carried no Luftwaffe markings but only a simple civil registration, was engaged in rescuing German pilots who had been shot down and were floating in the sea. No. 604 Squadron found it on the water near the French coast and had no compunction about destroying it. In mid-July Winston Churchill had ordered that these aircraft should be destroyed on the grounds that the pilots they picked up would otherwise be available to renew their bombing attacks on the civil population. For the same reason, Dowding, however careful he was to husband the lives of his 'boys', did not become enraged when he learnt that some of them had been fired on by German fighters while they were floating helplessly beneath their parachutes. They could, after all, be in battle the same afternoon shooting down Germans. Dowding pointed out at the same time that some German pilots had not shot at their unfortunate opponents but had rather flown past them with a wave of encouragement.

August 12th was a milestone. The battle now took on a new ferocity. 'Nobby' Clark, flying a Skua, an aircraft used by the British to spot their pilots shot down in the sea, was attacked by a Messerschmitt and tried to dive away vertically: 'I felt a sudden emptiness in my stomach as the never-to-be forgotten squat squareness of a white-nosed 109 slid into view. He was depressing his nose, trying to lay-off deflection, but his estimate of my speed was, as always happened, too fast. With blazing guns he flashed past ...'

From now on no quarter would be asked or given.

The second fact of significance concerned the cruel misfortune that befell Geoffrey Page. His squadron, No. 56 at Rochford, had just landed after a sortie when it was again ordered into the air to reinforce the Manston area. Page became involved in a villainous-looking yellow-painted Me 109.

'Everything blew up,' said Page. 'I was in a cone of fire ... I saw the "electric light bulbs" going by, I went on firing at a Dornier, then I was hit by the cross-fire. I simply went pummmmmmpfff ... I kicked the stick as she was rolling over and just went out.'

Page had pushed up his goggles to see more clearly and had also taken off his gloves to get a better feel of the controls. 'I was burned on hands and face, my trousers were completely blown off ...' Having abandoned his aircraft at 15,000 feet he made a free fall of over 1,000 feet, unable to pull the handle of his ripcord because of the pain in his hands. 'I was able to pull the ripcord. It was cold then; I had a long fall perhaps ten or fifteen minutes, before I would hit the sea.'

During this terrible fifteen minutes, Page had been sickened by the persistent smell of burnt meat. Now in the water, as he freed himself from his parachute harness, he noticed strips of flesh and skin floating around and slowly drifting away from him. Only then did he realize that the source of the horrible smell was himself.

He was picked up by a motor boat and taken to Margate Hospital. There, as they undressed him, he started to scream. His face, blackened with smoke, was raw; so were his hands and his back. A thick layer of tannic acid was applied to his wounds. Its purpose was to coagulate the blood that was oozing from the burns and also to reduce the frightful pain which could otherwise cause death from shock. It was a terribly disfigured pilot encased in a hard crust of tannic acid who was transported to the Royal Masonic Hospital in London. There he was given morphine.

Much later he awoke to find two people leaning over him, a nurse and her rather pretty assistant. They were taking off his bandages. As Page noticed the horror and sympathy in their eyes he found his own filling with tears. At last he found enough courage to look at what they were doing. From the shoulder to the wrist his arms were a mass of pus. His black claw-like hands might have been pieces of charred coral. The nurse smiled gently:

'It's the tannic acid that is black; it's not your skin.'

She handed him a mirror but he refused it. It was more than he could do to look at his own face. Several days passed before Page, who had been pressing the area round his eyes to clear them of pus and water, saw himself in the glass.

A monster.

Swollen to three times its normal size and as black as coal, his face bore no resemblance to any human features whatsoever.

Page recalled that at this moment – he will never forget it – he remembered that at the instant when they were about to attack the enemy he had looked across at his friend Maxwell and put his thumb to his nose.

Then he passed out.

7: The Thirteenth of August

Though August 12th had seen hundreds of aircraft fighting innumerable battles, it had been for most people in England just another day. The targets had been for the most part military installations and nothing had happened to change the life of ordinary people. The increased tax on spirits, beer and tobacco were more in people's minds than the damaged radar masts at Ventnor. In Parliament, certain members expressed their amazement that Noël Coward and Gracie Fields had been allowed to go to America. It was said in reply that their presence on the other side of the Atlantic would help the negotiations being held with President Roosevelt, but the members of the Opposition did not seem completely convinced. The B.B.C., hoping to paint a dramatic picture of England at war, transmitted a live commentary of a cricket match in its American and Canadian service. At the end of the match the commentator mentioned that the players had once more exchanged their bats for gas masks and their colourful club caps for steel helmets. But in this, their example was not followed by the public at large. In London there were queues at the theatre where Robert Donat was appearing in *The Devil's Disciple*. The weather was good but unsettled. There were a few patches of drizzle.

Over Germany, at dawn on August 13th, the sky was clear and its soft light gave promise of a glorious day. At Luftwaffe headquarters there was a feeling of eager expectation. By the order of Reichsmarschall Goering, the start of *Adlertag* had been fixed for 7.30 a.m. on August 13th. However, the weather reports from the Channel stations were giving cloudy conditions and morning mist. What was to be done? The problem was referred to Goering who, suppressing his fury, postponed all operations until the afternoon. At all events a start would still be made on the intended day and the chances of striking a spectacular blow would be greater when the morning mists had cleared.

When the order to postpone the attack reached Cap Blanc Nez, Johannes Fink was not there to receive it. He was airborne in a Dornier 17, one of sixty bombers that had formed up over Amiens at six o'clock to rendezvous with the Messerschmitt 110s of Joachim Huth. They were to launch a devastating attack against Eastchurch and Sheerness. Fink stared in amazement out of his cockpit window at the antics of the fighters. They were cavorting round the bombers like circus horses in their bright multi-coloured plumage, diving and rolling then climbing steeply back up again. The *Kanalkampfführer* did not waste time wondering what this extraordinary demonstration meant. No doubt it was simply the Messerschmitt pilots' way of greeting the dawn of *Adlertag*. The Dorniers set course for the Channel and disappeared into the clouds.

In the other camp the radar was again at work and Bentley Priory was calling up the squadrons. Fighter Command knew that three enemy formations were approaching and also approximately where they were making for. In the east there was Fink's formation of sixty from the *Luftflotte II* which had now split into two. Farther west there were two more formations which must have come from *Luftflotte III*. One formation of about one hundred aircraft had been picked up at Dieppe and another of about forty, to the north of Cherbourg. In addition there were several small groups scattered around the area of the Channel Islands. Fighter Command's response was immediate. In the east two squadrons of 11 Group from Croydon and Hornchurch were sent to patrol over the damaged airfields at Manston and Hawkinge and a section from Northolt took up its station over Canterbury. A squadron from North Weald was protecting a convoy at the mouth of the Thames and 11 Group had also taken the precaution of calling for a squadron from Tangmere and three sections from Kenley to stand guard over the estuary. Fink would find a warm reception waiting. Farther to the west three sections from Tangmere patrolled on a line between Arundel and Petworth. No. 10 Group summoned a squadron from Middle Wallop, an airfield it had just taken over from No. 11 Group, and stationed it nearer the coast at Warmwell. To this squadron was added a subsidiary formation brought up from Exeter. Altogether the British, who had to defend Kent and had a third of their forces committed to the Thames estuary, could muster some seventy fighters against two hundred German aircraft. A little later in the day four squadrons were brought in as reinforcements to meet a wave of simultaneous Luftwaffe attacks from Portland to Eastchurch; that is to say, practically the whole of the south of England except for the West Country.

But we must turn our attention to the bombers of *Luftflotte II*. Having formed up over Amiens and, with their Commodore Fink, crossed the Channel, they had been picked up by the Observer Corps. This organization had some 1,500 observation posts strung out behind the coast and situated on hilltops or in any position which afforded a good field of view. Two men were all that was required; one equipped with a tripod-mounted optical device that permitted him to estimate the height, speed and position of any enemy aircraft entering his area of observation, and the other with a telephone to maintain contact with the sector operations room. These men were the descendants of those who in earlier days had given warning of the arrival of the Danes.

The two German formations, Wing 2 under Oberleutnant Weitkus and Wing 3 commanded by Major Fuchs, were flying at 1,500 feet over the English countryside. Now and again they would see something through the mist; some fields or a cottage, a railway station, a crossroads or a country lane with a solitary cyclist. To their right lay the estuary with its marshes and islands, little flat villages and boats; an intimate union of land and water – it might have been Japan. Industry had come to the estuary, bringing its cranes and factories and smoke. On that pale August morning there was only a little light filtering through.

Fink was over Eastchurch, happy in the thought that if his luck held, he would be receiving Goering's congratulations that very night. As yet he was not troubled by the fact that he had not seen his escort again since their extraordinary ballet over Amiens. He was marvelling at his good fortune, for no British fighters had made their appearance. The Dorniers were now droning their way right over the airfield at Eastchurch. They released their bombs on the runways, hangars and store buildings. Fifty bomb craters and five Blenheims destroyed on the ground. Eastchurch did not belong to Fighter Command, but nevertheless it was getting the full treatment.

Just as the Germans were setting course for home the Spitfires and Hurricanes appeared. Usually they brought with them the Messerschmitts, but today the 109s and 110s were nowhere to be seen. Fink was furiously searching the sky, but he didn't have time to reflect upon his emotions, the mêlée had begun. The fighters were full of confidence. This was a glorious opportunity, the bombers were handed to them on a plate. If only the clouds had not been there. But there they were, lying thick and heavy and low over the Thames. It was these clouds, although Fink didn't know it, that had caused the operations to be postponed till the afternoon. Now they were to be his salvation. Even so the Germans lost four of their best crews.

As soon as he set foot on French soil, Fink rushed to the telephone. The smell of gunfire was still in his nostrils; he had seen the columns of smoke rising under his wings. He knew too that his men had died stupidly from simple lack of fighter cover. As soon as he got through to the fighter commander he started cursing at the top of his voice. What did the stupid bloody fighters think they were doing to disappear when the fight started. They were never there when they were needed. All they were good for was doing aerobatics where there wasn't an enemy aeroplane in sight. Oh yes! he'd seen them clowning about over Amiens, but this time they had gone too far! This time there was going to be trouble. He would report the matter directly to Goering so that he would know who it was who had sabotaged his *Adlertag*.

When Fink had calmed down a little, the man at the other end of the line gave him the news that *Adlertag* had been postponed.

'What! What rubbish are you making up? I received the message "AA".'

With great difficulty he was made to realize that 'AA' – *Angriff ausführen* – had been followed by a second message, 'AB', postponing the operation. Fink was stupefied.

'Why wasn't I told?'

Here it was a question of bad luck. Kesselring had given the order that all formations that were already in the air should be informed, but Fink's radio was unserviceable, and although Weitkus's was working, his radio operator was air-sick and in no state to copy the message. Hence he had continued en route to England.

'And what about the Messerschmitts?'

Precisely. They had received the message and their antics

over Amiens had been intended to warn the Dorniers. They had hoped that by constantly diving and climbing around the bombers the latter might deduce that 'something was up'. Kesslring himself came on the line: 'Wait there, I'm coming down.'

It was thus that Fink learnt that it had fallen to him, all by himself, to open proceedings on the so-long-awaited *Adlertag*. It was too much. He sat down and started to pull off his flying suit. *Kanalkampfführer!* Sewer-rat! Not a bad name for the job either.

Goering had made his decision – two o'clock.

It seemed as though even the weather was against him; it became progressively worse. But something had to be done, so he took the plunge.

The first aircraft to take off were twenty-three Messerschmitt 110s under Hauptmann Liensberger. They left from a field near Caen with permission to seek their targets anywhere they chose. They set course for Portland with high hopes of a surprise attack. The previous day the Ventnor radar station had been destroyed and they expected to reach the English coast undetected. But it was not to be. New aerials were in use and the trace duly appeared on the little green screen. Things started moving.

At Bentley Priory, Dowding was ready. His supicions had been aroused since August 8th and the events of the 12th had convinced him: the fight was now on in earnest. He was conscious that he had in reserve only 289 Spitfires and Hurricanes. Realizing the value of every single pilot, he had given an order that only bombers were to be attacked. In no circumstances was direct combat or dogfighting to be sought with the Messerschmitts. But though the radar stations could give an approximate idea of the size of a formation and could determine its direction, they could not detect what type of aircraft it consisted of. Dowding therefore had to decide what to do, knowing only the size of the enemy formation and where the battle would take place. He had no idea what opponents his pilots would find when they arrived. He scrambled three squadrons from Exeter, Warmwell and Tangmere and ordered them to proceed to Portland and St Alban's Head. If he had known that he was only up against Liensberger's 110s he would have kept his dogs on the leash.

Liensberger had just reached the coast when he heard one of his pilots call:

'Spitfires low.'

This was like an electric shock for the 110 pilots. They knew that their aircraft were less manoeuvrable than the Spitfires. Their only chance lay in their fire-power. Against the eight wing-mounted machine-guns of the British aircraft they could bring to bear four machine-guns and two 20-mm. Oerlikon cannon. On Liensberger's orders the 110s formed a defensive circle to present the Spitfires with the most difficult possible target. The leading aircraft went into a turn and one by one all the others followed him, forming a *carrousel* like a string of horses in a circus ring. In this way they ensured that they could not be attacked from the rear, their most vulnerable point. The German crews had a saying: 'The dogs eat the last man.'

Below, the Spitfires had understood what was going on. They climbed, hanging on their propellers, to catch the last Messerschmitt before the circle could be completed, but the German saw the danger and broke to the right. A burst of machine-gun fire passed to his left as the dog's teeth snapped shut on empty air.

The dance began.

From above the Spitfires dived into the ring like sea birds diving for fish. Their eights guns fired as one. An observer on the ground said: 'I could hear only a faint sound – the sort of sound you make if you run a stick along a line of railings.' Two of the fighter-bombers were shot down, but the circle was tightened to fill their places. The Spitfires were there again pressing home the attack. The German pilots, flying all the time in a level turn, would see from time to time a flash of roundels darting through their sights and they would fire. Some of the Englishmen left a plume of black smoke behind them and dived through the clouds towards the fields of Dorset. If their aeroplanes were still controllable they would force-land; if not, they would bale out. The Germans, on the other hand, were fighting over enemy soil with a hundred miles of sea between them and their base. They lost five aircraft and discovered, when they landed, that several others were riddled with bullets.

It had been a day of fierce fighting everywhere. The airfields of Hampshire and Kent, the Thames estuary – all had come in for their share of the attacks. Manston, where now only 600 (City of London) Squadron, equipped with Blenheims, was permanently stationed, had again been severely hit. Alan Deere found the airfield in a 'sorry state'. The telephone system was damaged, the hangars a shambles and the administrative buildings extensively damaged – 'Not that that mattered a great deal,' he added.

The 'boys' of 600 Squadron crawled out of the dust, white to the eyebrows. They had been attacked continuously and they were thirsty. One of their pilots said: 'When day dawns, like rabbits we return to our burrows to emerge again only when night brings peace and quiet.' They found some beer to celebrate the Messerschmitt 110 that they had shot down on the airfield with a Vickers gun mounted on top of their dug-out and another that the station defence Bofors had accounted for. The beer glasses were thick with chalk powder. Manston-in-the-Dust!

The final score for *Adlertag* was as follows. On the German side, 1,485 sorties for the loss of forty aircraft, and on the British, 700 sorties for thirteen aircraft lost, of whose pilots six were saved. The Germans could also claim to have wiped out some airfields that did not belong to Fighter Command and to have inflicted damage at Southampton and Castle Bromwich.

Night came on, warm and clear. In a few places the mist gathered as the island dozed off to sleep. It was said that that night Big Ben struck thirteen times at midnight.

The same night the Germans dropped a large quantity of military equipment over the Midlands and over the lowlands of Scotland. They released parachutes, radio transmitters, a small amount of very powerful explosives, maps, photographs and lists of highly placed public figures. It all made good hunting for British Intelligence. Later the Germans were to admit that this was a ruse to make people believe that a parachute landing had been made, but for the moment a British traitor, an announcer for the New British Broadcasting Station, which was an organization created by the Germans, read the following dire warning:

'We address this warning to our British compatriots. Take care. During the night German parachutists wearing civilian clothes or British uniforms have been dropped in the vicinity of Birmingham, Manchester and Glasgow. They carry capsules with which to produce fog and so avoid capture. Some of them are equipped with an electro-magnetic death ray.'

On August 14th, the Luftwaffe was exhausted from the two previous days' work and only flew 489 sorties against coastal towns and airfields. Over the Channel the clouds continued to pile up. The commanders of the three *Luftflotten* had all left their headquarters for an unknown destination.

To the north of Berlin lie a hundred thousand acres of moorland, forest and heath. Marshes and lakes with their reed fringes are scattered over the land like the fragments of a gigantic shattered mirror. Here roam the elk and bison brought from the cold lands to the north. Here too the deer, horses and wild boar; and on the lakes, swans. Paths of moss lead the wanderer through the cathedral groves of oak, beech and pine. This is Schorfheide, the domain of Reichsmarschall Hermann Goering, Grand Venerer of the Reich and Grand Master of Lakes and Forests. Here is Karinhall, the home of Siegfried.

Everything that is here, he conceived and designed, right down to the door knobs. A deep Germanic spirit pervades the place. The colossal and the romantic here clasp each other in a suffocating embrace; the granite melts under the flowers and thatch softens the Gothic stonework. The central façade bears the Reichsmarschall's coat of arms, a mailed fist holding a mace. All the windows open on to lakes or woodland and in the courtyard there are pools with water-lilies and bronze statues of wild boar. As you cross the threshold you find yourself in a hunting lodge such as Cecil B. de Mille might have imagined it, long rooms with beams, huge vaulted ceilings like the bottoms of great deep-water ships, vast open fireplaces. Underfoot are the skins of wild animals and on the walls trophies of the chase and paintings by the masters. The great hall is divided into two: the golden room and the silver. It is here that are kept the Reichsmarschall's fabulous 'presents'. But the secret of Karinhall lies elsewhere: outside in the park. There, beyond the place where two forest paths cross, beside the lake under a great tree, is the granite mausoleum where Karin sleeps. Goering has had the body of his first wife brought back from Sweden. On the coffin a simple wreath of white roses and the message, 'To my one and only Karin'. The coffin was taken down into the crypt where six candles were burning. Here Goering and Hitler stood alone, side by side, 'to pay homage to the woman who had suffered so much to help them on the road to power and glory.'

Karinhall was the repository of all that Siegfried held dear: the Germanic spirit, the love of nature and animals ('He who makes an animal suffer wounds the soul of Germany'), his worship of the dead goddess. At Karinhall he could feel secure. His fortune made him safe and the forest was his castle wall. The presence of Karin supplied the element of tenderness. He would wear a shirt of white silk, with flounces; a leather waistcoat and Tyrolean shorts. During his hours of sylvan melancholy he would read or fondle the dogs or, with his manicured fingers, play with diamonds in a crystal cup. And then, if the thought should come to him that after his contemplation of the past and his services to the cult of beauty, the true Knight should also make sacrifice before the altar of war, he had only to walk down a few steps to where he could shoot at moving targets until he was drunk with the fumes of powder. There, too, if his fancy should so incline him, he could plunge his elephantine body into an underground swimming pool. But it was not only the hero who found Karinhall so agreeable; it was a fine place for the invalid too. Here, there was nothing to prevent him following Doctor Kahle's cure. Here he could go to ground and take the cup that would plunge him for twenty-four hours in the most profound hypnotic sleep. The faithful Kropp was always there at his bedside, cloth in hand to wipe the sweat from his brow. For Siegfried would sweat. Sometimes he would sweat for two days as the morphine flowed from his hero's pores.

Goering had summoned Generalfeldmarschall Kesselring and Sperrle, the commanders of *Luftflotten II* and *III* respectively, to a meeting at Karinhall on August 15th. Both men were hardened and determined soldiers. Sperrle, bull-necked, with strong features and a monocle screwed into his eye, marched down the drive between the lawns scattered with Greco-Roman statuary, reminders of antiquity. Beside him Kesselring, a man who knew Goering well. He knew that 'when he sees that it is necessary, Goering can work with tremendous concentration and perseverance.' The man who was waiting to meet them was not the pearl-bedecked potentate, but the steel-grey commander of the Luftwaffe. Goering was under no illusion; he knew that the only thing that could save Siegfried was victory in the air.

The first thing to be recognized was that *Adlertag* had not been the great success that had been hoped. There were many factors to account for this. The weather had upset the plans, and then there had been the technical incidents of the morning that had delivered Commodore Fink and the bomber leader Paul Weitkus into the hands of the British fighters without their own fighter escort. By luck they had both returned and the day had finished with a net advantage to the Germans. At least that was the conclusion if General Halder's report was to be believed. 'The ratio of losses is three to one in favour of the Germans if account is taken of all types of aircraft. If we consider only fighter aircraft then the ratio becomes five to one.'

But the problem that seemed to preoccupy the Reichsmarschall was the protection of the Stukas. By now it was clear that Dowding had ordered his fighters to attack only the German bombers and more precisely to concentrate on the Junkers 87 Stukas. Goering judged that it would be necessary, from now on, to assign three formations of fighters to each formation of Stukas. The first would arrive at the target ahead of the bombers and engage the Spitfires and Hurricanes while the Ju 87s waited behind cloud cover. The second would fly in the Stuka formation and dive with it. The third would fly as top cover ready to intervene whenever the situation seemed most dangerous.

Kesselring and Sperrle sat and listened while their staff officers took notes. Goering repeated once more that his essential objective was the destruction of the Royal Air Force.

'Our operations must be exclusively directed against the enemy air forces and his aircraft factories.'

Serious losses among officers of the bomber crews had been reported to Goering and he signed an order to the effect that there should be only one officer in each crew. He also decided that Wing 100, a shock formation, should be thrown into the battle and once more expressed his displeasure at the poor results achieved by *Luftflotten III* on the previous day.

The discussion passed to the question of the *Funkmess*, the radar stations. Expert opinion was that these were extremely difficult to attack. The vertical masts made very poor targets; if the attack was made from overhead they were very hard to see, while if dive bombers were used, there was always the risk of their striking the mast with a wing. Furthermore, even if a bomb exploded close to the masts its blast passed through their metal trellis structure without causing serious damage. Finally was it worth asking the pilots to run such risks when on the day after the big attack of August 12th, General Martini's units had reported that the radar emissions were once more being detected.

Goering shook his head:

'It is doubtful whether there is any point in continuing the attacks on radar sites, in view of the fact that not one of those attacked has so far been put out of operation.'

It was hot. Goering had pressed the button that opened the windows by remote control. Now the scent of the forest was floating in. Siegfried was with his valiant men. He gave a sign and rose. These were his men, fresh from the field of battle, ribbons and Iron Crosses on their tunics. They walked with Goering past the canvases of Cranach without giving them a glance as they spoke to the Reichsmarschall of how they would wipe out the enemy. Sperrle's monocle gleamed and his boots pressed the furs underfoot. Goering was in his element. This was war as it should be fought.

'And the 27th?' he asked.

They gave him all the news of Galland and the Richthofen Squadron, his own command of the Great War, and as he listened it seemed easier to walk; his legs seemed to bear the great weight of his body better.

The boots ascended the stairway. Goering pushed open a door and the marshals stood staring in amazement. In an attic some eighty feet long, there was the most magnificent electric train set complete with points, signals, stations, locomotive repair works, tunnels and bridges. The straight alone was at least sixty feet in length. Goering turned round with a smile of pride and then walked over to a great red armchair and lowered himself into it with difficulty. There, under the fascinated gaze of his field-marshals, Goering's hands reached for the control panel that was placed beside his chair and in an admiring silence the Reichsmarschall began to play trains.

*

While the senior officers of the Luftwaffe were assembled at Karinhall with their Commander-in-Chief, the battle was raging over the Channel and the British Isles. Churchill was following every move with a passionate sense of involvement: he had said in May 1940, 'I felt as if I were walking with destiny, and that all my past life had been but a preparation for this hour and for this trial.'

At the headquarters of each of the three *Luftflotten* the maps of Great Britain had been brought out and targets were being selected. For the first time Stumpff's *Luftflotte V* was to take part in the battle. On every airfield from Cherbourg to Norway there was intense activity. Never before had there been such a deployment of forces as now, for the Luftwaffe had decided to launch a massive attack and knock the guts out of the Royal Air Force once and for all. Everywhere there were fighters being pushed out of the hangars, their yellow, orange and red noses shining in the sunlight. The heavy twin-engined bombers were being fuelled and bombed-up and checked for flight. The Messerschmitts, whose radius of action was short, were based at the coastal airfields at Guernsey, Caen, Le Havre, Dieppe, Abbeville, Wissant, Saint-Omer, Calais, and at airfields near Rotterdam and in the south of Norway. The Stukas were deployed immediately behind the fighters at Flers, Falaise and in the Pas de Calais. Farther inland at Tours, Orléans-Bricy, Chartres, Évreux, Villacoublay, Montdidier, Laon, Cambrai, Lille, Brussels, Amsterdam and to the north at Stavanger, there were the Junkers, Heinkels and Dorniers. Secure in the knowledge supplied by *Abteilung V* that the R.A.F. had only three hundred fighters left, the Luftwaffe prepared to fight.

Across the Channel, where in reality there were nearly six hundred fighters fully serviceable, the country had been divided into four great defensive zones all under the responsibility of Fighter Command. The whole of that part of England south and east of a line drawn from the Isle of Wight to Oxford, then north-east passing to the south of Cambridge and meeting the sea north of Norwich, was entrusted to 11 Group commanded by Keith Park and reduced now to twenty-one squadrons. To the west of the line from the Isle of Wight to Oxford and south of the line Oxford, Stratford-on-Avon, Worcester, Cardiff, the territory was the responsibility of 10 Group with nine squadrons under Quintin Brand. The extensive area of the United Kingdom lying to the north was divided into two areas. In the north, there was 13 Group under R. E. Saul, who still had under his command his original number of squadrons – thirteen. South of the line Lancaster-Scarborough was Leigh-Mallory's territory. From Watnall he commanded the fourteen squadrons of 12 Group. The blows were to fall everywhere at the same time.

At Hornchurch the pilots of 54 Squadron were woken up at four o'clock. It was a fine morning and the sky, in which the stars were still faintly visible, was clear. Half an hour later, having breakfasted and checked over their aircraft, they took off for Manston. There they refuelled and then settled down in their cockpits, half dozing, to wait for the first alert.

Now was the hour for doubts and hope and anxiety. Objects looked pale and fragile in the dawn. 'I climbed into the cockpit of my plane,' wrote Richard Hillary of 603 Squadron, 'and felt an empty sensation of suspense in the pit of my stomach. For one second time seemed to stand still and I stared blankly in front of me. I knew that that morning I was to kill for the first time.'

At seven o'clock came the order 'Scramble'. Alan Deere noted: 'I took off with two other Spitfires to intercept what was thought to be a weather reconnaissance flight at high altitude over the Channel.' The patrol found nothing, but no doubt Fink's pilots had been out to 'dip their toes in the water'. The preparations for the offensive were under way and it was going to require good weather.

At ten o'clock there was a new alert. This time 54 Squadron encountered Messerschmitts heading for Dover. A dogfight ensued and the British lost one pilot and two aircraft. At eleven o'clock a wave of one hundred aircraft consisting of forty Stukas heavily escorted by fighters, attacked the aerodromes of Hawkinge, Lympne and Manston. There was a long and furious mêlée in which 54 Squadron lost three aircraft but only one pilot, and the Germans had two bombers shot down. But on the ground the damage was severe. At Lympne the water and electricity was cut off and several buildings, including the sick quarters, were damaged. The airfield was out of action for two days. Hawkinge fared better, but Manston was once more devastated.

'On our return,' Alan Deere reported, 'instead of an airfield, we found a mass of bomb craters and burning hangars. The controller told us to land as best we could on the undamaged areas of grass. We refuelled as quickly as we could and took off again to meet the Stukas that were attacking Lympne.' No. 501 Squadron came up to help.

Galland, who was leading Wing III, had watched the battle but had not taken part in it. But now on the return journey, as soon as he knew that the Stukas were out of reach of the British fighters, he gathered his own formation together in mid-Channel and determined to take the measure of the Spitfires. The Spitfires he encountered must have been those of 54 Squadron. Galland shot one down and just missed a second who managed to turn tighter than he.

So far it had been Park's men who had been busy keeping the enemy at bay. Now it was to be the turn of Saul and his 13 group. Stumpff made the first move, slipping out from the fjords of Norway. Shortly after midday the radar picked up 'an enemy formation of twenty plus, some distance to the east of the Firth of Forth'. No. 72 Squadron at Acklington was the first to be scrambled and it was ordered to climb over the sea to 25,000 feet over the Farne Islands. Whilst 72 Squadron was climbing, Saul received more information. He now knew that there were three formations totalling more than thirty aircraft heading for the Northumberland coast. He called up the Hurricanes of 65 Squadron from Drem to patrol the Tyne valley and then immediately reinforced them with 14 and 79 Squadrons (the latter officially on leave) and the Hurricanes of 607 Squadron.

The commander of 72 Squadron, A. R. Collins, an expert photographer and brilliant squash player, had not flown Spitfires before and, taking part with considerable courage in a recent sortie, had nearly lost his life. Flight Lieutenant Ted Graham was now acting in command as his replacement. Graham had already crossed swords with *Kampfgruppe* 26 which had come out during December 1939 under the command of Klein, to seek combat over the Firth of Forth. Graham now began to give his orders, stuttering slightly as he always did. Deacon Elliott, who this time had his oxygen tube connected, heard Graham's voice and then suddenly, over the sea, he saw a sight that left him dazed. 'There were at least 200 enemy aircraft at about forty miles out to sea, made up of every type we knew. Led by He III and Ju 88 bombers with a long-range escort of Me 110s well to the rear. None of us had ever seen so many aircraft in the sky at one time.' Confronted by such an immense force, Graham, who had only twelve Spitfires, hesitated. He had just decided to order an attack on the right of the formation when the Germans were upon him. 'There was a gap between the lines of bombers and the Me 110s coming up in the rear,' explained Elliott, 'so in there we went. I do not think they saw us to begin with. When they did the number of bombs rapidly jettisoned was fantastic. You could see them falling away from the aircraft, and dropping into the sea, literally by the hundreds.'

In fact the German force was made up of one hundred aircraft: sixty-five Heinkel 111s from the 1st and 3rd Squadrons of *Kampfgruppe* 26 and thirty-five Messerschmitt 110s from *Zerstörergeschwader* 76.[1] When they found themselves being harassed by the Spitfires they became a little disorientated; especially when Saul's reinforcements arrived from Newcastle and joined in the fun.

'It really was a terrific scrap,' recalls Elliott. 'I saw two separate Huns literally disintegrate and later I was able to confirm them as having fallen to F/Lt. "Hiram" Smith and F/O Desmond Sheen.'

It was a great afternoon for Sheen. He hit one Ju 88 which blew up (this confirmed what Elliott reported) and then, flying through the wreckage, set a Messerschmitt 110 on fire. At this point the German formation broke up. Some of the bombers, having jettisoned their bomb load into the sea, turned and made off home at wave-top height. The sea was stained with great green patches made by the fluorescent sea-markers that the Germans carried in their survival kits to enable them to be easily spotted floating in the sea. Others of the German aircraft continued on their route, some towards the Clyde, others in the direction of Newcastle. 'We had hoped to get the stragglers on the way back,' wrote Deacon Elliott, 'but no luck. The squadron's original claim was 14 destroyed, but this figure was later reduced to 11 confirmed and 3 probables – for the loss of none.'

Altogether, Stumpff had the loss of eight bombers and seven fighters to mourn, without the slightest victory to put on the credit side. Air Vice-Marshal R. E. Saul and the anti-aircraft commander Major-General R. B. Pargiter could be

1. *Zerstörergeschwader*: destroyer group.

justly proud of having brought off one of the most brilliant victories of the war.

But the day was by no means over.

'You won't have any difficulty finding trouble,' said the commander of 603 Squadron, 'the only problem is how to get out of it.'

Luftflotte V was now turning its attention towards the south. It penetrated Leigh-Mallory's territory south of the line Lancaster–Scarborough. For several days now, Leigh-Mallory commanding 12 Group had been pestered with the demands of Bader to be allowed to intervene in the battle in the south. To every demand he had made the same reply:

'We cannot put all our eggs in one basket. The enemy would be delighted to see the aircraft protecting the Midlands being thrown into the big show. In any case until 11 Group ask for our help, we must wait."

Leigh-Mallory had just received a telephone call from Squadron Leader W. A. J. Satchell who commanded 302 Squadron at Leconfield. This squadron had been formed from the Polish pilots who had escaped to England and Satchell was telephoning to say that they were now ready for action. Leigh-Mallory immediately ordered them to fly to Driffield where an attack by *Luftflotte V* was expected. There they were to join 73, 264 and 616 Squadrons and were soon to be further reinforced by the Blenheims of 219 Squadron that had been transferred from 13 Group.

Satchell's Poles duly arrived at their appointed station over Driffield, but the controller, who was worried about their lack of experience, at once ordered them to land. In this way they missed what might have been a fine battle. The Germans were by now having a wonderful time. Houses were destroyed on the coast at Bridlington and a mushroom cloud of smoke indicated where a munition dump had been hit. But it was at Driffield itself that the heaviest blows fell. Twelve Whitley bombers were smashed on the ground and four hangars and the blocks of buildings were demolished.

And still the show went on. Quintin Brand's 10 Group, which had been spared so far, was now engaged against between seventy and eighty Messerschmitt 110s of *Luftflotte III*. Another attack again threatened Portland. It had just struck six o'clock when Keith Park had to call on 11 Group yet once more. 'Here we go again,' and up they went for the sixth time. Most of 11 Group's aircraft were on the ground, their pilots dead tired, red-eyed and trembling. Alan Deere remembers a young Spitfire pilot who had hardly climbed out of his damaged machine before he was told that he had to fly again. He seemed preoccupied, as if he was searching around in his clothing for something. Finally he found it: a bullet lodged between his neck and the collar of his shirt. 'Ah,' he cried, 'there, I knew there was something tickling me!' Nerves began to crack. Deere remembers a pilot rushing into dispersal and shouting at his flight commander: 'I refuse to fly again with that bastard and when he lands I'll tell him so.'[1]

Aircraft had fallen everywhere. Galland, scoring his third victory of the day, had hit a Spitfire and had watched it do a half-roll and fly along on its back. He had given it a second burst, after which it rolled back into its original attitude and only then plunged into the sea. Alan Deere met a German navigator who had leapt out of his burning Heinkel and had fallen a thousand feet into the Thames to escape with two black eyes. A Messerschmitt 110 had had its tail shot away and crashed on the airfield at Manston where it exploded. A survivor staggered groggily from the wreckage holding his head in his hands. Of the pilot and the aircraft nothing remained.

At Hornchurch three Spitfires were bombed as they were taking off. Two of the pilots were picked up in very bad shape and taken off in the ambulance. But although a careful search was made, no trace could be found of the third Spitfire. It had been blown by the blast and the explosion some five hundred yards and had landed on its belly, minus its right wing, in a little creek. The pilot had released his harness, opened the canopy and slipped to the ground. He walked back to the airfield.

Alan Deere ended the day with a miraculous escape by parachute. This was followed by a five-hour ambulance journey to hospital. After a night's rest and some medical attention he was released the next morning. There then followed a two-hour journey back to Hornchurch, and he was flying again in the early afternoon. His squadron had suffered badly. There

1. See page 157.

were only seven aircraft left intact and some good pilots had been lost – three of them killed.

Things had not been any quieter on the ground. At Rochester a wooden building, the factory where Stirling heavy bombers were assembled, was set on fire. At a near-by greyhound racing stadium, bombs fell on the track while a race was in progress. Some of the dogs were killed and others ran out into the street. It was easy to find them again simply by following the trail of blood. Later in the day it was the turn of Croydon and West Malling to be heavily bombed, following an attack on Martlesham.

'But where do the bastards come from?' exclaimed one squadron leader. 'They must be building a new lot of aeroplanes every day!'

Hauptmann Walter Rubensdorffer, who was leading Wing 210, was supposed to attack Kenley, but in fact took Croydon as his target by mistake. Croydon was the base of 111 and 1 Squadrons, the latter composed of Canadians who, like Satchell's Poles, had not yet received their baptism of fire – at least in this battle. However, their squadron commander, MacNab, was flying with his opposite number of 111 Squadron, Thompson. They found two Dorniers over the Thames and shot them down. When Rubensdorffer made his attack on Croydon, which was London's airport at the time, the Canadians were away, but the British pilots of 111 Squadron were patrolling overhead at 10,000 feet. The leading Messerschmitt 110 released its bomb and immediately the storm burst in all its force. A hangar containing fifty training aircraft burst into flames and a well-camouflaged group of factory buildings received a stick of bombs. Eighty people were killed or injured.

Thompson took the opportunity of adding a Messerschmitt 110 to his earlier victim. Rubensdorffer failed to return.

One squadron leader, describing the dizzy sensation produced by the apparently endless succession of enemy aircraft, said: 'It was like watching the moving stairway at Piccadilly Underground station.'

Elsewhere a squadron adjutant slammed down his telephone receiver and rushed in to his squadron commander's office:

'Great news. Toby came down in a vicarage garden. He'll be with us this evening.'

'Fine. That'll be one vicar with a new vocabulary; that is if he has a chance to talk to Toby about what has happened.'

'Nightfall', as Alan Deere wrote, 'brought blessed relief to the weary pilots.' But the bombers were back again. Seventy aircraft attacked Birmingham, Boston, Kirton, Beverley, Southampton, Crewe, Yarmouth, Harwich, Bristol and Swansea. In twenty-four hours the Luftwaffe had flown 1,786 sorties and the R.A.F. 974. Seventy-five German and 34 British aircraft had been shot down. For the German air force this was *schwarzer Donnerstag*, black Thursday. The most remarkable fact was the severe setback inflicted on Stumpff. In a single day *Luftflotte V* had lost one-eighth of its bombers and one-fifth of its long-range fighters. It was clear that raids from Norway were impracticable and also that Messerschmitt 110s were not fit to take part in the battle without an escort of 109s.

The senior officers of the Luftwaffe saw the Messerschmitt 109 as a 'killer' aircraft; a magnificent fighting machine whose primary function was to bring the British fighters to action and to dispatch them with one clean blow. From now on the 109 was to play the part of a sheepdog. It was never allowed to leave the bombers it was guarding; no more searching for combat, now it must play the waiting game. This was the exact reverse of its intended role. Galland wrote: 'The German fighters found themselves in a similar predicament to a dog on a chain which wants to attack the foe, but cannot harm him because of his limited orbit.'

The following day, August 16th, 72 Squadron at Acklington held a party. 'Firstly,' wrote Deacon Elliott, 'to celebrate yesterday's victories, next to say farewell to the Station Commander, Wing Commander Caswell, and finally to welcome his successor, Wing Commander Pringle. My head aches at the thought of it.'

It was an unforgettable day for Flight Lieutenant J. B. Nicholson of 249 Squadron too. A German formation split up to make individual raids on Ventnor, Tangmere, Lee-on-Solent and Gosport. Nicholson intercepted a Messerschmitt 110 near Gosport, a Coastal Command airfield. The German got in a burst which set his Hurricane on fire and very quickly he found his cockpit walls glowing red and the flames licking around his flying suit. But Nicholson was stubborn. Before going down he intended to have that shark-shaped form with its pale camouflage and black crosses. So the duel went on: one burning aeroplane chasing a twin-engined machine that was spraying it with gunfire. Now he had him! The 110 was right in the centre of his gunsight. A long burst and a shout of Triumph! – No. The German had slipped out of his sights. Round again for another attack; but again no luck. Surely now was the time to get out! But not Nicholson. He absolutely *must* get his bandit. He tried again, but this time as he pulled, the Hurricane no longer responded to the controls. The machine had failed before the man. It dropped away and Nicholson, falling vertically, slid back his cockpit canopy screaming with pain as he did so and took to his parachute.

He hung bobbing about beneath in his parachute harness and as the other noises died away he was aware of the sound of the blood pumping through his veins flooding his burns. Then suddenly there was the sound of firing. Could it be the Messerschmitt 110 returning to finish him off? But the firing was coming from the ground. The spectators of the fight had become confused and had thought that it was the German aircraft that had been brought down. They had cheered when it hit the ground and now a member of the Home Guard was loosing off three or four rounds at the 'Hun'. Nicholson felt one of the bullets hit him. No, this was really too stupid for words. He closed his eyes.

When Nicholson reached the ground the error was discovered and he was picked up and taken to hospital. He became the first pilot of Fighter Command to receive the Victoria Cross and he remained the only one to do so throughout the whole of the Battle of Britain.

But what of the fate of German pilots who were forced to make parachute descents over Britain? The British pilots had strict instructions about this. They were fighting on their home ground and this advantage entailed a responsibility to observe certain rules that were in any case in accordance with their own feelings of humanity. Air Chief Marshal Sir Hugh Dowding acknowledged, although he deplored it, that the Germans might shoot at British pilots descending over England who could be recovered immediately and put back into battle. At the same time he forbade the British pilots to treat their opponents in the same way, since it was only necessary to wait a few seconds for them to drop into the safe hands of their captors. One squadron commander, Billy Burton, addressed his pilots in dispersal:

'I'll court-martial any member of my squadron who shoots at anybody on a parachute.' Then he added:

'But as long as the bastard's still in his cockpit give him everything you've got!'

This was a matter for pilots to settle between themselves.

What happened on the ground depended on the behaviour of people who were not directly involved in the fighting. There were many things that might explain, though not justify, bad conduct: fury at seeing British aircraft shot down in flames and sympathy for their pilots. Even so, there do not appear to be any records, even on the German side as one might easily have supposed, of airmen being mishandled once they had landed, or being actually killed while descending by parachute. Nevertheless, the accounts of British pilots who became members of the Caterpillar Club[1] and who had been mistaken for Germans, perhaps only for a few moments, show that the reception they received was not exactly welcoming. What happened to Nicholson must also have happened to pilots who really were Germans. Some of them met with more amusing adventures. One German airman came to earth unobserved in a field. He got rid of his parachute and, taking a deep breath of English air, his last as a free man, decided to walk to the nearest house to give himself up. In the sky above, vapour trails marked the battle in which he had just taken part and which was still going on. Yet here he was now among the green fields of Sussex, looking at the orchards heavy with fruit and listening to the birdsong. He started walking in the direction of a magnificent country mansion. Suddenly he was

1. The Caterpillar Club is an association of airmen who have had to abandon their aircraft at least once by parachute. Edmond Rostand's line in *L'Aiglon* seems to apply to them: 'Can the butterfly become once more a caterpillar?' The membership of this club, as of so many British clubs, is a highly sought-after privilege. It is said that a French pilot serving with a British squadron was so keen to become a member that he took his Spitfire up to 10,000 feet and deliberately jumped out. According to the story he was placed under arrest but admitted to the Caterpillar Club at the same time.

surrounded by farm workers and captured. The group climbed the steps and rang at the great door. It was opened by an old retainer who, if he was surprised at such an extraordinary gathering, allowed no sign of it to show on his face. He inquired who the visitor might be; then showed him into the drawing-room and, inviting him to be seated, went off to inform his master.

'My lord, there is an officer waiting to see you.'

'What goes he want?'

'I don't know, my lord.'

'Then go and ask him.'

'I can't, my lord. He doesn't understand me. He's a German officer, my lord.'

A few moments later Earl de la Warr formally arrested his guest and offered him a cup of tea.

Another German was captured by Betty Brown, an alert and decisive young lady of fifteen. Unable to believe it, he remarked, 'I never thought that I should end up in England like this.'

A farmer's wife, Mrs. Norman Cardwell, having captured her prisoner and given him a drink, suddenly found she couldn't prevent herself saying: 'What the devil do you think you're doing here anyway?'

One can imagine how these young men felt. Within the space of two hours they had been breakfasting on *Kaffee* and *Brötchen* and *Marmelade* in a Luftwaffe mess in Normandy or the Pas de Calais, had flown the Channel, fought like dogs and after knowing for a few long seconds the fear of death, had found themselves in an unknown and hostile country, surrounded by strangers who could not speak a word of their language. Some of them, the proud ones, would light a cigarette and, smiling, announce: 'My comrades of the Wehrmacht will soon be here to set me free.' Others allowed themselves to be led away quietly. Whichever way it was to be decided, for them the war was over.

But it was not only the living who fell from the skies; there were corpses too. Pieces of aircraft, strips of parachute silk and twisted metal fragments rained down on the woods and roofs and gardens. An inhabitant of Lee-on-Solent noticed something odd floating in the pool of his garden. He fished it out. It was a human hand. A photograph taken at the time shows us a tin-helmeted soldier with his rifle slung over his shoulder standing on the wing of a German aircraft, his boots firmly placed on the black cross. Or again we see ordinary simple people holding up shattered pieces of a wing and giving the thumbs-up sign. A sergeant of the R.A.F. had his photograph taken as he examined the equipment of a German pilot he had just pulled from his smashed machine. The British Isles were building up a collection of grim trophies of the enemy who had invaded their skies.

And still they came. On August 16th the airfields of Kent, Hampshire and Sussex were attacked and serious damage was caused, especially at Tangmere where a raid by Junkers 88s destroyed three Blenheims on the ground and damaged three more, as well as seven Hurricanes and a Magister. At No. 2 Flying Training School at Brize Norton, forty-six training aircraft went up in smoke. The radar masts of Ventnor in the Isle of Wight were once more attacked and the station was put off the air.

Targets in Essex and Suffolk were also attacked and at night there were raids on Bristol, Newport, Swansea, Portland, Worcester, Chester, Tavistock, Farnborough and upon several airfields.

August 17th was relatively quiet with raids only on the Midlands, Merseyside and South Wales.

In a broadcast on the B.B.C., the Minister of Information gave news of the Luftwaffe's defeat.

Heavy leaden sunshine beat down on Bentley Priory. The lawns had been watered and the green scent of wet grass filled the air.

Dowding received at last an Air Ministry authorization he had been waiting for: permission to have a certain number of Bomber Command and Army Co-operation pilots transferred to Fighter Command. In addition, the Poles of 302 and 303 Squadrons, the Czechs of 310 Squadron and the Belgians and French scattered around in other squadrons would be allowed to take part in the battle.

They did not know this as yet. René Mouchotte, who was still under training, wrote:

'We were doing nothing here in Odiham; the camp is a long way from anywhere. What a waste of time! Can it be the traditional slowness of the French administration General de

Gaulle is said to have brought over? We spend our time wandering round the aircraft, listening to the news, learning English and eating.'

Then suddenly the orders arrived:

'We are off at last. They are sending us to the centre of England, to Sutton Bridge. There we shall handle the famous Hurricane, the English fighter; after that, posting to our squadron.'

So that was the state of affairs in the R.A.F. at the start of the second half of August; on the one hand an Air Chief Marshal crying out for pilots and on the other the pilots themselves crying out to be allowed to get into the fight.

On the airfields, where the W.A.A.F.'s had already earned the admiration of the pilots because of their conduct under fire, all efforts were being made to repair the destruction. Perrin, one of the few Frenchmen who were lucky enough to have been posted to a squadron, hurried over to help a group of girls who were struggling, bent double, to push an aircraft into a hangar. He was immediately sent away.

'Leave it to us; it's our job.'

At Tangmere, even as the dead were being collected around them, they were busy erecting trestle tables and benches so that they could serve a meal from an old field kitchen for the 'boys' between sorties.

Alan Deere, shot down on the 15th, rejoined his squadron the next day. There he gave a detailed account of his adventure. His engine had been hit and he jettisoned his hood with the idea of making a forced landing. But then the engine caught fire and he decided to roll on his back and bale out: a method of abandoning an aircraft that had been successfully tried by one of his friends. He had undone his straps and pushed forward on the stick to raise the nose of the inverted Spitfire. He was duly thrown out of the cockpit but his parachute fouled some part of the cockpit. Deere tried to climb back in but the force of the slipstream pinned him where he was. As he had forgotten to trim the aircraft fully forward, the nose now dropped and he went into an inverted dive. He was still pinned to the fuselage and now also in the grip of panic, with a feeling like a jet of icy water splashing down his spine; the ground was coming up when, struggling, he at last broke free, smashing his wrist against the tail plane. The rip-cord worked and the parachute opened. A few seconds later he hit the ground not a hundred yards from where his Spitfire was burning. He was still disentangling himself from his parachute harness when the two airmen appeared on the scene.

'Where did you two spring from?' Deere asked.

They turned out to be the driver and nursing orderly of an ambulance on its way to Kenley. They had watched him fall and had hurried over to see if their help was needed. 'Can we do anything for you?' they had asked.

Deere's wrist was hurting terribly. The orderly pointed out that his wrist-watch was broken. The works had been somehow scooped out leaving only the case and the strap. Across his wrist was a red weal where a bullet had grazed him.

'That was a perfectly good watch,' thought Deere.

He got into the back of the ambulance which had been parked not far away behind a clump of trees, and, with his silk polka-dot scarf round his neck, lay down on one of the stretchers and dozed off to sleep. When he awoke it was dark. He was vaguely aware of the ambulance stopping and hearing directions. Then it started again. Deere could no longer bear the pain in his wrist. He knocked on the window. 'Where are we?'

The driver was lost. He thought they must be somewhere near East Grinstead where there was a hospital for the pilots of the area. Deere gritted his teeth and sweat broke out on his brow. He was cold, then hot, then cold, until he didn't know what he felt. The ambulance started off again with a jolt. It was in fact East Grinstead. Deere thanked his rescuers. They had been well-intentioned if somewhat clumsy. He was in terrible pain. A night nurse examined him and gave him an injection to calm him. The wrist was very swollen and inflamed; it would have to be X-rayed first thing in the morning. Deere fell into an uneasy sleep.

The end of the story he was to learn much later from the mouth of Sir Archibald McIndoe, the chief surgeon of the hospital. For Deere all that happened was that he left the hospital and went back to his squadron minus a good watch.

What had happened was that McIndoe, having examined him, had telephoned his station commander. Deere had a fractured wrist and looked absolutely all in. McIndoe asked if he could keep him in hospital for a few days. The station commander had said that he would be grateful as it was otherwise impossible for him to stop Deere flying.

The surgeon put down the receiver and went to find Deere, but the bird had flown.

Some months later Deere was compensated for the loss of his watch from public funds.

There had now been enough air fighting to provide the bases for discussions about tactics. On all the airfields these were being hotly pursued. Pilots all over the world use hand language. Generally the left hand represents the enemy aircraft and the right is used to demonstrate the manoeuvre. Wing Commander Blake hit on a striking formula: 'Don't fire until you can see the rivets.' Glasser of 65 Squadron thought the greatest danger lay in hesitation: 'You have to go at it flat out; just like rugby. It's just when you think you may get into trouble and hesitate, that you do get into trouble.' Richard Hillary was seeking something more in aerial combat; perhaps the same thing that Saint-Exupéry and Mermoz hoped to find in airline flying. He wrote: 'I realized in that moment just how lucky a fighter pilot is. He has none of the personalized emotions of the soldier, handed a rifle and bayonet and told to charge. He does not even have to share the dangerous emotions of the bomber pilot who night after night must experience that childhood longing for smashing things.'

And what were his emotions as a fighter pilot?

'Those of the duellist – cool, precise, impersonal. He is privileged to kill well. For if one must either kill or be killed, as now one must, it should, I feel, be done with dignity.'

On the other side of the Channel Galland's words echoed those of Hillary: 'By its intrinsic properties the fighter arm belongs to the elite. The almost unbelievably expensive product of clever designers, precise technicians and specialized workers, given into the hands of scientifically chosen and comprehensively trained experts, constitutes an arm of the highest efficiency, but also of great delicacy. It can be compared with a razor blade, which must be guided by a sensitive hand. The man who uses it like a hatchet must not be surprised if it turns jagged and finally becomes useless.'

It certainly seems that the pilots were becoming weary with all the blows they had delivered and received. Perrin, writing about his English comrades, noted: 'We were dead. We were too tired even to get drunk. You simply never saw a pilot drunk.'

And here is Galland: 'We complained of the leadership, the bombers, the Stukas, and were dissatisfied with ourselves. We saw one comrade after the other, old and tested brothers in combat, vanish from our ranks. Not a day passed without a place remaining empty at the mess table. New faces appeared and became familiar, until one day these too would disappear, shot in the Battle of Britain ... You could count on your fingers when your turn would come. The logic of the theory of probabilities showed us incontestably that one's number was up after so many sorties.'

On the evening of August 16th, Alan Deere, who had just turned up again at 54 Squadron, watched his friend Gray landing.

'I've had enough today,' he said as he flopped down in the grass. 'I reckon the Huns have too. Perhaps they might let us return in peace to Hornchurch. I'm just dying for a beer, a good meal and bed.'

Hardly were the words out of his mouth when the warning bell sounded. The telephone orderly came rushing out of the dispersal hut:

'Scramble.'

There were only nine Spitfires left serviceable. Immediately their engines started and in moments they were off and lost to view in the sky and the first hint of dusk.

Both sides shared the same experience and both camps were filled with tired heroes. The attackers were taking their rebuff badly. At the beginning of July the German pilots were convinced that they would never have to meet the R.A.F. in battle. A month later they were being told that it would all be over in a few days. 'I shall see to it myself with my Luftwaffe,' said Goering. But still they were meeting implacable resistance and wearing themselves out in bitter fighting from which every day some of their comrades failed to return. Orders and counter-orders followed one another and now finally the fighter pilots were required to wait to be attacked by the enemy they should have been hunting down. What had become of the bowler hats and umbrellas that had been used to ridicule Chamberlain, or the fat cigars to make fun of Churchill? Where were the broad jokes and the laughter?

So give me your hand, your pretty white hand,
For tonight we march against England . . .

Marching is one thing, when would the victory come?

Dowding's 'boys' had an answer to this question. They might sleep only four or five hours a night on their shattered airfields. They might have to mark the names of their friends with black crosses, but their answer was 'Never'. In ten days Fighter Command had lost one hundred and fifty-four pilots killed, missing or severely wounded. Only sixty-three new pilots had been produced to replace them. Dowding's hour-glass had been turned once more.

The Channel, separating the two sides, had at last become clear. The little waves of summer lapped on the holiday beaches, which were now disfigured with block-houses, watch towers and camouflage netting.

At Cap Blanc Nez where Commodore Fink kept watch, the sea was blue.

9: So Few

In the south of England the corn was ripe. From time to time some camouflage-dappled aeroplane would crash and explode in a great fireball. Then the crops would burn and the air be filled with a scent of a bakery. The farmers set great store by their wheat crop and waited to greet the Huns with pitch-forks.

On the airfield the W.A.A.F.s were clearing up. Not all of them had yet been issued with their blue-grey uniforms and flat caps. Some of them were equipped with what was available, a beret and blouse. One less fortunate wore a black satin skirt and high-heeled shoes. Jean Mortimer, a girl of twenty-eight, was promoted sergeant. She was to be seen, after each raid, walking alone across the airfield with a bundle of flags under her arm. Her graceful, self-assured figure would lean forward over the bomb crater as she looked for unexploded bombs. When she saw one she would plant one of her little flags beside the crater, for all the world like a caddy marking out a golf course.

Lord Beaverbrook gave a tremendous spurt to aircraft production. All was grist that came to his mill. 'Clear out your old bones. They will make glue for aeroplanes.' He learnt that an interned German Jew named Loew was an aluminium expert. He had him released and sent him on a tour of other internment camps to recruit scientists who might be able to assist the war effort. One of the American pilots who delivered aircraft from the factories to the squadrons was killed when making a belly landing in a Spitfire.[1] In St. Paul's Cathedral, not far from the bust of Washington, there is a plaque bearing the inscription: 'An American citizen who died that England might live.'

There must be some way to beat the radar! That at any rate was the conviction of Leutnant Lamberty of *Kriegsgeschwader* 76. On August 18th he decided to lead his Squadron 9 on a low-level attack. Early in the afternoon his nine Dornier

1. Pilot Officer W. M. L. Fiske had volunteered for combatant service.

17s set course over the Channel at one hundred feet like a shoal of hunting shark. They soon swallowed up the English coast and flew on between the hills, their slipstream cutting a swathe across the countryside. They passed over a great country house at East Grinstead – no doubt the hospital to which Alan Deere had been taken three days earlier – then on over more fields, hedgerows and trees. Suddenly there was Biggin Hill.

The Bofors gun crews were taken completely by surprise as the Dorniers rushed over them with a deafening roar and began dropping their bombs. Then the guns opened up. Rockets soared into the sky and from them little parachutes opened, like the tiny Japanese flowers that open in water. From the parachutes hung cables in the path of the bombers. Lamberty had part of a wing cut away. Another Dornier crashed, while a third, whose pilot had received a bullet in the heart, flew round and round the airfield by itself.

Lamberty's left wing was now on fire and he decided to make a forced landing. The temperature inside the cockpit was already unbearable. His Dornier hit the ground, bounced three times and crashed into a hedge, its wing jammed against a tree. He saw a detachment of the Home Guard already taking aim at him. Fire was now consuming everything in the cockpit and the metal was glowing red and beginning to twist and melt. Lamberty had to pull himself out of the furnace by grasping the metal with his bare hands. He had no sensation of pain as he staggered, dazed, down on to the grass. The British were there with their rifles raised. Would they shoot? Lamberty made a gesture towards them and then rubbed his hands on his flying tunic. The Home Guards saw strips of flesh falling from his hands and drew back.

At last they came towards him again and led him away with one of his crew, as badly burnt as he. Lamberty asked them to help him get one of his cigarettes and they searched his pockets and brought out a packet of English cigarettes that Lamberty had bought in Guernsey. They lit one for him. He smiled bravely and merely said:

'What really makes me sad is that I think it will be a long time before I fly again.'

At that moment there was a tremendous roaring sound as the second wave of Dorniers, escorted by Messerschmitt 109s, arrived to drop a hundred bombs on the airfields of Biggin

Hill and Kenley. The blast was so great that Home Guards and the wounded airmen flung themselves down on the ground and stayed there while the deluge of metal fell. At Kenley ten hangars, four Hurricanes and four other aircraft were destroyed and many more damaged. The operations room too was destroyed.

When the prisoners and their escort got up again the roads were already becoming crowded with fire engines. Columns of smoke were rising over Biggin Hill and Kenley. Croydon and West Malling, too, were in the same state.

Of the nine Dorniers that had slipped surreptitiously past the radar screen, two were shot down and the other seven set off home, hedge-hopping as they had come. All had been hit and it was an unfortunate little group that limped away towards its nest. Two had to ditch in the Channel, their crews being later picked up by rescue boats. Then there were five, flying in the spray blown off the waves, trying to make the coast. They made it, and three of the five force-landed where they could, bringing off their landings more or less well. The last two reached Cormeilles-en-Vexin. On the ground a few French peasants were delighted to see only two return. 'The English must have given them a hard time,' they thought.

One of the two aircraft that had escaped was the one that had been turning in crazy circles over Biggin Hill. The crew had pulled the dead pilot out of his seat and the engineer succeeded in getting the aircraft back to base. It was his first flight and for his remarkable achievement he received the Iron Cross.

Flight-Lieutenant Peter Townsend, of 86 Squadron, was patrolling over Debden. 'Ginger' Lacey, the red-headed Yorkshireman, was airborne with seven Hurricanes of 501 Squadron. These aircraft encountered about fifty bombers and fighters not far from Hawkinge. There then began a battle in which two Messerschmitt 110s were shot down and in which Flight Lieutenant Stoney was killed.

No. 85 Squadron encountered the enemy a little before six o'clock to the east of Chelmsford, a region where land and sea met in marshland. This time it was a 'Valhalla'. The term 'Valhalla' was used by the Germans to describe a large formation of bombers which had a preceding fighter wave, a close escort and top cover. In this case it was a group of Junkers 87 followed by a formation of Heinkel 111s two thousand feet higher, and higher still, at about fifteen thousand feet, Junkers 88s and Messerschmitt 110s. Over them all was the top cover of Messerschmitt 109s.

When they saw the British fighters coming into the attack, the Germans split up their 'Valhalla'. Townsend, leading Red Section, and Hemingway, leading Blue Section, were treated to a spectacle worthy of the finest days of Barnum and Bailey. The Stukas were heading out to sea while the Junkers 88 and Heinkels had started to climb to form a great defensive circle turning counter-clockwise at eighteen thousand feet. Two thousand feet higher the Messerschmitts were doing the same. There was no chance now of biting off the last man's tail.

Townsend attacked. This was the moment he loved, the moment when you had to take a grip on yourself and when danger brought a keener taste to being alive. He got within range of a Messerschmitt 110 and gave it some three-second bursts. With a smile of satisfaction, he saw it enter a spiral dive towards the sea, but already he was kicking his rudder pedal and breaking away to the left.

The leaders of all four sections, Red, Blue, Yellow and Green, were by now engaged. Hemingway, who had taken on a single-handed combat with the circle of Junkers, was caught in the machine-gun fire of two of the aircraft which were flying in close formation. His motor was hit and Hemingway could smell the distinctive smell of glycol. Soon the engine began spitting oil and there was a grave risk that at any moment the whole aircraft might catch fire. But Hemingway had no time to think about this, for the Hurricane had gone into a spin and he was fully occupied trying to make it recover. He succeeded at about seven thousand feet and was looking round to see if he could reach the coast when, suddenly, the motor caught fire. A parachute descent into the sea was clearly the better choice. The canopy opened and Hemingway duly found himself in the water. Above him the fight continued; he was fished out of the water by a boat an hour and a half later.

Back at Debden the following day, he made an entry in his log-book: 'August 18th, shot down by a Ju 88. Descended by parachute in the sea 12 miles off Clacton.'

No. 85 Squadron's score for the day was six Messerschmitt 110s, three Messerschmitt 109s, one Heinkel 111 destroyed;

four probables and six damaged. This was achieved for the loss of two Hurricanes and a third damaged.

No. 54 Squadron had been busy too. In four sorties it had achieved its best score ever: fourteen enemy aircraft destroyed without loss. This earned the squadron a telegram of congratulations from the Chief of Air Staff: 'Well done, 54 Squadron.' The squadron was back at Manston-in-the-Dust which had been bombed yet again. This airfield had the misfortune to lie on the route of the German squadrons as they returned home. If they had any bombs left, they would drop them on Manston where they had a good chance of exploding amongst the Spitfires as they landed.

August 18th had been a glorious day. Seventy-one enemy aircraft had been destroyed for the loss of twenty-seven Royal Air Force machines; but the pilots were at the end of their strength. On the previous evening, in 54 Squadron's mess, there had been the usual discussion which always followed a day of particularly hard fighting. Colin Gray was telling the story of one of his successes during the afternoon and Alan Deere, frowning slightly, was listening. His attention was attracted by the unusually vague expression on the face of George Gribble, sitting not far from him. Gray's account went on and although Alan was still listening to him, all the time he was watching as Gribble's head pathetically nodded lower and lower towards the plate of bacon and eggs in front of him. As Gribble's nose was almost touching the plate Deere made a sign to Gray who, turning from his account, called out: 'Hi, George, you are meant to eat those eggs, not put your face in them.' At this Gribble sat up with a start and, holding his head erect, looked round at his friends fiercely.

Now on the evening of the 18th, the pilots were bearing an almost intolerable burden on their shoulders. The strain of mastering their fears, the accumulation of fatigue and the intoxication of victory, all seemed to have built up at once into a mountain of weariness. They would have given anything to be sent away for a rest, even for a few days, just enough time to recover a little before starting again. But it was not to be.

In the Air Ministry the loss figures for the ten days between August 8th and 18th were being closely watched. They amounted to ninety-four pilots killed or missing, two hundred and forty aircraft destroyed in the air and thirty on the ground.

In Berlin, Beppo Schmid was making his calculations. He did not spend much time on the German losses, although these came close to the figure of seven hundred aircraft during the ten days' period. He was concerned with the enemy's position.

To help him in his appreciation, he had the reports in which the commanders of the three *Luftflotten* described their victories, but apart from these only some fragmentary information about the movements of the British squadrons. Thus from the fact that 255 Squadron moved from Wittering to Hornchurch on August 9th, he deduced that the squadron at Hornchurch had been destroyed. What he did not know was that 74 Squadron was due to leave Hornchurch for Wittering on the 14th, simply as part of the policy of rotating the squadrons. As for the British losses, he arrived at a figure of 644 aircraft. Putting this against the basic assumption of his 'Study in Blue', he was able to assert that the Royal Air Force had now only 430 fighters of which, at the most, 300 could be brought into action at the same time. In fact the Royal Air Force had about 650.

What can be the explanation for a specialist in intelligence matters being so wide of the mark? The British figures are 270 aircraft destroyed and 650 available. According to the Germans, these should be 644 and 300 respectively. In each case we are concerned with figures intended for the information of the Chiefs of Staff; not for propaganda. In fact, if we look at the matter honestly, we must admit that, in furnishing these figures to the Air Ministry, Fighter Command had an interest to serve; it needed a rapid recruitment of pilots and faster delivery of new aircraft. There was therefore no reason to be optimistic. On the other hand, although Schmid was trying to show that the Battle of Britain was being won, his figures are much more conservative than those of the German operations bureau.

But both sides were working on figures which were largely illusory. The British were fortunate in being able to count the wrecked aircraft that were littering their countryside. As for the Germans, although it was an easy matter for them to know how many of their aircraft did not return, they had to rely upon the reports of their pilots where British losses were concerned. The pilots were often genuinely mistaken. They knew they had fired and seen smoke come from the enemy aircraft. They would see it diving towards the ground or the sea and therefore believe that they had shot it down. In many cases the aircraft had merely dived away to break off the engagement and had returned to base.

The British pilots had been ordered not to break formation in order to follow a damaged aircraft. They were therefore obliged to make their claims without further investigation. Again, it frequently happened that two or more fighters from different squadrons had all fired on the same enemy aircraft. Although this aircraft would be well and truly destroyed and although each pilot, making his report, would be claiming an authentic victory, nevertheless it would be counted several times. The officer whose duty it was to substantiate the claims faced innumerable problems: the pilot would be posted to another squadron, or he might be shot down or flying when a report was wanted. In fact, with the best will in the world, it was not possible to be strictly accurate when the figures were published, they were exaggerated for propaganda reasons 'to maintain civilian morale'.

'I remember', wrote Dowding, 'being cross-examined in August by the Secretary of State for Air about the discrepancy. He was anxious about the effect on the American people of the wide divergence between the claims of the two sides. I replied that the Americans would soon find out the truth; if the Germans' figures were accurate they would be in London in a week, otherwise they would not.'

The figures given in the news bulletins were not taken literally by the pilots. Alan Deere mentions that he and his colleagues realized that the claims were too high. In August and September the most experienced pilots were too fatigued to get these sort of results, and the new pilots were not yet capable of them. They knew also that the claims of certain squadrons were very dubious, but for the most part inaccuracies were due to inexperience. Earlier, in July, when the pilots had all been experienced veterans of the fighting over Dunkirk, the claims had been much more precise.

It had now become urgent to establish the facts. The order

was sent to the commanders of the German fighter units calling them to a meeting with the Reichsmarschall. Galland, who was at this time thoroughly demoralized, wrote of his astonishment and disquiet at receiving his order calling him to Goering's luxurious residence, Karinhall. 'Had he summoned me in order to inform me personally of my disgrace, or did he simply want the opinion of one of his fighter leaders engaged in the battle?'

Galland arrived in Berlin wearing his best uniform and smoking a cigar. Here there seemed to be very little sign of war. The Channel was far away and the daily battles of a handful of men were not enough to capture the imagination. The Reich was still enjoying the taste of its victories. Galland took a train to Schorfheide. Perhaps he travelled with Mölders; in any case Mölders, the Germans' greatest ace, had also been summoned. A 'sumptuous limousine' was waiting at the station to drive them to Karinhall, but in what sort of mood would they find the Reichsmarschall? They would of course exchange news and hear the latest gossip, but in general Goering was known to be permanently ill-tempered. He had said, 'According to my estimation and the official figures, the British fighter force should no longer exist.' How then would he welcome his pilots?

We have conflicting accounts of what was said, but we must suppose that Goering took his senior commanders severely to task and then showed himself in a more amiable light to the leaders of the squadrons. He advised the senior officers to 'attack the aircraft factories and not the Dover lightship'.[1] During the last four days the atmosphere had changed. No more electric trains now. The Commander-in-Chief of the Luftwaffe demanded from his generals more carefully worked-out plans than he had received in the past. He also instructed them to improve the quality of their staff. It is clear that the German Air Force was too recent an institution to have built up an administrative and tactical structure. What it had, had been borrowed here and there from the other services. Since the Royal Air Force clearly did exist, whether the Luftwaffe liked it or not, it was necessary to take certain decisions. First of all, in order to conserve its strength, the Luftwaffe placed the Stukas in a state of virtual

1. Translator's note: There is no Dover lightship. The Varne lightship which was attacked lies almost in mid-Channel off Dover.

retirement. They were too vulnerable and suffered severe losses, which meant that many pilots were killed. Secondly, it was decided to make no more massive raids like those of August 15th across the North Sea. Whenever it was necessary to bomb factories, this would be done at night or, if by day, by a small formation, or even by a single aircraft which could take refuge in the clouds. *Luftflotte V* whose bases were too far from their targets would no longer be used by day.

The Reichsmarschall decided that until further orders, the principal task of *Lutfflotten II* and *III* would be to inflict the greatest possible losses on the British fighters. To this task would be added the secondary one of attacking the enemy's bomber airfields, but this task would be carried out in such a way as to avoid as far as possible the loss of human life.

And what of *Luftflotte V*? Goering was coming to that.

'There will no longer be any restrictions upon the choice of targets. I reserve only the right to order the bombing of London and Liverpool.'

In co-ordination with the other *Luftflotten*, which were preparing for night attacks, *Luftflotte V* was getting ready to mount one against Glasgow.

And now Goering turned to his pilots, wiping away all traces of severity from his puffy face as he did so. Having done his duty as Commander-in-Chief, he could now allow himself the pleasant task of congratulating his brave warriors. These were the men who were doing the actual fighting; dealing out blows and receiving them. Well, they should not be neglected; when they came back battered and shaken there would be a girl and a soft bed to soothe them. And if they never came back at all, the answer was just as easy: a posthumous Iron Cross. As Goering had remarked to the British Ambassador, Sir Nevile Henderson, one day, 'The Englishmen I really admire are the pirates like Francis Drake. The others haven't enough brutality.'

Galland, who with Mölders received the gold and diamond insignia which Goering had created for his best pilots, admits that it was a great relief to find his corpulent commander in excellent humour. Having thus satisfied at one and the same time his taste for investitures and for jewellery, he promoted both officers to the rank of commodore. This was an important gesture which symbolized the Reichsmarschall's new intention of introducing young men into the higher echelons of the Luftwaffe and placing the real professionals in positions of command.

The atmosphere became relaxed and Goering was at his most charming. At such moments he could show an unusual side of his character. 'He is not only accepted in Germany,' wrote Ciano in his *Memoirs*, 'but perhaps even loved for it. That is because he has a dash of humanity.' According to Galland, who was the person most closely involved, it was then that the famous incident of the Spitfires took place. All the other sources say that it occurred on the Channel coast two or three days later. Whoever is right, the date, as such, is of little importance, but the story has a different psychological feel according to whether it is set in the atmosphere of Karinhall or at the front line. Galland's account of it is so precise that one cannot imagine him having invented it. Why indeed should he? No doubt he had boasted about it when he returned with Mölders to his wing, and as 'fat Hermann', once again furious, arrived the following day, the officers who were present at this visit may have superimposed the scene which took place on the 19th upon their recollection of the 21st. This is what Galland writes:

'Finally, as his time ran short, he grew more amiable and asked what were the requirements for our squadrons. Mölders asked for a series of Me 109s with more powerful engines. The request was granted.'

One can imagine the scene: a summer evening with the thatch turning gold in the last light of the sun and the coming night already invading the impenetrable forests. Above the door the mailed fist holding aloft the mace. In the great rose-clustered courtyard stands the long car, its chauffeur waiting at attention for the three iron-grey silhouettes – those of the two pilots, young and straight; the Marshal's, obese. Goering turned to Galland:

'And you?'

'I should like an outfit of Spitfires for my group.'

'After blurting this out,' wrote Galland, 'I had rather a shock, for it was not really meant that way . . . Such brazen-faced impudence made even Goering speechless. He stamped off, growling as he went.'

If Galland is correct and the incident really took place at Karinhall, then it has a special significance. As he walked back into his mansion, the palace of excess built as a memorial to his extravagant tastes, the Reichsmarschall must have felt himself a poor man. He might growl at Galland, but underneath he knew that although he could give his men the golden insignias so dear to his own heart, he was not in a position to provide them with the aircraft they wanted.

Siegfried had taken command of the greatest air force in the world, but in so doing he had condemned himself never to speak the language of the pilots again.

The limousine drove off towards the station and in the distance a deer, crossing the road, was caught for a moment in its headlights.

Goering was alone.

At Uxbridge it was Air Vice-Marshal Keith Park who was busy with figures. It was as though the combat of the last ten days had turned the Chiefs of Staff into chartered accountants.

The instructions that came down from headquarters on both sides allow of only one interpretation: on both sides the men were tiring.

At Uxbridge, the operations room was a model of efficiency: a submarine or a sunken fortress with its serpentine air-conditioning trunking and its looms of telephone wiring. Keith Park's office was next to the stairway leading to the shelter, which was also a communications nerve centre. With his pointed nose, bushy eyebrows and typical R.A.F. moustache, he was the classic Royal Air Force senior officer. But this is not to say that he was always in agreement with the commanders of the neighbouring groups. The disagreements were to last almost as long as the battle itself, and they grew stronger until the autumn, when Dowding intervened in his stiff and quiet yet firm way and announced his decision. It was on Park's 11 Group that the worst of the enemy attacks fell. Park therefore decided on a series of measures which he issued to his controllers on August 19th as his 'Instruction No. 4'.

The general aim of these instructions can be expressed in one phrase: 'economy of pilots'. Park at Uxbridge and Goering at Karinhall had both taken the same decision. As far as the use of pilots was concerned, they would henceforth be misers. Neither man could be blind to the terrible reality that underlay the dazzling reports of victories. This battle on which, in the final analysis, the fate of millions depended, was a confrontation of specialists. Triumph or defeat lay in the hands of a few men – less than three thousand in all – who knew how to sit in a fighter cockpit and press a firing button. Such men were suddenly and quite literally worth more than their weight in platinum, let alone gold. The conclusion to be drawn might have come from a fairy-tale. All the magic in the world was powerless; only the Knights could save the princess. Strangely the Knights did not seem to realize this. Their courage had something left over from childhood about it. They were happy to be given toys to play with – the toys were called Messerschmitts and Spitfires. 'In a Spitfire,' wrote Richard Hillary, 'we're back to war as it ought to be – if you can talk about war as it ought to be. Back to individual combat, to self-reliance, total responsibility for one's own fate.' For this responsibility, however fleeting it might be, men were ready to undergo anything. They had the stimulus of fighting men of their own kind, neither showing the other any pity, all facing death with a gleam in the eye. This was the last thing Goering or Park wanted; they knew how irreplaceable the pilots were.

This must not be confused with any idea of respect for human life. If either of the two countries had possessed a few thousand pilots in reserve, it would have been a matter of duty to use them up in action if by doing so the battle could have been ended sooner and in the country's favour. For a soldier, once he has accepted the horror of war, the worst crime is not to use all his means to win it as quickly as possible. The sooner it is won, the sooner it is over. But this was a battle between paupers.

'Avoid all unnecessary loss of human life,' ordered Goering. 'We cannot afford to lose pilots through forced landings in the sea,' noted Park. On both sides the search went on for tactical economy.

'Dispatch fighters', wrote Keith Park, 'to engage large enemy formations over land or within gliding distance of the coast.' The commander of 11 Group was using everything he had; the cloudy weather, the assistance of the other groups, the Polish and Canadian squadrons (of which more later), local superiority of numbers. He was fighting like a gambler committed to the table, knowing that he was playing with the last of his money and therefore taking care to eliminate all foreseeable risks.

The bombers, which were less dangerous as targets than the fighters, were to be given priority, Dogfights between fighters had become a luxury and in this game it was up to the Germans to raise the stakes. The R.A.F. would only pay to see. Park expressed a wish that the enemy formations should be attacked before they had dropped their bombs. This may seem self-evident, but there was another school of thought that affirmed that it was preferable to attack them later when there had been time to build up large formations of fighters rather than to try to surprise them earlier with insufficient forces. Neither side would move from its position. What was incontestable was that every effort must be made, even by sections of one or two fighters, to protect fighter squadrons on the ground, refuelling, when they were at their most vulnerable.

The Germans and the British were playing the same game. Neither would play an ace for fear of having it trumped. The fighter, an essentially attacking aircraft, was packed away in cotton wool like precious glass.

On August 20th, Winston Churchill rose in the House of Commons:

'The gratitude of every home in our island, in our Empire, and indeed throughout the world, except in the abodes of the guilty, goes out to the British airmen who, undaunted by odds, unwearied in their constant challenge and mortal danger, are turning the tide of the world war by their prowess and by their devotion. Never in the field of human conflict was so much owed by so many to so few.'

And he concluded:

'All hearts go out to the fighter pilots, whose brilliant actions we see with our own eyes day after day.'

10: A Small Question of Bombs

There is no substitute for a visit to the front if you want information.

On August 21st Goering was on the shores of the Channel. Whether he came by road or in his special train 'Asia' is in dispute, and the documents also disagree on where he was. Some say Cap Gris Nez at the advanced headquarters of *Luftflotte II*, others, with Johannes Fink and Paul Weitkus at Cap Blank Nez. The two places are only about ten kilometres apart and so there is no reason why he should not have gone first to one and then to the other. One fact is certain, Goering was furious.

The Commanders-in-Chief at the front found themselves in the embarrassing position of schoolboys meeting the headmaster during the holidays. They had developed their own ways of doing things; built up their own folklore. Feeling themselves far from the eye of the master they had become proconsuls. But now the ogre was there and he looked severe, irritable and grave. He was wearing the white Luftwaffe summer cap and the collar of his tunic cut into his neck. An Iron Cross hung between the points of his collar, and his binoculars, held in place by a leather strap, were propped against his belly. He stood upright, pushing down on the pommel of his sword. Beside him, Kesselring, obviously uneasy, adopted the oriental expression he reserved for the bad days, while Lörzer affected a light-heartedness that he clearly didn't feel.

And Goering was blowing his top. 'A few days would be enough!' That's what they had said at the beginning of the battle. Well now they'd better start winning it! And what about those people who had complained that it wasn't started sooner: were they going to swear that they had always agreed with General Felmy? Two years earlier Felmy had said that the Luftwaffe would not be capable of undertaking the task, but at the time Goering had thundered:

'I did not ask for a hypothetical study which merely emphasizes our weakest points. I know these well enough myself.'

Jeschonnek was fretting too:

'If Goering threw all the squadrons of the Luftwaffe at England at the same time, the sky over London would be black with aeroplanes.'

All right, where were these squadrons? That was what Goering had come to find out. And what did he see but a lot of overdressed puppets who spent their time chasing women and getting so attached to the easy life that they had become scared of losing it? But the worst thing was that everyone lied to him. Everyone from the engineers and technicians to the senior officers. Well if they thought they could treat a Reichsmarschall as an incurable invalid who couldn't be told the truth they would soon learn that they were wrong!

What were they waiting for? There was England right in front of their faces. The generals followed Goering's example and adjusted their binoculars, standing all in a row, their faces stinging with the salt air, looking at the cliffs of Dover.

It never entered the heads of the radar operators just across the water that their masts were being scrutinized by all the brains of the Luftwaffe. If a motor torpedo boat had taken a trip across the Channel just then, what a fine target it would have found!

With a few brief orders and a slamming of car doors Goering was gone. It does not appear that the sight of the radar masts provoked him sufficiently to change his order of August 15th in which he had forbidden all attacks on those installations.

Galland was waiting with the others at Cap Blanc Nez, standing to attention. Here the whole landscape was warlike, with fortifications, camouflage netting, coastal artillery and observation posts. It was an unpleasant cloudy day with rain in places. Goering's experiences at Cap Griz Ncz had done nothing to calm him and now his temper was even worse. These were the men who were responsible; these silent figures standing stoically in the rain. Now they would hear what he thought of them. Of all the cowardly, useless, good-for-nothings . . . !

'He flushed like an enraged bull,' reported an eye-witness. Galland, who knew the score, managed to keep looking straight ahead with no more than a trace of a smile on his lips. He wrote: 'Goering came to inspect us and stayed to insult us for more than an hour.' Weitkus, who had a naturally mocking expression, was silent, and Fink, knowing that all that was required of him was to be a good sewer-rat, simply accepted things.

'You have the best fighter aircraft in the world,' shouted Goering, 'what more can you ask for?'

It was then that Galland's reply is supposed to have come. And one must admit that it was most apposite.

'Spitfires, Herr Reichsmarschall.'

Goering is reported to have made a frightful grimace and to have turned gruffly away without waiting to hear more.

The false note that this story strikes lets us decide the point. Every junior officer has a story about his colonel which ends, 'So I said . . . and that shut him up!' Every bank clerk has, at least once in his life, prevented the managing director making some irreparable mistake; but it is a very different matter to imagine Galland trying to make an infuriated Goering look ridiculous in front of his troops.

In any case Galland never claimed that he did. It was the others, who were silent, who said so.

It was almost as if the weather had decided to take an active part in the battle. Goering had summoned his generals to Karinhall on August 19th, the day on which Keith Park had issued his Instruction No. 4. On the 20th Churchill had made his speech, and on the 21st Goering undertook his tour of inspection of the Channel coast. On these three days and on the 22nd and 23rd, the weather bulletins continued to announce 'generally cloudy conditions'.

The rains of August brought relief to the men worn out by fighting. In five days the R.A.F. destroyed thirty-two German aircraft and lost eleven. On August 22nd, during a meeting at the Air Ministry, Air Marshal Harris managed to obtain twelve Lysanders to assist in the rescue of aircrew shot down in the sea.

In France the Germans were busy with plans for increasing the severity of their offensive. The Messerschmitt 109s of *Luftflotte III* were placed under the command of General Lörzer and incorporated in *Luftflotte II*, turning the Pas de Calais into a modern version of the famous pistol pointed at the heart of England.

General von Richthofen noted in his journal that as a result of Goering's intervention: 'We have to change our tactics and attack Great Britain with redoubled energy.'

At last on the 24th the forecast read, 'Fine clear conditions in the south.'

A decisive phase of the Battle of Britain now began. After so many changes of plan and so much bitter fighting the object of the battle had become forgotten. None of the accounts we have makes any mention of Operation Sea Lion, but that was what it was about. It will be recalled that it was scarcely a month since Goering had said: 'Give me just five days of good weather.' Now he had them. Would he at last destroy the R.A.F. and leave the way open for the invasion of Great Britain?

In Berlin, Halder had already expressed the greatest of reserve about the chances of success of such an operation: 'I reject categorically the proposals of the Chief of Naval Staff. There can be no question, as he has suggested, of disembarking on a narrow front. We might as well pour the troops into a sausage machine.'

Despite this sort of reticence, the problem could be stated quite simply. Could the Germans wipe out the Royal Air Force and thus permit a landing before the end of the summer? For this to be done it was necessary to strike at once and decisively against Fighter Command. It was necessary to smash the fighter airfields around London. This would compel the fighters to show themselves and enable the Luftwaffe at least to 'knock the guts out of the R.A.F.'.

There is no doubt that so far the Luftwaffe High Command had been lacking in audacity. It had been over-anxious to protect the bombers and had therefore demanded caution from the fighters. We recall Galland's famous remark about 'chained dogs'. On the other side Keith Park's orders to his Spitfire pilots amounted more or less to saying, 'I am not asking you to shoot down Messerschmitt 109s, but to draw them away from the Heinkels and Junkers, leaving them for the Hurricanes to deal with.'

Although both sides were trying to fight the battle as economically, even as miserly, as possible, both were now to find that it was becoming very expensive and that the destruction on the ground was really terrifying. Leigh-Mallory was the advocate of more offensive tactics, but Park's policy must be evaluated in the light of his situation. It was he who was under siege. The German tactics are at first sight much less easy to understand. For them it was absolutely necessary to act quickly. If the invasion had not taken place before the end of September, the unfavourable weather conditions would force them to postpone it for six months. Who could say what might happen in that time? Possibly Roosevelt might have finished his eel-fishing and America might have awoken. The Germans, who had numerical superiority and who were engaged in a struggle that was vital to their destiny, should have been going for the jackpot. The battle might appear to be insanely confused, but in fact they were winning.

Of course it was not as simple as that. The change of a single variable altered the whole equation. For example, it was decided to go right to the heart of the problem and destroy the hornet's nest of airfields surrounding London. But this brought serious problems, especially for the Messerschmitt 109s. If they were asked to penetrate farther into the United Kingdom they at once became more vulnerable, for they were now operating close to the limit of their range. They would no longer be able to confuse the opposition by approaching their target with many changes of course, but would have to fly straight to their objective. During the actual fighting the Messerschmitt pilots would now have two enemies: the Spitfire and their own petrol. It is not easy to fight with one eye on the fuel gauge. After a long dogfight there was no guarantee that the pilot would not now have to ditch or make a forced landing on the sand dunes. This happened more than once. Colonel Viek records the case of a formation of two hundred and fifty fighters of which only eighty managed to land back at base. 'Because of the inadequate radius of action of our fighters,' wrote Galland, 'the battle took place over less than one-tenth of the British Isles. In the other nine-tenths the R.A.F. was left in peace to have its aircraft built, train its pilots and build up a reserve ready to be brought down to the very small area of actual operations at the most suitable moment.'

If this picture is somewhat simplified, it has nevertheless a certain truth; a truth of which Dowding at Bentley Priory ever lost sight.

In the crucial month of August 1940, England remained, as always, an island.

Manston-in-the-Dust received its final blow.

It was now no more than a ghost airfield. Buildings destroyed, communications cut, a lunar desert.

Ramsgate, too, suffered for its proximity to the doomed Manston. On the sea front, a row of houses was knocked down from one end to the other like a pack of cards.

Fighter Command crossed Manston off the list of its airfields. When, later, it was to be repaired, it became no more than an emergency landing ground. It is said that when Churchill was told about this he said: 'Such a disgrace must never occur again.'

North Weald.

No. 151 Squadron took off to intercept a large enemy formation reported approaching the airfield.

There were 109s everywhere and as these aircraft were more than a match for the Hurricanes, it was not possible to attack the bombers. Even whilst they were in action, the British pilots took the risk of an occasional glance back at their airfield. It was no longer recognizable. Smoke was rising everywhere as the Dorniers and Heinkels made their attacks. 'Of the hangars that stood on the southern side, nothing remained. The whole place is completely changed.'

When the squadron was returning to base it received a warning from the control tower, 'Caution when landing. Bomb craters and unexploded bombs.'

At Manston-in-the-Dust three electricians worked on among the half-buried unexploded bombs which might at any moment go off. They were trying to repair some of the two hundred and forty-eight telephone lines that had been cut.

They refused to admit that Manston was dead.

The air-raids of the afternoons caused a cricket match at Lord's to be interrupted; a sacrilege without precedent in the history of the game. As the sirens wailed the players walked slowly from the field and with regret the spectators left their places. All, that is, except one. Wrapped in a great red overcoat, one man remained impassively in his place. The Scots Guards were bowling and he did not intend to miss a single ball even if it meant being blown sky-high.

It was no joke. An interrupted cricket match meant that

the damned Germans could do more than just invade England; they could interfere with its daily life.

During the course of a performance of *A Midsummer Night's Dream* in Regent's Park, London received three air-raid warnings, the eleventh, twelfth and thirteenth of the day. Then came nightfall.

That night one hundred and seventy German bombers raided Northumberland, Kent and Lancashire. Bombs fell in Rochester and on the outskirts of London, at Kingston.

But this was not all. The German pilots, whose target was the petrol depot at Thames Haven, dropped their bomb loads on the City. The church of St. Giles, Cripplegate, was hit and the blast from another bomb blew Milton's statue off its pedestal. For the first time since the Gotha raids of 1918, the soil of London shook with the blast of enemy bombs.

In itself, this raid was of small importance. It appears to have been due to an error of navigation and the damage sustained was minimal. On the other hand, it was to have serious consequences, for during the night of August 24th–25th, the Germans took a decisive step along the path of 'escalation'. So far the *Luftflotten* had not been authorized to attack London. During his recent staff conferences, Goering had merely asked that preparations should be made for raids on London, Liverpool and Glasgow; he had not given the go-ahead. Had the bomber crews given an accurate account of their raids? What we know of the interrogation that German bomber crews underwent after night raids indicates that they were extremely searching. Major Horst Quednau, the pilot of the Heinkel 111s of K.G. 27, who was based first at Avord and then near Rennes, recalls:

'I have heard crews say "the raid went off all right, but the interrogation . . . !" '

Each man spent half an hour alone with the chief of his bomber group. He would be questioned about the enemy's interception tactics, the location of the searchlight batteries, the quality of radio communication etc.; but the greater part of the questioning woud be concerned with the precision and effects of the bombing.

'At this time,' wrote Horst Quednau, 'we were not allowed to attack any but military targets.'

How did they get on then that night? Were the crews who

had bombed the wrong targets able to reply to the questions they were asked?

'To be unable to reply involved you in disciplinary action,' wrote Horst Quednau. 'So I know of many cases where air crews made false reports which they had agreed upon beforehand.'

In other words, it may be asked whether the High Command of the Luftwaffe knew on the morning of August 25th that it had been, quite unintentionally, responsible for the bombing of London. But we possess documentary evidence which shows conclusively that it did. In his book *Angriffshöhe 4 000,* Cajus Bekker wrote,

'Major Josef Knobel remembers very clearly the telegram from Goering which arrived early the next morning. It was sent to all the bomber units which had been in action the previous night. "An immediate report is required identifying those crews who dropped bombs within the perimeter of London. Luftwaffe High Command will itself undertake the punishment of each aircraft captain involved. They will be posted to infantry regiments." '

Bircham Newton. Dusk on the evening of August 25th.

Squadron Leader Oxley, leader of a group of eighty-one Hampdens, twin-engined bombers, was preparing to take off. His destination, Berlin; his official target, the Siemens-Halske factory.

A full account of this raid was published in *The Times* of Tuesday the 27th. It is a very relaxed, particularly British piece of work by one of Oxley's pilots. To read it, you would think its young author thought no more of going to bomb Berlin than of making a trip to the Henley Regatta. In March 1940 the bombers visited the German capital five times. The author of this report was using his season ticket on the London–Berlin express for the twenty-fifth time.

'Until then we had only been dropping leaflets. When at the briefing before we started the intelligence officer mentioned Berlin, everybody was pleased. We were very keen to have a crack at it, for we had been hoping to do so for some time. So far as the general details were concerned it was just another trip. After the "briefing" we went to the crew room and worked out our course and how we intended to go in. Then we had a bit of dinner. The weather was bad right from the start, and as soon as we gained any height at all we ran into heavy cloud.

'It was the same the whole way, and during the journey we caught sight of only three small gaps in the cloud. For at least two-thirds of the way there was very heavy anti-aircraft fire, much more than usual. One might almost have thought that the Germans were expecting us. Twice I had to take evasive action to escape the shells. When we arrived over Berlin there was a formidable concentration of guns and searchlights. We cruised round for half an hour before we located the target and all the time the guns were popping off at us and accurately. Then suddenly we saw a small gap beginning to open in the clouds three or four miles away and we made for it. First of all we thought we could see the main road junction. Then the hole in the clouds widened still more and we saw that we were right. Next we caught sight of the reflection of the moon on a lake and these two points gave us our position.'

Oxley was far less certain. He descended to 5,000 feet without being able to identify his target. Even if he had gone down to 500 feet he would still have seen nothing. He summed it up like this:

'I was keen, but not that keen. I could have brought my bombs back, of course, but I didn't, *I left them in Berlin.*'

The italics are mine and I use them intentionally. If, that night, Berlin received its first bombing, apart from the bombing of military targets, which it was not possible to identify, it was because the squadron leader, understandably, did not wish to return with his bomb-bays full. Anyway, many aircraft which had not got rid of their load were to disappear over the Channel on their way home and were never to be seen again. There is no reason to suppose that the previous evening, those few bomber pilots lost over London had not had *exactly the same reaction*, and simply jettisoned their bombs. If such was the case, then within twenty-four hours the two opposing capital cities, which had so far been inviolate, were both bombed *for want of anything better to do.* This illustrates how statesmen, though they may conceive subtle plans and weigh carefully questions of peace and war, lose control of events once they let their warriors play with fire.

The pilot interviewed by *The Times* continued his account:

'More flak ... so we did a preliminary canter. We went away and two or three minutes later we came back ... having dropped our bombs we turned away, dodging violently because the guns were getting warm again. We could see a large red fire burning and then the clouds finally closed over the scene.'

On his way home Oxley was in trouble. Near the English coast one of his two engines failed. He continued on the other until it in turn cut. Fortunately Oxley was over Leconfield. He glided in and landed. The first person he met was the controller who gave him a telling off for not taxiing his Hampden to the hangar. This gentleman was a Pole with an incredible accent – explanations were impossible. Exasperated at being unable to make him understand that both the engines had failed, Oxley flung him the remark:

'Taxi it yourself because I can't.'

There was still his report to write and he was dropping with fatigue.

Dawn was rising on August 26th, 1940.

Nothing can alter facts.

London had been bombed for no reason on August 24th; Berlin on the 25th.

These two useless raids were to bring matters to a head. Did Churchill order the raid of the 25th as a reprisal for that of the 24th? *The Times*, on August 28th, asserts that he did not, but this was wartime and the desire for justification took priority over the observance of truth. 'The Royal Air Force attacked clearly defined military objectives which had been selected a long time before.' Even so, it seems that Churchill was taking a gamble. Was not the bombing of London, even accidentally, for him, like an act of providence? Was it not this that he had been waiting for when, at Chequers, he had raised his fists to the sky and cried out: 'So they won't come!' Great Britain could not win this war alone. Churchill knew it. What he wanted, at any price, was to force America to come in. If Milton's statue had been knocked down, then bombs must fall on Berlin before it was back on its pedestal. Out of an incident he would make an event. The enemy's act of clumsiness would be turned into a political act. The Prime Minister ordered the raid against the unanimous opinion of the Royal Air Force Chiefs of Staff.

It seems that German pride was genuinely hurt. Had not Goering once said, 'If a single British bomber attacks Berlin you can call me Meier!'?

There is no doubt that by the interplay of chance and fate these two shoddy and futile raids were to lead the Germans to hurl themselves upon the towns, pointlessly destroying buildings, while their one real chance of winning the Battle of Britain lay in continuing their merciless attacks upon the aerodromes, the aircraft factories and the R.A.F. itself.

But that is another story.

11: Dogfight

'All hell is let loose when you press the button!' Thus René Mouchotte at the controls of a Hurricane for the first time.

Early in the afternoon of August 26th, twelve Hurricanes of 85 Squadron intercepted a formation of fifteen Dorniers not far from Eastchurch. The bombers were protected by about thirty 109s flying ten thousand feet above them. In accordance with their orders, the Hurricanes went for the Dorniers and shot down three of them. One of them went down with pieces of its structure breaking away, but the pilot pulled it out of its dive and crash-landed in a field. Townsend and Hemingway were involved in this action.

After this excellent opening, Hemingway decided to climb and try his luck with a Messerschmitt. He was to regret it. A burst hit his fuselage and set fire to his engine. Hemingway was getting quite used to this. He undid his straps, unplugged his oxygen tube and slipped back his cockpit canopy. There could be no doubt about *his* qualifying for membership of the Cat Club. For the third time, the second in eight days, he dived overboard.

Hanging from his parachute he had the leisure to notice that the Dorniers had a new camouflage colour scheme. The undersurfaces of their wings were painted sky-blue. There was just one that was sooty black; no doubt a night bird that there had not been time to repaint. All change! Hemingway had arrived. He found himself splashing around in the marshes near Pitsea. Back at the airfield he noted in his logbook, concisely enough: 'August 26th. Shot down in flames by Me 109.' As for the unfortunate Hurricane No. 3966, Hemingway had only received it two days before.

'Towards the end of August,' wrote Johnny Johnson, 'I was called into the adjutant's office and told to report to 19 Squadron at Duxford, near Cambridge.'

Johnson had a grand total of 205 flying hours. Recently he had been engaged, with several other pilots, in trials on a Spitfire equipped with two cannon instead of eight machine-guns. It was hoped that this might be the answer to the

Messerschmitt 109s, some of which were armed with machine-guns, some with cannon. Beppo Schmid had stated in his 'Study in Blue' that the Spitfire was inferior to the Messerschmitt 109. In any case the results of the trials were disastrous and Fighter Command suspended them for the time being.

Johnson had twenty-three hours on Spitfires. He recalls: 'The day I flew a Spitfire for the first time was one to remember. To begin with the instructor walked me round the lean fighter plane, drab in its war coat of grey and green camouflage paint, and explained the flight-control system. Afterwards I climbed into the cockpit while he stood on the wing root and explained the functions of the various controls. I was oppressed by the narrow cockpit, for I am reasonably wide across the shoulders and when I sat on the parachute each forearm rubbed uncomfortably on the metal sides.

"Bit tight across the shoulders for me?" I inquired.

"You'll soon get used to it," he replied. "Surprising how small you can get when one of those yellow-nosed brutes is on your tail. You'll keep your head down then! And get a stiff neck from looking behind. Otherwise you won't last long!"

Johnson was posted to Duxford in the extreme south of 12 Group's area, almost on the line dividing it from 11 Group. Frequently patrols of 242 Squadron, based farther north at Coltishall, would land there. No. 242 Squadron, most of whose pilots were Canadian, was led by Wing Commander Douglas Bader. He had lost both legs in an accident in a Bristol Bulldog nine years earlier, but he had lost none of his authority. He had decided opinions about the value of the standard fighter tactics. He had a 'thing' about the classic VIC formation which he abandoned in favour of the pair, a loose formation of two aircraft. The leader of each pair would seek out the enemy and the number two would guard his leader's tail. These pairs were rather like the links of a watch chain; they could be hooked on to each other to make a chain of any length. The Germans had adopted this formation at Mölders's instigation and they used it in conjunction with their normal section. In the course of the fighting, ideas about the tactical positioning of aircraft had developed and the rules had been made less rigid. Sometimes a squadron would operate with four sections of three aircraft, sometimes with three sections of four. In the latter case the three sections were like snakes weaving about. This presented a dreadful problem for the number four, 'tail-end Charlie', who, as he was usually the most junior pilot, would be so obsessed with not losing his leader that he had scarcely time to look behind. Sometimes there would be a short burst and he was finished, without seeing what hit him.

For his first flight with Bader, Johnson was flying number three in a section of four. 'Ahead of me were Cocky and the Wing Commander,' he writes. 'Behind me, in the unenviable tail-end Charlie position, was an apprehensive Nip.'

Johnson stifled a cry; there, just ahead and not a hundred feet above him, were three Messerschmitt 109s. It was too good to be true! They were flying on the same heading as the Spitfires and appeared not to have seen them. Johnson thought for a second what he should do. No. 145 Squadron was up at a higher altitude and the Messerschmitts would make a perfect target for them. Should he warn them? But Bader's reputation was great and he was always keen to add to his score. Johnson called his own leader, but in doing so, instead of giving him the necessary information, he called out the warning: 'Look out Dogsbody.'[1]

What had he done? Around him the formation exploded!

'They took swift evasive action and half-rolled, dived, aileron-turned and swung out in all directions.' Johnson realized the mistake he had made. He had given the danger signal exactly as if there were 109s about to bounce them from behind. When he returned to dispersal he didn't know where to put himself. Bader was wearing his black expression:

'Close the door, Billy.'

Someone closed the door. God, but it was hot! His shirt was sticking to his back and his flying suit weighed a ton.

'Now,' Bader said, 'who's the clot who shouted "look out"?'

'I did.'

'Very well. Now tell us what we had to "look out" for?' demanded the angry Wing Commander.

'Well sir, there were three 109s a few hundred feet above ...'

'Three 109s!'

1. 'Dogsbody' was Bader's code name, based on his initials D.B.

The Wing Commander repeated the phrase, lingering over it with a fierce expression as if every word tasted bitter. He must have been thinking, 'If those blasted Huns saw us they must have thought we were chicken!' He forced himself to be calm.

'Your girlish scream made us think there were fifty of the brutes behind.'

And as they had lost three easy targets he might have gone on to say: 'I'm wondering if you don't deserve an Iron Cross for your little exploit; many German pilots have won it for less!'

'In future', writes Johnny Johnson, 'the words "look out" would not be used. In dire emergencies we would cry "break port, blue section" or even "break port, Ken", for Bader preferred the use of Christian names . . . In all other instances enemy aircraft would be reported according to the clock code, with full details, thus: "Dogsbody from red two. Six 109s at two o'clock, high. About 2,000 yards." '

As he left the dispersal hut on his two artificial legs, Bader winked at Johnson and gave him an encouraging grin. That was the worst of all.

'I never forgot that lesson,' admits Johnson.

The war was becoming increasingly bloody.

Fantastic rumours were spreading beneath the surface. It was said that German corpses, terribly burnt, had been washed up on the beaches. It was even said that people in Paris, living in avenue Friedland, rue du Faubourg Saint-Honoré and rue Beaujon, could not sleep for the screams of the wounded in the Beaujon Hospital. According to the sensation-mongers there had been an attempted landing on the English coast which had been repelled with such heavy loss of life that the Channel was 'white with corpses'.

There's no smoke without fire.

What had happened was that the British had been carrying out a spectacular experiment on the south shores of the Solent. Vast quantities of petrol had been poured into the sea and then set on fire by rockets containing petrol and caustic soda. The flames had leapt high into the air, reaching up above the cliff tops, while below, the sea had boiled. This no doubt was what the apocalyptic rumours were based on.

'We took no steps to contradict such tales,' wrote Winston

Churchill, 'which spread freely through the occupied countries in a wildly exaggerated form and gave much encouragement to the oppressed populations.'

At Uxbridge, Keith Park concealed, beneath the infinite dignity of a senior British officer, his continuing rage and anger. Everything was against him; first and foremost the topography. The area under his command was the most exposed part of the whole of Great Britain. It was literally 'invasion country'. Because of the way in which Fighter Command had split the country up into the different group areas, almost the whole of the enemy offensive fell on him alone. Furthermore, the experience of the raid on Debden had taught him that if he could always rely on a helping hand from No. 10 Group, the same could not be said of No. 12 Group. When he complained about this he was sure that he was putting into words the feelings of the pilots of No. 12 Group who were itching to get into the fierce fighting to the south of them. One of the results, among many others almost as hard to bear, of the excessive respect paid to the lines of demarcation drawn between the groups, had been the destruction of Manston. From now on Park grew weary of applying to his colleague to the north. He put his request directly to Bentley Priory.

Officially, the disagreement was regarded as merely a lack of co-ordination between the commanders of two groups, but in fact it was a complete break between Park and Leigh-Mallory. There can be no more serious difference between operational commanders than a total difference of theory. To simplify the issue we may say that Park's methods were above all defensive, while Leigh-Mallory's were offensive. As both men were convinced that they were right (and indeed they were both right in the sense that together their views represented a complete strategy), neither would give an inch. It so happened that it was Leigh-Mallory's view that convinced Air Vice-Marshal Sholto Douglas, the Deputy Chief of Air Staff. Park's insistence on his own theory was to cost him the command of No. 11 Group when the battle was over. On August 27th, 1940, all that had happened was that a new instruction, more biting in tone than that of the 19th, was issued from Uxbridge. The experience of the coming week was to harden attitudes all round.

Let us try to make an objective assessment of the practical results of the two theories. The first thing we notice is an apparent paradox; Park, the more defensive, preferred to operate with small formations. This meant that his squadrons had to go at once into the attack as soon as they had reached the appropriate point and altitude. He was so keen to get as many prompt interceptions as possible that he instructed his formation leaders to accompany their cries of 'Tally-ho' with as much information as they had time to give without worrying about the formalities. He was very happy to receive such calls as:

'There's at least two dozen of the bastards. 109s. They're at 12,000 feet, three miles east of Hornchurch.'

For the controller in the Ops Room, such information was invaluable. It enabled him to intervene as quickly and as effectively as possible. And Park, husbanding his resources, wanted immediate action.

Leigh-Mallory, the advocate of attack, wanted to be sure that when his aircraft gave battle, they did so in force. To ensure this he was prepared to take his time. One by one his squadrons would take off and climb to join up, behind the threatened area if necessary, and only then, when they were in a large and well-knit formation, would they set upon a 'Valhalla'. To some extent this method owed its inspiration to Bader. He had made the suggestion at wing level, proposing to join up No. 242 Squadron and the two Duxford squadrons, Nos. 19 and 310. This, according to him, would make a formation of thirty-six aircraft that would be at once powerful and flexible. Leigh-Mallory looked forward to trying Bader's experiment but on a vast scale. In this way he hoped to strike two or three really heavy blows at the Luftwaffe before it had time to exploit its advantages.

To get into action early, strike a few blows and get away, avoiding contact with the deadly 109s as far as possible; or to concentrate the forces and strike a heavier but later blow: these were the two alternatives. Park, who was always under attack, was like a man running round putting out fires with small buckets of water. Leigh-Mallory, who with 12 Group had to meet fewer attacks, would bring up all the fire-engines and then start pumping. There was the risk that in the meantime the fire would have destroyed everything and that the attackers would have got away scot free.

When they came across each other in a pub, the pilots of the two groups found their own way of continuing the tactical argument:

'We thought we could see four unhappy-looking Spitfires in the middle of that vast enemy formation. Couldn't have been you by any chance, could it?'

'There, we *knew* it must be you,' the pilots of 11 Group would reply. 'I must say it was a magnificent sight, that great aerial armada flying wing-tip to wing-tip in the setting sun. We were even more sure it was you because by the time you arrived the Germans had been gone for hours.'

Park or Leigh-Mallory? Dowding knew that he had to mix fire and water. With his own unyielding personality why could he not appreciate the same characteristic in his group commanders?

During August 24th, 25th and 26th, the R.A.F. scored ninety-nine victories for the loss of sixty-nine of its own aircraft. The score was getting closer. An order from the Air Ministry forbade the staging of a large exhibition of shot-down German aircraft; a large public assembly was considered too much of a risk. Instead a series of small exhibitions were mounted at different places around the country.

The hop-pickers worked with their gas masks over their shoulders. However, the daily reports from R.A.F. Station Kenley always concluded with the words: 'No poison gas used.'

Lord Beaverbrook was continuing his campaign to increase the level of aircraft production. He sent a letter of thanks to General Dobbie, the Governor of Malta, who had forwarded to him the sum of £6,000 raised by popular subscription on the island. 'It is our sacred duty to produce in our factories a fighter capable of meeting and annihilating those who are attacking our fortress!'

Following on his appeal for pots and pans and, later, bones, the Minister of Aircraft Production was now asking for 'gold for Spitfires'. Soon in the small-ads columns appeared notices that said: 'Sell your gold and give the proceeds to your local Spitfire fund.' 'Help bring victory nearer; sell us your unwanted jewellery; highest prices paid for diamonds and other precious stones, silver and plate.'

In addition to the advertisements seeking houses in the

country 'with a view to evacuation', there had now appeared, for several days, an advertisement which offered 'Superbly constructed cellars which make an ideal air-raid shelter'. The company Ciment Fondu Lafarge, 298–302 High Holborn, W.C.1, was ready to undertake immediately the repair of any damaged roads, defence works, factories or public utilities.

The war and its train of problems was beginning to take its place in the daily life of Great Britain. The butter ration was reduced, there were constant appeals by the Red Cross, and in *The Times* the obituary columns grew longer. 'This conflict', wrote *The Times*, 'is more than a difficult struggle for the army, it is a test of character for the whole nation – the ultimate test, in which the courage, endurance and spirit of self-sacrifice of a free nation are opposed to the despotic dictatorship of its enemies.'

In Parliament, a Member rose and said:

'If an archangel appeared before all the members of the War Cabinet at once and said, "There is one red-headed man in England who, unless care is taken, will do something to injure the State," I think it would be the duty of the War Cabinet to see that all red-headed men were interned.'

The strain of war affected people in various ways. It will be remembered that the government had forbidden the ringing of church bells. At Burton-on-Trent, after two months of silence, Michael Dooley, an Irishman of twenty-six, could not stand it any longer. One Friday he climbed to the belfry of St. Paul's church and rang all the bells as hard as he could. Panic in the villages, doors locked and barred – scandal. Dooley pleaded guilty. He wanted to hear what it sounded like. Three months in prison.

In the small ads, below the advertisements for tombstones and funeral masonry, appeared bargain offers of tulip and daffodil bulbs. At Richmond the cricket fortnight opened.

Deacon Elliot of 72 Squadron records that on August 27th, No. 79 Squadron left Acklington to change places with No. 32 Squadron: 'No. 32 had a good record – most of their pilots were decorated – under the leadership of Squadron Leader Mike Crossley – better known as the "Red Ace". He had twenty-two confirmed kills.'

At Rochford, Alan Deere of 54 Squadron saw the arrival of his new squadron commander, Don Finlay, the Olympic hurdler. It looked as though things were starting to move in the squadrons.

Over the Channel August 28th was bright but cool. During the night Portsmouth had been bombed. The Germans were clearly carrying out Goering's instructions and launching small raids in all directions. These consisted of small formations or even single aircraft slipping through at dusk or using cloud cover for their marauding missions. Wromsky, a warrant officer who had been with Lufthansa at Croydon, but was now a Heinkel 111 navigator in *Kampfgeschwader 55,* had been making calculations. He wrote, 'Every time I fly, a million people take to their shelters.'

This was a matter of the air-raid warning system, which was still the subject of considerable controversy in Great Britain. It consisted of three phases: yellow alert which Fighter Command issued to all regions that the bombers might eventually reach, violet alert which was used at night and which meant, among other things, that lights which were still in use at the docks, in factories and marshalling yards, were switched off. Finally there was red alert when the sirens would be blown. Most English people grumbled about the system. The men of the Observer Corps tended to be overconscientious to the point where they would almost get on the telephone to Bentley Priory to report a swarm of bees. There was always the same dilemma: whether to give sufficient notice of a raid and thus disturb a vast section of the population, or, on the other hand, to leave it until the last moment and risk exposing a smaller number to far greater danger.

On that day, August 28th, Winston Churchill was watching the battle through a pair of binoculars from the ramparts of Dover Castle. Fink, in his bus on the other side of the Channel, had already called up his squadrons. It looked like being a great day!

Galland was out with his 109s, escorting a formation of Heinkels. There was a lot of grumbling in the German fighter bases. What was the point of having won the battle of France and being two hours by car from Paris if you weren't allowed to go off in search of girls? A blonde, a Spitfire, another blonde, another Spitfire; a very pleasant prospect indeed. *Verboten!* The pilots were confined to their bases and made to do drill under army drill sergeants. The pilots played up and collected vast herds of stray dogs that drilled with them. Galland watched them, a grin beneath his moustache. He could understand. They were just kids. At their age he'd have done the same. Still holding his cigar between his lips, he climbed into his cockpit.

> So give me your hand, your pretty white hand,
> For tonight we march against England . . .

He crossed the Channel, scanning the sky. His windscreen was misted up. Strange weather for August 28th. There was some sunshine, but it seemed to give the sea a heavy look; very dark, almost opaque. Then, suddenly, below the Heinkels, Galland spotted a formation of strange-looking aircraft. For a moment he thought they were Stukas. In fact they were Defiants of 264 Squadron from Hornchurch. The other Defiant squadron, 141, was still at Prestwick in 13 Group.

The Defiant was a two-seater, single-engined, low-wing fighter with a gun turret behind the cockpit. It was the guns of these turrets that were now trained on the Heinkels from below.

Galland dived for the kill, his 109s following him. It was a massacre. One of the Defiants broke up like a jigsaw puzzle. It turned into a glowing brazier and, stripped of both its wings, dipped through the sky like a red-hot sword blade. Another was shot down and four damaged aircraft returned to their base.

By now the Spitfires of 79 Squadron had arrived. Having flown in the previous day from Acklington, their pilots had not yet had time to taste the pleasures of the mess at Biggin Hill before being thrown into the fray. Galland's wolves had scattered the unfortunate Defiants and were now turning their attention to them. Meanwhile the bombers were blasting Eastchurch.

Another formation of twenty Dorniers was pressing an attack home on Rochford. The Defiants were put into the air again, but there were several squadrons already in the area. No. 54 Squadron was around and Don Finlay took part in two engagements. He managed to come out of the first unscathed, though it was a near thing, but in the second he was knocked out. He was new to the battle and, as was often the way with fresh pilots, he was to be shot down within a few days, for the early days were the most difficult. Later a pilot would pick up a few tips, become hardened, learn all the dirty tricks; then you had to run into a really tough customer or have a bit of bad luck to get yourself shot down. But Finlay had not had the time to learn these things. Colin Gray flew over him and saw him standing in a field waving. He flew off, reassured, believing his squadron commander to be unhurt. In fact, he was to spend many weeks in hospital before getting another squadron, No. 41, also at Hornchurch.

While this was going on, Rochford was bombed again, but the damage was very slight; a few bomb craters on the airfield. Alan Deere landed there and was happy to have the chance of making a call on the boys of 65 Squadron. They had a marvellous story to tell. The medical officer from Hornchurch was at Rochford on a routine inspection when the fun started. Seeing a Dornier which had crashed on the airfield, he rushed up and with great difficulty pulled out the pilot who was in a very bad state. He had just laid him out on the grass when he turned round to be confronted by a most terrifying sight. Inside the gun turret he could see the figure of the gunner. The turret swung round until the guns were pointing straight at him. He shuddered and, so that there could be no mistaking his intentions, bent over the wounded man and made a great show of attending to him. When he stood up again, the guns were still pointing at him. He made a leap for the shelter of the wing and then crept along the fuselage towards the turret. When he reached it he breathed a sigh of relief. The gunner had fired his last shot.

While Alan Deere was listening to this curious story before taking off again, Morris of 79 Squadron was out over the Channel with a section of two aircraft. They attacked a Heinkel 59 which was clearly marked with red crosses, and after two passes, sank it. When he returned, Morris was worried. Should he have done it? He and his number two were assured that their action was perfectly correct.[1]

What he did not know was that his neat piece of work had been executed under the eyes of Winston Churchill.

After his inspection of the battle from the cliffs of Dover, the Prime Minister went on to Manston. With his staff, he walked among the piles of rubble. Everywhere there were

1. Alan Deere had had a similar experience with 54 Squadron on July 11th.

craters and a layer of chalk covered the whole place. He walked on in silence.

The airfield was scattered with little yellow flags indicating places that were unsafe to land. Alan Deere observed that from a distance it looked like a field covered with little yellow dots.

Was it a matter of superstition? Or perhaps of not giving way to the enemy? Who made the decision? The Prime Minister? The Air Ministry? Fighter Command? The end of the war shed no light on the question, but somebody decided that 54 Squadron should take off from Hornchurch every morning and position itself at that cursed airfield, Manston. Pilots who were new to the squadron often had to make two or three low passes before they could find a place to land. Manston was being kept alive only by artificial respiration while overhead in the criss-cross pattern of blue sky and contrails, the battle continued.

Alan Deere was flying again for the third time. He was now leading 54 Squadron. Towards the end of the afternoon three large formations of German fighters were picked up over the Thames estuary at 25,000 feet. Deere was worried. The squadron was in terrible shape with Finlay shot down, not more than four pilots capable of leading a section, and now the incident with Jack Coleman.

Deere had wanted to give him a chance. He had been noticing him in action and thought that with a little practice he would make a good section leader, but when he gave him the news, Coleman's reaction was disappointing:

'I would rather not fly again today, Al, I don't feel well.'

'What do you mean, not well? You're probably just overtired like the rest of us. I'm sorry, but you will have to fly, there's no one else capable of taking the second section.'

Coleman controlled his feelings, contenting himself with the abrupt reply:

'If you say so.'

Sitting in his cockpit Deere was wondering whether, under the strain they were all feeling, Coleman had not become another Dennis. 'Dennis' is a fictitious name used by Deere when he is talking about one of the squadron's sergeant pilots whose nerve went at a very inopportune moment. The squadron was attacking a formation of Stukas when some Messerschmitt 109s appeared on the scene. In the middle of the fighting 'Dennis's' Spitfire was seen heading off home. This was on July 25th, the day of the battle over the convoy C.W.9; the day 'Wonky' Way was killed. And if 'Dennis' hadn't turned yellow and fled, 'Wonky' might still be there, in the mess, looking sour, for sure, but at least still there. Nobody could manage a smile at meals any more; they made a sad-looking squadron. Gribble's good humour was gone, Colin Gray was hollow-cheeked and some of the others looked like ghosts. Deere had lost weight and his forehead was heavily lined.

To return to the question of 'Dennis'. He had been nailed on his return and made to explain himself. He claimed that his motor was not working properly, but when it was tested it was perfect. He just wasn't the right type and, confronted by the steady gaze of the others, he did not make much of a showing. He was given one more chance and then posted as 'operationally tired'. It was with 'Dennis' that one of the pilots of 45 Squadron refused to fly.[1]

Deere thought of 'Dennis' and then of Coleman, but not for long. The 109s were back and the whole sector was buzzing with them. Over Herne Bay, 56 Squadron from North Weald, always a game crowd, was already engaged. 'Al' immediately got on the tail of a 109 and was just about to open fire when he saw a Spitfire diving down from a much higher altitude to move into position on his tail.

'Good!' he thought, 'he's coming to give me a hand.'

He had three of the bastards right in front of him. Fine! He'd make them dance a nice foursome! Then things started happening so quickly that Deere had no time to realize what was going on. He heard a series of explosions and his aeroplane pitched. Deere looked behind and there was the Spitfire which had just finished firing at him breaking away and moving out of sight. 'Al' hung on to the stick and tried to keep the aircraft flying straight and level, but the bullets had cut his control lines and the port wing and fuselage were riddled with bullet holes. Impossible. Up ahead, the 109s had taken advantage of this miraculous and unexpected bit of help and were making off. What a mess! 'If only I could get my hands on that chap,' thought Deere, as he realized with rage that there was no way he could save his old Spit. In a few

1. See page 109.

minutes it would be a heap of scrap. There wasn't even a chance of rolling it on its back before baling out; it was a really sick aeroplane. Deere rolled it very slightly to one side, slid back the canopy, undid his straps and in a flash was dangling ten thousand feet over Kent.

Beneath him in the sunlight, the countryside was green and lush, suggesting ripe fruit and long summer evenings. To one side, he could see the Canterbury–Gillingham road cutting straight through the fields; the Watling Street of earlier and happier days. He then thought of the past, and of New Zealand; a contrast to his present life of dogfighting. As the ground grew closer, he pulled on his parachute lines and side-slipped to avoid a farmhouse, ending up instead in the middle of a plum tree, not without some nasty and embarrassing scratches. As he sat there in the top of the tree that he had pruned fairly harshly with his arrival, he heard an angry voice shouting to him to stay where he was and not move. He looked down. Between him and the voice was a gun barrel and behind the voice an irate Kentish farmer, holding his shotgun in the manner of a man who knows that he holds the strategic position and is also at the right end of the gun.

Deere did not lose his head, but for a moment he wondered whether the farmer might not misinterpret his New Zealand accent. Finally he announced that he was British. 'Oh,' replied the voice from behind the gun, 'and did you have to choose my best plum tree to land in?'

Hemingway wrote an entry in his log-book:

'Dogfight with 20 Me 109s.'

And again, the same day:

'Dogfight with 3 Me 109s.'

Flight Lieutenant Townsend scored hits on a 109 which made a forced landing. The pilot was taken prisoner.

At Lewes, to the north-east of Brighton, a German aeroplane landed, in perfect condition, on a race course. It was a great mystery how he came to be there. The aircraft was a training machine, a Gotha 145.

The young pilot's face was worth seeing. He was stupefied. He was carrying a load of mail from the German airmen stationed on Jersey and Guernsey and was supposed to land at Strasbourg. But instead, here he was on an English race course surrounded by a detachment of Home Guard volunteers who were very proud of their prize. Some error of navigation!

That evening the interpreters of the British Intelligence Service would have some interesting reading.

All was grist that came to Bill Coope's mill!

Deere arrived back at base to find that his old squadron commander, 'Prof', was back. 'Prof' suggested very sportingly that he should continue to lead the squadron, which he had been doing since Finlay's accident. The New Zealander refused. 'Prof' then mentioned that Coleman was in hospital very ill with malaria which he had been developing for some days.

A dark shadow passed across Alan's face. He might have sent a brave man to his death. But then he smiled. Jack Coleman wasn't another 'Dennis' after all; that was what counted. A few weeks in hospital and he'd be back, just as good a companion as ever.

During the night of August 28th–29th, Alan Wright of 92 Squadron, flying a Spitfire, shot down a Heinkel.

This was a real achievement. Only one pilot had bettered it by shooting down two German aircraft in a single night. But since this exploit, his name had begun to leap from the pages and the chronicles.

His nickname was 'Sailor'.

It was Group Captain A. G. Malan.

In late August 1940, aerial reconnaissance photos taken by the Royal Air Force gave grounds for great concern. Large concentrations of merchant ships were observed at Kiel and Emden. In addition to the ships there were large numbers of barges intended for landing operations. Later others were found at Ostend and Terneuzen.

On August 29th, *Luftflotte II* was out in force. They were 564 Me 109s and 159 Me 110s, a huge pack of fighters with yellow, red and orange noses all sniffing the air for the scent of a Spitfire. Keith Park sent his fighters up believing that this huge force must be escorting bombers; but no, this time the Messerschmitts were having an outing on their own. 'A free sweep over England', what they had always dreamed of. But 11 Group was no young fox and if its prey wasn't there it would take no risk. The British fighters had orders to knock down bombers and not to get knocked down themselves by 109s. With a very few exceptions they slipped off, sliding between the rain showers, diving through the blue sky into the curtains of rain, refusing combat. A few did give battle. They broke, turned towards the enemy, exchanged a few bursts as they might have exchanged insults and then made off to their lairs.

The result of the match was released for the newsvendors' blackboards as 'England 17, Germany 9'.

Alan Deere, returning from Rochford, landed at Hornchurch to find that the station had a visitor: a German bomber pilot who had been shot down the day before or that morning. He was a dark, rather short officer, wearing flying boots, and he was rather pleased with himself. He sat smoking one of those horrible so-called 'Turkish' cigarettes of which the inhabitants of occupied France used to say 'they're made of hay,' and did not seem at all put out to be looked at as though he were some strange animal in the zoo. His eyes seemed to say, 'You can stare, but it will be my turn soon!'

One of the squadron pilots interpreted and astounded his fellows by reporting what the German had said. As fighter pilots they regarded any bomber pilot, of whatever nationality, as a mere manual worker, a dropper of bombs, a bus driver. So they were staggered when this one, sitting comfortably in his chair, announced:

'Hitler will be in London within two weeks.'

He paused for this to sink in and then showed the little case he had with him:

'That's why I only bothered to bring a few toilet requisites with me.'

The German pilot clearly believed this. Despite wind and tide, the preparation of Operation Sea Lion went ahead in the German staff offices. The landings were scheduled for the end of September, either the 21st or the 27th. Raeder had asked for ten days of working up to prepare his fleet, and so the Battle of Britain had to be won by the 17th. The Luftwaffe had only two weeks left.

Its objective was to smash the shield of airfields surrounding London. The British capital would then become 'the biggest target in the world'.

On the morning of August 30th there was good visibility over the Channel. The game of cat and mouse began with some attacks on shipping in the Thames estuary and other isolated raids which were intended to divert attention from the big blow that was to fall. The attackers were fortunate. The clouds had lifted and formed a thick layer at about 7,000 feet, hiding from the watchers of the Observer Corps a force of a hundred aircraft forming up over the Pas de Calais. When at last they were detected, Fighter Command sent off sixteen squadrons against them.

Alexander McKee[1] gives an account of what happened to Teddy Morris of 79 Squadron. According to him, Morris was leading a patrol of six Hurricanes. Basil Collier in his book *The Defence of the United Kingdom,* which the British regard as the Bible on anything to do with the Second World War, states that 79 Squadron, which was stationed first at Acklington, then at Biggin Hill, was equipped with Spitfires.[2] In any case, Hurricane or Spitfire, Morris dived on a

1. Alexander McKee's book *Strike from the Sky* is the most fascinating work written on the Battle of Britain. It cannot be too highly recommended.

2. Translator's note: So does the official history of the Royal Air Force.

formation of Heinkels. He passed through it and came upon a second.

'All I saw was a grey blur, and felt an awful thump on my right wing. I immediately went into a violent spin,' he wrote.

Very soon Morris was hanging beneath his parachute, and looking up saw three other open canopies in the sky: the occupants of the Heinkel which he had hit had managed to jump from their burning aircraft.

'There the bastard is!' cried a farm labourer who was carrying a pitch-fork as Morris landed. Beside him was another armed with a shotgun.

'I remember letting go a volley of Elizabethan epithets to indicate I was friendly.'

Recognition, effusive welcome. Kisses from an elderly farmer's wife and a splendid lunch. Morris was back at Biggin Hill 'for the second attack of the day'.

The first attack had severely shaken the airfield which, luckily, remained in service. The second was more scattered, with aircraft being sent to attack Shoreham, Kenley, Tangmere and, once again, Biggin Hill. Attacks were also made on six or seven radar stations on the coast.

The game was by no means over. Biggin Hill, among other airfields, caught it for the third time in one day. Detling was set on fire as the Luftwaffe redoubled the force of its attack upon the shield of airfields around London.

At six o'clock in the evening a group of ten raiders flew up the Thames estuary at wave-top height. Clearly they were going to bomb shipping. But no, they made a sharp turn and keeping very low, roared across country at full speed towards Biggin Hill. The demolition contractors were working shift work.

The officers' mess is a most attractive red-brick building surrounded by greenery. In late August the front of the mess is covered with Virginia creeper. Behind there is a terrace which looks down on a large garden descending in a series of steps towards the open country. Later a swimming pool was to be built there. The main road separates the airfield from the mess. The mess was not hit, but its walls shook.

Across the road everything was wrecked; the workshops, the transport section, the stores, the long brick-built barrack blocks, one of the hangars with its great sliding doors, even the W.A.A.F.s' quarters ... There was no water, no gas, no electricity, no telephone; nothing but fire and ruin everywhere. Thirty-nine people were killed and twenty-six wounded, and even while the corpses were being pulled out of the wreckage, the work of clearing and repair was begun. Biggin Hill remained in action.

Better still, it was reinforced.

'It was on the evening of August 30th,' writes Deacon Elliott. 'Some of us were showing the "32" pilots the haunts when the phone rang in the office of the manager of the Ashington dance hall – he was entertaining us – "All pilots of '72' return immediately to prepare to leave for Biggin Hill in the morning." '

*

At dinner time, Leigh-Mallory, the Air Officer commanding No. 12 Group, landed at Coltishall. He came to congratulate the pilots of 242 Squadron who had shot down twelve Germans in the course of the day. Of these, one pilot, MacKnight, had accounted for three.

Bader came forward on his artificial legs. Two of the victories had been his.

'As a matter of fact, sir, if we'd had more aircraft we could have knocked down a lot more.'

Bader appealed to Leigh-Mallory to be allowed to increase the size of his formations still more. Leigh-Mallory found the idea attractive, but replied that he would need time to think about it.

But the final picture was black. In the air twenty-five British aircraft had been shot down for thirty-six Germans.

The sand was running again in the hour-glass.

In beautiful weather, on August 31st, fifty balloons were burning over Dover. Messerschmitt 109s hacked them down with bursts of machine-gun fire and the great elephantine shapes grew flabby and then sank, one ofter another, in a blaze of light. Some of them had been moored out to sea, others over the land. Not one was left.

But this was not just a destructive game; it was also a signal for an attack.

North Weald, Duxford and Debden were pounded by

Dorniers with fighter escorts. The Spitfires of 19 Squadron took off to intercept. J. B. Coward was in action and fighting above his own house. He found the sensation 'exalting'. He was hit by a burst of fire which tore his foot almost completely away from his leg and was obliged to bale out. As he did so his wounded foot smashed against the side of the cockpit and his nerves blazed with pain. Gritting his teeth, Coward looked at his leg. Blood was pouring out and as he fell it was floating up past him. Quite literally, he could watch his life's blood drifting away. Realizing that he would be empty when he reached the ground, he managed to get at the radio lead that was attached to his helmet and tighten it round his thigh.

Coward tried to avoid letting his gaping leg come in contact with the ground, but the landing was dreadful and his reception not much better; he too was confronted with a pitch-fork.

Teddy Morris of 79 Squadron was shot down by a 109 just as he was finishing off a Dornier. His legs were riddled with shell splinters, but he managed to get back to Biggin Hill and make a belly-landing.

Hauptmann von Eschwege, with his *Jagdgruppe* I/JG 52, continued on course towards Eastchurch.

Meanwhile, 72 Squadron, which had taken off from Acklington, was flying south. And a glorious flight it was too. On Fighter Command's map of the British Isles dated July 1940 there were three little black patches. They looked as though they might indicate outcrops of coal. All three were in the northern half of Great Britain between Edinburgh and Leeds. They were the 'unobserved areas' where, in theory, one could sleep in peace at night. Not far away was Catterick, where pilots were sent to rest; or to be more exact, used to be sent. It was at Catterick that Gribble had left behind his little W.A.A.F.

The squadron stopped at Bicester in Oxfordshire to refuel. 'The station commander', wrote Deacon Elliott, 'was simply terrific; like the party he had organized. Our eyes popped open wide; the luxury of a starter trolley and an airman for each aircraft was incredible. Then there were drinks, fruit and food served with loving care by the wives. All this under the blazing sunshine of early afternoon on Saturday, August 31st, 1940.'

The Huns were there again. A hundred aircraft crossed the coast at Dungeness, the place that must have seen more German aircraft fly overhead than any other in England throughout the battle. The 'Valhalla' split into two parts, one turning away to the north-west, whilst the other, KG2 led by Oberst Fink, continued straight on to the north.

The first group steered for Croydon and Biggin Hill.

'We landed at Biggin Hill at 1530,' wrote Deacon Elliott. 'As we flew in, No. 610 – or what was left of them – flew out; they seemed in a hell of a hurry and we were soon to find out why. We were ordered to readiness as soon as refuelling was completed. Then within minutes we were to take off on our first mission in what we now all know as the Battle of Britain.' Already the first explosions could be heard. 'I saw at least two dispersed aircraft burning from the direct hits with incendiary bombs. Bomb craters everywhere.'

At Croydon, twelve bombs destroyed a hangar and damaged several buildings. In a brief engagement the Hurricanes of 85 Squadron shot down two 109s and one 110 but lost two of their own machines in doing so. Peter Townsend was wounded. Hemingway, who flew on three sorties that day, made two attacks on a large formation. On his first sortie he fired at a 109 and, seeing smoke pouring out of it, expected to have it included in his list of victories. He wrote in his log-book, 'August 31st. Dog-fight with Balbo. [A large formation of aircraft was sometimes called a 'Balbo', after the Italian general of that name.] One Me 109 possible.'

Pilot Officer Allard was adding to the series of exploits that were to make him the ace of the squadron. He scored hits on a Dornier 17, a Dornier 215 and a Messerschmitt, but did not have time to see what happened to them.

When the pilots of 72 Squadron landed back at Biggin Hill, they realized the extent of the damage. The previous day's raid had destroyed almost everything. It was now known that most of the victims were W.A.A.F.s. The operations room had been blown to pieces and Group Captain Grice wounded. In today's raid another seven people had been killed. The telephone system was cut and field telephone lines were laid. The neighbouring aerodrome Kenley, no longer having contact with Biggin Hill, made an urgent request for the call signs of 72 and 79 Squadrons, so that it might establish direct contact with them. But the Observer Corps post at Bromley, to which the inquiry was addressed, had no contact with Biggin Hill either. A dispatch rider had to be sent.

'The most amazing thing about it all', writes Deacon Elliott, 'was the human factor – no panic – everyone doing their utmost to keep the aircraft in the air. Bomb craters on the airfield being quickly filled in, food being delivered to dispersals to avoid waste of time returning to messes.'

But he admitted:

'But Biggin was hit very hard and conditions were at a low.'

In this, its baptism of fire at Biggin Hill, 72 Squadron destroyed three enemy aircraft and damaged two. Willie Wilcox was killed. Squadron Leader Collins crashed between two trees and a haystack. 'He was very shaken, but he came back to continue flying,' noted Deacon Elliott. Smith was shot down and terribly badly wounded. A cannon-shell splinter entered the back of his neck, grazed the spinal column and came out of his left ear. Desmond Sheen was reported missing, but it was soon learnt that he had landed at another airfield.

Fink's formation reached Hornchurch, where its arrival took everyone by surprise. So far, as Deere noted, the morning had been 'strangely and ominously quiet ... particularly in view of the good weather.' About lunchtime came the order to scramble. The pilots of 54 Squadron ran to their aircraft and had just taxied out into the position for take-off when they received a counter-order. No doubt this was the moment when the German formation split. It had been supposed that Croydon and Biggin Hill were to receive its undivided attention. So 54 Squadron taxied back to dispersal and stopped their engines.

Richard Hillary, who had spent the whole of the previous day in the air, turned over in bed. He found the noise irritating. He was sleepy and the morning was his to do with as he pleased. Fortunately the noise of the motors ceased. He got up, dressed and went out to find 'the heat haze forming a dull pall over everything'. One of the squadron's lorries offered him a lift, but he refused, preferring to walk across the airfield even though it was forbidden.

Scramble! 'In a matter of seconds,' wrote Alan Deere, 'all twelve aircraft were again taxi-ing to the take-off and urged on by the controller's now near-hysterical voice shouting over the R/T:

'"... Get airborne as quickly as you can, enemy in the immediate vicinity."'

Hillary could also hear the controller. To him the voice did not sound hysterical, but he is alone in this. Alexander McKee speaks of a 'frantic controller'. Hillary, who was himself exceptionally calm, remembers the 'emotionless voice of the controller'. Perhaps it depended upon whether the listener was taking part in the action or was merely an eye-witness. Hillary looked up.

'I saw them – about a dozen slugs, shining in the bright sun and coming straight on.'

Alan Deere had turned his Spitfire into wind and was just about to open the throttle to take off when he noticed that his No. 2, Sergeant Davies, was blocking his path.

'Get to hell out of the way, Red Two.'

There were one or two seconds of delay, but that was enough. As Deere careered across the airfield in pursuit of his squadron the first bomb fell. 'At the rising scream ...' wrote Hillary, 'I instinctively shrugged up my shoulders and ducked my head.' 'Good, I have made it!' thought 'Al'. Afterwards all he was able to remember was that 'A tremendous blast of air, carrying showers of earth, struck me in the face.'

'Out of the corner of my eye,' wrote Hillary, 'I saw the three Spitfires. One moment they were about twenty feet up in close formation; the next catapulted apart as though on elastic. The leader went over on his back and ploughed along the runway with a rending crash of tearing fabric ...'

This was 'Al' Deere, still hanging strapped in his seat as his inverted Spitfire slid along the ground, scraping his helmet and spattering him with stones. At last with a horrible crunching sound the aeroplane stopped.

'The No. 2', wrote Hillary, 'put a wing in and spun around, on his airscrew, while the plane on the left was blasted wingless into the next field.'

Watching this, Hillary had one of those stupid thoughts that the sight of a catastrophe so often provokes. When we look back, we cannot believe that we thought as we did; but nevertheless it is true. Hillary remembered thinking, 'That's the shortest flight that he's ever taken.'

At the precise moment his feet were nearly knocked from under him and he found that his mouth was full of dirt. He caught sight of a friend shouting at him from the shelter entrance,

'Run, you bloody fool, run!'

Deere, meanwhile, was hanging in almost total darkness. Bombs were exploding all around, but they did not worry him. It was what he could smell that was terrifying. The smell of petrol, at first scarcely apparent, then growing stronger and finally overpowering. He looked around him; he was hanging in a bath of petrol. One spark and he would be a bonfire.

'Al, Al, are you alive?'

God how good it was to hear a friend's voice. He could not tell where the voice came from, but it was near, friendly, rough – a man's voice. It was Eric Edsall, his No. 3.

'Yes, but barely. For God's sake get me out of here quickly!'

They had to work at it together, one pushing and the other pulling. For a moment Deere thought that he was not going to be able to release his parachute harness. At such a moment the smell of petrol seems like the smell of death; and it was still there, more tenacious than ever. At last they managed it and Deere wriggled through the tiny opening of the cockpit door. He was out, out in the fresh air, out into life . . .

'Come on, let's get off the airfield quickly, our "Mae Wests" will attract the Hun fighter pilots,' said Eric breathlessly.

He was in no fit state for hurrying, the poor fellow. Hit in the leg, he had had to crawl across to Alan's Spitfire. Now he supported himself around his leader's neck and together they struggled through the bomb craters until they reached the sick quarters. These had been hit too, but treatment was still being given, as well as possible, to a queue of injured airmen. Deere left his No. 3 in capable hands and went off to the mess where he threw himself on his bed. He was dead tired and would rather wait for the Medical Officer to come and see him later. The accumulated fatigue of all the days that had just passed it him now, all at once. He had had enough; more than enough!

Hillary came out of his shelter to find his Spitfire covered with a shower of grit and rubble.

'Will you get hold of Sergeant Ross and tell him to have a crew give her an inspection.'

The aircraftman who was standing beside him pointed out where the lorry lay 'grotesquely on its side'. The roof had been blown about twenty yards further on.

'Sergeant Ross won't be doing any more inspections,' he replied.

Ross was the driver, who, less than a quarter of an hour before, had asked Hillary if he wished to climb up beside him.

Lying in bed, Deere began to feel his injuries. The skin had been torn off above his right temple and his face had been torn by pebbles. His face felt as if it was burning and his head was heavy; he could not turn it on its stiff neck. He felt rigid, frozen like a statue. He did not know whether it was anger or disgust or exhaustion that had hold of him; he just felt, what a bastard of a war!

Colin Gray, as he landed, saw the remains of Alan's Spitfire. He groaned to himself:

'Poor old Al, he's had it.'

And where was Davies, Deere's No. 2? His aeroplane was there lying outside the airfield boundary in two pieces, just as Hillary had described. A search was started and the wreckage was examined. But there was no sign of him. Perhaps he had been blown to pieces.

Late in the afternoon he arrived, carrying his parachute. He had been blown still sitting in his cockpit into the river Ingrebourne. He had climbed out unhurt but had had to walk two miles round the outside of the aerodrome fence before he could get back in.

The bodies of the four men killed in the lorry were taken away and then, after the wounded had been bandaged, the craters filled in and the unexploded bombs marked with little yellow flags, there was time to pause and take breath. 'Six o'clock came and went . . .' wrote Hillary. 'We started to play poker and I was winning. It was agreed that we should stop at seven: should there be a "flap" before then, the game was off.'

At 6.55: scramble!

'603 Squadron take off and patrol base: further instructions in the air.'

The twelve aircraft formed up over the airfield in four

sections of three. Hillary was flying No. 3 in Blue Section. Following their instructions they climbed to fifteen thousand feet and then turned onto a heading of 110°. They were being vectored to intercept the Ju 88s and Me 110s heading for Hornchurch with another load of bombs. The enemy formation was reported at about twenty thousand feet and so they continued their climb.

'And then', wrote Hillary, 'quite clearly over the radio I heard the Germans excitedly calling to each other. This was a not infrequent occurrence and it made one feel that they were right behind, although often they were some distance away. I switched my set to "send" and called out "*Halt's Maul!*" and as many other choice pieces of German invective as I could remember. To my delight I heard one of them answer: "You feelthy Englishman, we will teach you how to speak to a German." '

Whilst this new battle was building up in the air, Deere, not yet recovered, received a visit from Gribble.

'I can only stay a minute . . . Must tell you about my cow before I go . . .'

'I can't see how a cow can have any connection with what's going on, unless you have bought one to supply early morning milk to the pilots.'

'Not a bit of it, old boy,' replied George. 'Norwell and I fastened on to a Me 109 which we chased at tree-top height right across Essex, taking a pot shot at him whenever the trees would allow. In the course of our chase we crossed a meadow full of grazing cows and unfortunately for one of them I chose that moment to fire a burst. A cow was right in my line of sight and took the full blast. It went up vertically for about twenty feet, just as if someone had ignited a rocket tied to its tail, before plomping back to earth. I bet there's still a look of amazement on that cow's face when the farmer finds it.'

'Al' came out of his torpor and, moving his stiff neck with difficulty, replied:

'I take it you're claiming one cow destroyed in your combat report.'

Hillary landed with 603 Squadron. 'There was to be a concert on the station that night,' he wrote, 'but as I had to be up at five the next morning for Dawn Readiness, I had a quick dinner and two beers, and went to bed, feeling not unsatisfied with the day.'

Saturday, August 31st, was the most deadly day of the whole Battle of Britain for Fighter Command. Thirty-nine aircraft were lost and fourteen pilots killed. The Luftwaffe had forty-one aircraft shot down.

If we recall the disproportion of the forces involved – at least four to one – we can see why this first day of the 'worst weekend' should be marked in black in the calendar.

During the night of August 31st–September 1st, Liverpool suffered its fourth successive night raid. The Heinkel in which Wronsky, the former Lufthansa employee from Croydon, was flying was hit on its outward voyage just as it crossed the English coast. It turned back and crashed in France.

When the sun rose on September 1st, the ring of airfields around London presented, for the most part, a scene of desolation. At six o'clock 72 Squadron took off from the ruins of Biggin Hill to land at Croydon. 'Here', wrote Deacon Elliott, 'facilities were very limited but Croydon had not received the punishment of Biggin Hill.'

Field kitchens were set up right on the airfield and at every take-off grass and bits of earth were thrown into the soup. But the pilots, refugees from Biggin Hill, did not mind. They were happy. They were taken to the Airport Hotel where, for the first time in three days, they were able to have a bath and a shave.

If only it had been bad weather! Just one or two little clouds would have been better than nothing, but the sky remained relentlessly blue. There were one or two whitish patches over the Channel, but these were soon burnt off when the sun rose.

'At 0955', wrote Deacon Elliot, 'we were scrambled – squadron strength – and soon in the thick of it again. Enemy aircraft were everywhere it seemed. A terrific scrap with Me 109s.'

These were a formation of one hundred and twenty aircraft of *Luftflotte II*. They crossed the coast at Dover and spread out for Eastchurch, Detling, Tilbury and Biggin Hill. To meet this threat, Bentley Priory put up fourteen squadrons and one flight. No. 72 Squadron was among those scrambled and received a mauling. Oswald Pigg was reported missing. He was later found, buried beneath his Spitfire in a little wood in Kent. Happy Thomson was wounded and sent to hospital. Desmond Sheen had to descend by parachute. During his descent he saw a 109 pilot in the same situation. As he watched, the German pilot slipped from his harness and dropped towards the earth like a stone. When Sheen landed he was met by an army officer brandishing a revolver. 'I ignored the revolver, continued to pick up my parachute, and started as normal a conversation as possible under the circumstances,' wrote Sheen. Sergeant Pocock was seriously wounded in the leg by a cannon-shell splinter and in the hand by a bullet.

Meanwhile the Dorniers had been blasting Biggin Hill. Such persistent and savage attacks had not been seen since Manston was wiped out. The airfield was covered with craters and the pilots of 610, who were just getting into the buses which were to take them off for a rest period at Acklington, ran for cover in the woods. One of them was ordered to remain where he was by an 'excessively keen' officer holding a pistol. He obeyed and stood helplessly watching as his Spitfire went up in flames. No. 72 Squadron returned but were unable to land and were diverted to Croydon. At that moment Biggin Hill looked deserted, all its squadrons gone.

At Croydon, 72 Squadron had just the time necessary to refuel and were off again. This time they were flung into the attack against a force of one hundred and fifty German aircraft coming in from Cap Gris Nez. Deacon Elliott wrote, 'We were split up by enemy fighters as we closed with a bomber formation and now it was every man for himself. In the process my aircraft was badly mauled by an enemy fighter, tearing a gap the size of a dinner plate in the port wing, damaging the tail-plane and punching numerous holes in the wing.' He limped back to Croydon and landed. His aircraft was a complete write-off.

Hawkinge, Lympne, Detling and, once again, the balloon barrage at Dover were all attacked, but it was Biggin Hill that took the worst punishment. For the seventh time it was bombed flat. Everything that had been more or less repaired after the morning's raid was once more mercilessly knocked down again. The sector operations telephone exchange was smashed. Two W.A.A.F. telephonists kept the system working until the very last moment. Lying flat on their stomachs amid the broken glass and plaster they continued replying 'Yes sir,' as if nothing had happened until the last lines were cut. Both Sergeant Helen Turner and Corporal Elspeth Henderson received the Military Medal. When the bombing was over, it was decided to remove whatever equipment was still usable from the shattered buildings, where it might be damaged by walls or roofs falling in. Technicians had been working in conditions of incredible discomfort and danger since the previous day, trying to re-establish communications; but every time they succeeded, a new attack would render their efforts useless. With aircraft burning and the air unbreathable because of the smoke, the dust and the gas leaks, Biggin Hill resembled the ruins of some chaotic open-air fairground that had been reduced to a pile of wreckage. It bore no resemblance to an airfield. Alexander McKee records a remark made by an engineering officer: 'Pilots who were on the ground when there was a raid couldn't get into the air quick enough. When you can hit back it's a build to morale. But to sit on the ground, without a gun, unable to hit back, and just get blasted, is a terrifying experience.'

Some of the pilots got results.

Hemingway wrote in his log-book:

'September 1st. Dogfight with Balbo. 1 Me 110 probable.'

Deacon Elliott drew up the day's balance sheet for his squadron: 'Did four missions on that day – all interceptions and claimed six Me 109s confirmed and a Do 17 in addition to several damaged.' But 72 Squadron had on its own accounted for half the British score and the final result was bad. For the first time since the start of the battle, the Germans had shot down more aircraft than they had lost. The London news-vendors wrote on their blackboards on September 1st:

Germany 15, Great Britain 14.

'Fine and warm.' 'Fine and warm.' 'Fine and warm.' The weather forecast began with the very same words on September 2nd, 3rd and 4th.

The Luftwaffe was now intent upon the destruction of the defences of 'the biggest target in the world' and redoubled its attacks on the ring of airfields shielding it. Shattering blows were delivered against Eastchurch, Rochford, Debden, Biggin Hill (yet again!) and North Weald. It was at this last airfield that the most serious damage was caused; the hangars were set on fire and the telephone system put out of service. The operations centre suffered a direct hit . . .

No. 72 Squadron spent September 2nd going up and down like yo-yos. After the excitement of the previous day, the squadron passed a quiet night and in the morning moved to

Hawkinge. The pilots were pleased to be joined by Wing Commander Lees who was to spend a week with them. On the first sorties Squadron Leader Collins was shot down with serious injuries in the knee and hand. Ted Graham took over the command of the squadron; but not for long. He was shot down over Lympne. And what of Wing Commander Lees? Soon afterwards, he crashed at Hawkinge and it was only with great difficulty that he was extracted from his cockpit. He took off again and plunged into a swarm of Me 110s. When he emerged it was with an aeroplane that was only fit for scrap and with his thigh laid open. 'This was bad luck,' wrote Deacon Elliott. 'We had hoped he would be with us for a whole week.' Sergeant Norfolk was more fortunate. He crashed-landed his burning aircraft and walked away unhurt. A hell of a day just the same!

*

The squadron claimed eighteen victories, but the final score was very close; thirty-five German aircraft destroyed for the loss of thirty-one.

As on the previous nights Liverpool was bombed. Goering's orders were being carried out to the letter.

On September 3rd, in the course of their attacks upon the airfields, the Germans experimented with new 'mixed-bag' tactics. They had realized that the British fighters were trying to isolate the bombers to make it easier to shoot them down. They now countered this by flying in an assorted formation of bombers and fighters together. This experiment was not conclusive and the Luftwaffe soon returned to its familiar method of having the faster 109s fly above the Dorniers, Heinkels and Junkers, ready to dive when they saw the bombers being attacked.

'Still at Croydon,' wrote Deacon Elliott, 'out on the airfield by our aircraft listening to the constant wailing of the air-raid sirens. As the raids came and went it was difficult to differentiate the distant "all clear" from the adjacent "take cover" warnings and vice versa.'

And he concluded:

'Other than rapidly constructed slit trenches we had no

other form of protection at Croydon – anyway by now we were all getting a little blasé with the whole affair.'

A drawn game; the score for the day: Germany sixteen, Great Britain sixteen.

'September 3rd marked the final day of operations for 54 Squadron in the Battle of Britain,' wrote Alan Deere.

After four sorties and some violent engagements with 109s and 110s, late in the evening 54 Squadron was relieved by 41. The close of a chapter in history.

A curious incident took place that day which had nothing really to do with the air fighting or the bombing attacks. Two Dutchmen, working for the Germans, came ashore at Hythe, to the south-west of Folkestone. They had set out from Le Touquet and their task was to provide information for the German invasion troops. Apparently the attack was imminent. They were found by a patrol, wandering along the sea-shore, each with a spare pair of shoes strung round his neck. They had with them a radio transmitter.

A little later two other spies landed at Dungeness and then split up. One of them, a German, working alone, succeeded in setting up a radio aerial in a tree and began to transmit messages. The second, whose nationality is not known, was captured when he stupidly went to a pub and asked for cider outside licensing hours. His companion was arrested the following day.

All four were tried. One of the Dutchmen was acquitted; the other three were hanged.

September 4th.

'First early patrol at 27,000 feet,' wrote Deacon Elliott, 'saw nothing. The weather was still hot and cloudless.'

The Germans kept up their raids on the airfields, but now, in accordance with the Luftwaffe operations bureau order of September 1st, they attacked an aircraft factory. Their target was the Vickers-Armstrong factory at Brooklands where the Wellington bombers were built. Fourteen Junkers 88s were strung out in a clear line on the operations room table, but then disappeared as they slipped into the confused pattern of all the other formations that were airborne. They followed the Southern Railway line and burst on Brooklands like a thunderbolt. Fortunately the sergeant in charge of the anti-aircraft defence of the Vickers aerodrome was keeping a vigilant watch. The first two attacking aircraft were brought down. To the noise of crashing aircraft was soon added the sound of bombs. The Junkers formation had been thrown into disorder, but still their bombs found the mark. Six of them struck, killing eighty-eight people and wounding six hundred more. The factory was out of production for four days.

The Hurricanes caught the bombers over Clandon on their way home. Air fighting had now broken out everywhere. Deacon Elliott watched his friend Dutch Holland landing at Hawkinge after a tussle with a 110. He observed with malicious humour:

'His machine looked more like a pepper pot than a Spitfire – there were even several holes in the blades of his prop.'

It had been a hard day. Some of the pilots went up to London in the evening but found they couldn't get going and so, in Deacon Elliott's words: 'we bathed, fed and tumbled into bed very early, feeling rather exhausted.'

Great Britain beat Germany twenty-five to seventeen.

Liverpool was bombed.

There was much bustling about among the men in the steel-grey tunics with broad white lapels. There was the slamming of car doors; shouted orders in the conference rooms, much consultation of the wall maps – the Luftwaffe was in a state of great agitation. Major the Baron von Falkenstein had started it on September 1st. He reported that since August 8th the R.A.F. and the Luftwaffe had lost 1,207 and 467 aircraft respectively. He went on further to say that the R.A.F. losses had probably been significantly higher. His report concluded:

'The British fighter force is in very bad condition. If our attacks continue during the month of September, and if the weather permits, we may expect to be faced with only the weakest opposition and we shall thus be able to make greatly intensified attacks upon ports and industrial areas.'

Two days later, more slamming of car doors, more Nazi salutes; this time with great pomp at The Hague. From one of the limousines flew the personal flag of Reichsmarschall Hermann Goering. Accompanied by his faithful Beppo, the supreme head of the Luftwaffe had summoned Field-Marshals Sperrle and Kesselring, with all their staff officers, to a conference.

Without any doubt, it was on this day that Germany lost the Battle of Britain. On May 16th, when he prevented the dispatch of further squadrons to France, Dowding had provided Great Britain with the means of resisting the enemy's first violent attacks. On 3rd September, Goering, by making a fundamental change in the instructions he had given to his three *Luftflotten*, allowed Fighter Command to take breath at a crucial moment and so saved the British fighter force from destruction. This change – called by the Germans the *Zielwechsel*: the change of objective – was the greatest error of the Reichsmarschall's career. We must, however, recognize that he had two excuses for what he did: Hitler's burning impatience to attack London and Kesselring's supreme self-confidence.

Let us look a little further into the matter. On the previous day, Hitler had given the order for 'reprisal raids on London'. The time of havering was over. In a single week the political and psychological framework of the problem had completely changed. By the end of August Hitler's famous 'patience' was 'exhausted'. Eight days earlier the pilots who had carelessly dropped a few bombs on London had been posted to infantry units. Now Hitler was preparing a fiery speech to be delivered the next day before the Reichstag. Goering knew well enough what it contained. 'For three months', Hitler was to say, 'I did not reply because I believed that they would stop, but in this Mr Churchill saw a sign of our weakness. The British will know that we are now giving our answer night after night. We shall stop the handiwork of these night pilots.'

Churchill! He was the man, the shadow whose influence finally determined the outcome of the game. His gambler's master-stroke of the night of August 25th–26th had had the effect he desired; his enemy's heart now ruled his mind. The Führer of the Reich was enraged. On his orders the invasion fleet had been assembled for all to see in the North Sea ports. He had sent spies into the enemy's territory. He acted on his 'intuition', the intuition that, against the advice of the Wehrmacht's high command, had achieved the breakthrough at Sedan. After that anything, anything at all, even a miracle, was conceivable.

When he arrived at The Hague, Goering knew very well what the Führer wanted. He had accepted it although it certainly wasn't how *he* would have acted. All his previous instructions are there as proof. He had never ceased insisting on the obliteration of the R.A.F. before all other objectives. He would not have wished for the *Zielwechsel*, but he was ready to submit to it.

Perhaps he was hoping to be given sound reasons to delay. The fact that Schmid was there with his 'Study in Blue' tucked, figuratively speaking, under his arm, seems to indicate that this was the case. Beppo could hardly fail to be astonished that 1,200 British fighters had been shot down in less than a month when the R.A.F. had only had 675 of them three weeks earlier. This would mean that the monthly production of the British aircraft factories had exceeded, and by a very handsome margin, the supposed figure of 180 to 300 aircraft.[1] And then, when all was said and done, the resistance that Fighter Command was putting up every day provided striking proof that if it had suffered heavy blows, it had not yet been rendered harmless.

'What is your opinion of the present state of Fighter Command?' the two Field-Marshals were asked.

Kesselring's reply was clipped:

'The British fighter force has been liquidated.'

Sperrle removed his monocle and put it back before replying:

'They still have a thousand aircraft.'

Goering listened while Kesselring expanded his plan. The airfields to the south of London have been wiped out. If it is desired to strike a decisive blow at the British capital now is the time to do it; now or never. The majority of the British squadrons, or what is left of them, have had to take refuge to the north. The British have therefore lost one of their key trump cards: they can no longer intervene sufficiently quickly, and it is now their turn to face the problem of the short range of fighter aircraft. Goering agreed; the Führer was calling for London to be punished. The only question that the supreme commander of the Luftwaffe asked was:

'Do you consider that the enemy fighter force has been

1. The true production figures were 496 aircraft in July, 476 in August and 467 in September.

sufficiently reduced to allow such an operation to take place without serious risk to the bombers?'

Sperrle cut in: 'No!'

'Yes,' said Kesselring.

'We must persevere with the attacks on the airfields,' Sperrle continued. Schmid, thinking of his 'Study in Blue,' heartily agreed with him.

'Certainly not,' Kesselring retorted. 'We shall never destroy the English fighters on the ground. If you want to have done with the R.A.F. you must force it into the air. There is only one thing that will do that: massive attacks on London. If you do that, the remaining Hurricanes and Spitfires will be forced to give battle. We shall strike the final blow only in the air.'

Kesselring won.

Dowding was right in June when he prophesied that it was the very fact that London was so *near* that would make the Germans lose the war.

The meeting closed. Decision: top priority for attacks on London. Papers were gathered up, brief-cases locked. Everyone stood up.

Once more, orders, car doors, steel-grey uniforms with white leather facings. This was the departure of a Reichsmarschall...

On the devastated airfields of England, where the pilots still fit to fly and the aeroplanes as yet undamaged by bombs were being counted like a miser's hoard, no one knew that Fighter Command had just won its most glittering victory – around a green baize table. All they knew was that today it had been a draw, sixteen all; that, and that they were tottering with fatigue.

This was the turning point.

Liverpool was bombed.

On September 5th a German agent, who was to remain undetected throughout the war, sent an accurate and detailed report on the damage done to targets on Tunbridge.

In fact he was not at Tunbridge, but at Camber-on-Sea, not far from Hastings. The reason he was misled was that the shopkeeper who ran the grocery and sub-post office had obeyed the government's instruction to paint out the name of the village on his sign. He left only his name which, unfortunately for the German agent, happened to be Tunbridge.

'Only nine Spitfires left,' wrote Deacon Elliott on the morning of September 5th.

Keith Park said in his report:

> 'The daily German raids have caused serious damage to five of our advanced airfields and six or seven of our operational centres. By about September 5th, the results of these attacks had appreciably reduced the defensive potential of the British fighter force. With large numbers of telephone links out of service and the necessity of using improvised operational headquarters furnished with bits and pieces of equipment; with the almost total dislocation of the defensive organization, the direction of the squadrons called up into action became an extremely delicate matter.'

It was at this precise moment that Dowding intervened. The Air Chief Marshal had never seemed more austere, more withdrawn, more occupied with his thoughts. He had inherited from his grandfather, the Reverend Benjamin Charles, a profound distrust of everything that was not essential. Still Dowding entered into the heart of the battle. He *knew* that his squadrons were decimated, his airfields destroyed. He *suffered* for his 'boys'; but he continued to think and to act with cold lucidity, shunning emotion. He writes:

> 'It was possible for the Germans to put one or two aerodromes like Manston and Hawkinge out of action for a time, but we had so many satellite aerodromes and landing grounds available that it was quite impossible for the Germans to damage seriously a number of aerodromes sufficient to cause more than temporary inconvenience.'

Certain of his officers felt that he wasn't living the battle *from the inside*. This was true. He had to be the buttress from without.

The sun was hot. At Bentley Priory it burnt down, casting the shadow of the tower and the great cedar over the vast lawn. Dowding learnt that the chief of 11 Group had obeyed his instructions. The Air Chief Marshal had ordered that a particularly close watch be kept on aircraft factories. For a long time he had been waiting for them to be attacked; the thing seemed inevitable. To start with, the Germans had tried to destroy his aircraft in the air, and then, when that had failed, on the ground. Having gone through these stages and finding that they were meeting just as many British fighters as ever, they had decided to go to the heart of the problem and strike at the factories. Park announced that he had established patrols over Kingston, Langley, Brooklands and Southampton. Dowding confirmed his order that whenever enemy aircraft were reported south of the Thames. No. 10 Group should send up squadrons to reinforce the lines Brooklands–Croydon and Croydon–Windsor. Park was particularly insistent about the protection of Southampton.

In the Ops Room the pieces were already starting to move on the chequer-board.

'To Hawkinge for the day,' wrote Deacon Elliott. 'First patrol ran into two lots of Me 109s at 27,000 feet and into lots of trouble.'

The Luftwaffe adopted a new ruse. To divert attention from its principal objective, Biggin Hill, it launched a bomber attack on Croydon. On their return, the bombers were bounced by half a dozen Spitfires. Von Selle, leading the thirty escorting Me 109s, gave the order to attack.

At exactly that moment a Spitfire fired its first burst. Von Selle had dived and it had missed him, but hit his right wingman, Leutnant Franz von Werra. His Messerschmitt shuddered and he rolled to the right, dropping out of the pack like a wounded animal. The English pilot followed him, clinging to his tail, looking for the perfect shot to finish him off. Von Werra was flicking switches; his radio had gone dead. He tried his luck and pushed the throttle wide open; the damaged motor backfired. He glanced behind. Yes, the Spit was still there. He hit the throttle again – nothing. His Messerschmitt was now struck by a series of short bursts. The ground was getting closer and he could see orchards and oasthouses. A row of trees, a farmhouse roof, and he touched and bounced back into the air. Some farm labourers who were loading crates of fruit on to a lorry watched him thresh his way into the straw in a cloud of dust, and then stop...

A few seconds passed. The cockpit hood opened and the pilot stepped out, unhurt. He took off his helmet, jumped on to the wing and then to the ground. He looked about him.

What was he going to do? Run for it? No, he was bending down. What was that, a flame? There was a searchlight crew near by and it was the cook who saw it and came running.

'Quick, he's going to burn his aeroplane.'

When they reached him he was still holding his burning flight documents between the tips of his fingers. He had unfolded them so that they should burn better. A few black fragments fluttered to the ground.

They surrounded him and searched him. He was quiet. As they led him out of the field, he stretched out a hand and picked an apple. He munched it and spat out the core. A little farther on he started playing up again, but one of the soldiers stuck his rifle in the small of his back. Von Werra shrugged his shoulders. He was taken in a car to the County Police Headquarters at Maidstone.

The two guards who remained with the Messerschmitt were intrigued by the painted symbols below the swastika on its tail. There were six broad vertical bands, marked with eight roundels, two French and six British. Above the swastika were painted five arrows in the British colours. The captured pilot therefore had thirteen victories to his credit. Clearly one of the Luftwaffe's aces!

John Terence Webster who had brought off this coup had fourteen confirmed victories to his credit. He had just been decorated with the D.F.C., but he was not to celebrate his final victory. He was killed the same afternoon.

Desmond Sheen of 72 Squadron was shot down by a burst of fire from astern. He had the greatest difficulty in escaping from his cockpit and fell free at the very last moment. He landed in a wood and his parachute got stuck in a tree. He freed himself and, wounded, crawled to the road. There he was found by a policeman who took him to the nearest town.

The town was Maidstone, where von Werra had been taken.

Overhead the battle continued.

London was quiet. The war had just entered its second year. Three million men had been called to the colours and everybody seemed to have forgotten that the status of the city of Danzig was what had brought it all about.

On Thurday evening the 5th New Zealand Infantry Brigade was giving a concert in Trafalgar Square. Life went on.

At the Arts Theatre Jean Cocteau's latest play *The Infernal Machine* was being performed, and at the Institute Français there was a revue in French and English. *The Magic Bullet* with Edward G. Robinson was the latest success on the screen and a film made in Czechoslovakia before the invasion was being shown in the trailers; its title, *The Fall of the Tyrant*.

Lord Beaverbrook's Spitfire campaign continued and passed all the targets set. Someone called it 'the cemetery of the enemy's dreams'. Mrs. Joseph Kennedy, the wife of the American ambassador, had just founded the American Ambulance.

Nobody paid much attention to Hitler's threats. After all, he could scarcely do any more than he was doing already! His Reichstag speech simply proved that the R.A.F. raids were getting on the Germans' nerves. Hadn't they set the Black Forest on fire? Anyway, it was easy to snarl into a microphone, but if he was as strong as he said he was, how had he let 350,000 British soldiers slip through his fingers at Dunkirk?

There were more immediate problems to think about. There was the shortage of iron rings for tethering horses, for example. Horses became panicky during air-raids and if they weren't secured, there was the chance that they might injure themselves and passers-by as well. It was interesting to study the behaviour of birds too. Pheasants would give the alarm before the sirens blew and frequently a chicken house would set up a cackling early warning of the bombers' arrival. The swallows and swifts, on the other hand, seemed to take no interest in what was going on above them. Some had been seen darting about quite normally beside a burning aeroplane as four parachutes dropped around them.

The Air Ministry issued an important notice to the public concerning airmen dropping by parachute. Evidently there had been too many encounters with guns and pitchforks recently. The public was reminded that although it was necessary to remain vigilant, it was wrong to suppose that every parachutist was automatically an enemy. Force should not be used against him unless he adopted a menacing attitude or tried to commit some hostile act. Not only was it possible that he might be a British fighter pilot, but equally, the notice went on, he might be 'one of our Polish, Czech,

French or Belgian allies who is unable to speak a word of English'.

There was boating in Hyde Park.

It was very hot.

What was there to worry about?

Liverpool was bombed.

On the evening of September 5th, Deacon Elliot summed up how things stood for 72 Squadron which had just received a telegram of congraulations from 13 Group for its recent success.

'Apart from one Me 109 destroyed by P/O Dutch Holland I have no record of other claims. Our losses once again were tragic. P/O 'Snowy' Winter was shot down, tried to bale out but left it too late and was killed. Sergeant 'Mabel' Gray was seen to catch a terrific packet from a Me 110, apparently being killed instantly, his aircraft dived vertically into the 'deck'. Sergeant Gilder's aircraft was a write-off from enemy fire but he managed to get away with it. F/O Desmond Sheen was wounded once again, and taken off to hospital in Sidcup.'

Richard Hillary was in hospital too.

He had been shot down on the morning of September 3rd, while attacking a Messerschmitt. Terribly burnt, he had fallen into the Channel where he remained for a long time floating in his Mae West. Unlike the Germans, the British did not yet have dinghies. Eventually the Margate lifeboat picked him up, 'a brandy flask was pushed between my swollen lips; a voice said, "O.K., Joe, it's one of ours and still kicking"; and I was safe. I was neither relieved nor angry: I was past caring.'

He came out of his nightmare. He was in a bed and someone was holding his arms.

' "Quiet now. There's a good boy. You're going to be all right. You've been very ill and you mustn't talk."

'Gradually I realized what had happened. My face and hands had been scrubbed and then sprayed with tannic acid. The acid had formed into a hard black cement. My eyes alone had received different treatment: they were coated with a thick layer of gentian violet. My arms were propped up in front of me, the fingers extended like witches' claws, and my body was hung loosely on straps just clear of the bed.'

Another client for McIndoe!

He ended up like Geoffrey Page in the famous Ward 3 of the hospital at East Grinstead, the home of the Guinea Pigs.[1]

September 6th.

'Only five Spitfires available first thing today – the lowest number the Squadron had operated since the war began,' wrote Deacon Elliott.

No. 72 Squadron took off with four aircraft and joined up with 66 Squadron. Together they intercepted a formation of bombers heavily escorted by fighters and, despite the disproportionate odds, attacked. Deacon Elliott got in two bursts at a 109 and saw it go down leaving a long trail of black smoke. It crashed near Marden. But his Spitfire had been hit too. The windscreen was gone and great holes had been torn in the wings. At 1,000 feet the engine cowlings flew off and the aircraft caught fire.

'I baled out from about 800 feet,' wrote Deacon Elliott, 'landing in a hop field only to find I was being covered by a shotgun in the hands of a member of the Local Defence Volunteers.' Things were then sorted out and the hop-pickers offered him their last bottle of beer – 'how refreshing', he notes. Then as they sat on the ground waiting for the army lorry to come and collect him, the conversation turned to the weather and above all the battle. The hop-pickers were not happy about the way things were going. They wanted to see more Huns shot down and fewer R.A.F. boys. Elliott finished his beer and said how sorry he was to have disappointed them.

Churchill gave the casualty figures for the month of August. German air-raids had killed 1,075 civilians including 335 women and 113 children.

It had been cooler in London on September 6th. That night the city slept in peace. For the last time.

1. The Guinea Pigs Club was not founded until July 20th, 1941, but I have used the expression in an anticipatory sense to describe burnt pilots.

14: The Gala Opening

Through the canals and navigable waterways of Europe had come an armada of small craft. They had assembled at the ports of the Channel, the Pas de Calais, Holland and Belgium, and there had joined up with the deep-sea ships. In all the armada numbered 168 transports, 1,910 barges, 419 tugs and about 1,600 small motor vessels.

On the night of September 6th–7th, Blenheims were sent to bomb the fleet. The Joint Intelligence Committee felt it necessary to inform the government, 'Attack probable within the next three days.'

That morning the weather was fine in the south with a slight mist. The start of a beautiful day.

At Bentley Priory, Dowding was at his accounts. His squadrons now had an average of only sixteen pilots instead of twenty-six. The number of Spitfires and Hurricanes immediately available was, according to report, one hundred and twenty-five.

On the Operations Room blackboard he could read the position at each station, but where would the enemy strike? Where would the yellow counters indicating enemy bombers start to appear on the great chequerboard? Dowding did not stay long in the round room. He crossed the hall and went into his office where he set to work on his 'plan of stabilization'. The squadrons were worn out and now they seemed to be crumbling away before his eyes. He decided on a new classification system, like a hotel guide, but instead of one, two or three stars he would give them letters: A, B or C.

The A squadrons were those of 11 Group. To reinforce their flanks, he took some squadrons from the Middle Wallop sector of 10 Group in the west and from the Duxford sector of 12 Group in the north. Five squadrons of 10 and 12 Groups were allocated the letter B. They were to relieve any of the A squadrons that required total replacement. The remaining C squadrons were those composed of five or six experienced pilots whose task would be to train the newer pilots of Fighter

Command. They constituted a sort of reserve behind the front line.

This 'plan of stabilization' was dated September 8th. It came at exactly the right time. What it meant was that Dowding had decided to back Keith Park. It was his group, No. 11, that he made the linchpin of the aerial defence of Great Britain. 'I must pay a very sincere tribute to the Air Officer Commanding No. 11 Group, Air Vice-Marshal K. R. Park,' he wrote later. Backing Park meant the acceptance of his tactic of small formations. On this point Dowding was quite specific. 'I think that, if the policy of big formations had been attempted at this time in No. 11 Group, many more bombers would have reached their objectives without opposition.'

Having received this support, Park, on the morning of the 7th, began to impose his tactical theory. For the 'gala opening' Fighter Command would be wearing the 'Keith Park style'. Precise instructions went out from Uxbridge to the controllers in the operations rooms. They were to transmit the altitudes reported by the pilots without commentary. For some time it had been stated that the controllers tended to minimize the altitudes of enemy formations, no doubt to encourage the squadrons sent to intercept them. Too often the fighters found that they had to make their attack from below, which put them at a great disadvantage. So to compensate for this, many of the pilots had got into the bad habit of passing exaggerated altitude reports to the ops room. In this way they thought they were rendering a service to their fellow pilots in other squadrons that might be sent up to intercept later. Now Park firmly stated the requirement that on both sides what was reported should be the simple truth.[1]

To the squadrons he gave the following instructions: 'Whenever time permits squadrons are to be put into battle in pairs. The enemy's main attack must be met at maximum strength between the coast and our line of sector aerodromes.' The higher flying Spitfires were to harass the escorting fighter

1. Or rather, the simple false truth. Dowding had decided that false 'angel' reports would be given to mislead the enemy monitoring service. Thus 'angels 18' would no longer mean 18,000 feet, but 21,000 feet.

screen, while at a lower level the Hurricanes would tackle the bombers.

Keith Park was ready. He realized that the most important period in his life was about to open. What he did not know was that it was coming in a matter of hours.

During the morning, no doubt prompted by a report from the Joint Intelligence Committee, the Air Ministry signalled to Bentley Priory:

'Landing considered imminent.'

The train 'Asia' drew to a halt.

Marshal Goering stepped down: Siegfried had come to be with his Knights at Cap Blanc Nez. The air smelt of salt spray and seaweed. Fink was there dressed in his flying suit, ready to leave. On the airfields the 'gallant warriors' stood by their armoured steeds, whose names were 109, 110, Dornier and Heinkel. Their armour had been dulled or painted blue so that it would not glitter in the sun. Their lances were machine-guns or the 20-mm. cannon, their maces, bombs. In the clear blue sky they would spread their banners: the white contrails.

Now that the decision was taken, Goering had no more doubts. He wanted victory and, looking at all the confident faces around him, he was sure that he would get it. Perhaps on his finger he wore the solitaire that his father had given him. There was a story to this ring. During the First World War, Goering was made *chevalier* of the order *Pour le Mérite.* This gave him his first piece of military jewellery, and he at once sent his batman off to Munich to collect the ring which his father had promised him. Now, with the sea breeze lifting the fine blond locks that stuck out on either side of his cap, his binoculars hanging at his neck, his steel-grey uniform plastered with decorations, he stood with his sword planted in front of him, sniffing at the air. Now, as in the days gone by, he smelt – war. It was only a pity that he had had to bring along his nurse, Christa Gormanns, with her syringe.

Goering stood on top of a dune with Kesselring and Lörzer beside him. Fink had left with the first wave. For a quarter of an hour there had been a noise of engines in the air. Certainly aircraft engines, but they were nowhere to be seen. In another direction perhaps. The party turned round. Over that way? No. The sky was empty. The great cats were prowling, but as yet only their growls could be heard. The pack was forming in some secret place in the sky, like the lion packs of Africa which meet no one knows where. Then, suddenly, there they were. Three hundred bombers escorted by six hundred fighters passing right over the Reichsmarschall in two separate waves. The noise, by its sheer terrifying power, seemed no longer to exist. The sight was all that mattered. Jeschonnek was right when he had said: 'The sky of London will be black with aeroplanes.' Goering nearly broke his neck with looking. He dreamt he was up there at the controls of a Messerschmitt, leather-helmeted, earphones clapped to his ears, his face covered with an oxygen mask, his finger resting on the gun button. He was airborne and flying against England. All around him, ahead, behind and to both sides, was his aerial armada; the yellow, red and orange noses, the dappled camouflage and the black crosses. He was flying against London – here they come, the enemy with the red, white and blue roundels. In the distance he could see the black puffs of anti-aircraft shells.

The telephone rang. A message for the Reichsmarschall. Goering sent Frau Gormanns to take it for him.

The radar operators couldn't believe their eyes. The screens were covered with two huge traces. There was no room for doubt: this was not just another raid. At 4 p.m. the order went out from Bentley Priory. Twenty-three squadrons were scrambled.

Paul Weitkus, leading the second formation, reported, 'All the way from the French coast we could see ahead the tall columns of smoke rising from the oil tanks that had been bombed the day before.'

Those were the petrol installations at Thames Haven.

The listeners to the B.B.C. had just heard a talk by Major W. H. Osman, editor of the *Racing Pigeon*, on 'Practical uses for Racing Pigeons'. Then a few records were played. The most popular hit of the day was 'A Nightingale sang in Berkeley Square'. It was known to be the fighter pilots' favourite tune. Suddenly the sirens started to wail.

At 5.30 the British Chiefs of Staff of all three services were at a meeting in Whitehall. They could hear the roar of the enemy force. This time it was the real thing. He's coming!

And there was no one to stop him! To the south of London, the squadrons were guarding the airfields and aircraft factories of the 'biggest target in the world'. They could not be everywhere at once. The German armada was flying at between 17,000 and 25,000 feet. On each flank and to the rear it was protected by a fighter escort and up above and farther away it had a top cover ready to come down to its defence. All the fighter sheepdogs knew exactly the part they had to play. If the attack came from one side they knew who was to take the place of the flank escort that was engaged. In the face of multiple attacks they knew they were to form a great defensive circle round the bombers. Four British squadrons came and blunted their teeth against the great German formation. Fink saw a Dornier falling in flames to his right.

Over Redhill, the Hurricanes of 111 Squadron tackled a vast 'Valhalla' with an attack from the side. They continued their attacks as the bombers flew on to the outskirts of London, but the 109s came down on them from above like arrows, forcing them to split up. Then the Poles of 303 Squadron from Northolt appeared. They had heard one of the British pilots call 'Tally-ho!' This was what they had been waiting for since the dark days of Warsaw, through all the dangers of their journey into exile: the hour of revenge! They didn't let their chance slip. They were the heroes of the day. 'We gave them all we'd got,' wrote Squadron Leader Kellett, 'opening fire at 450 yards and only breaking away when we could see the enemy completely filling our gunsight. That means we finished the attack at point-blank range. We went in practically in one straight line, all of us blazing away.'

There were twelve of them against forty Dorniers heavily escort by 110s and with a following escort of 109s. But their blood was up. Very nearly every Polish pilot got his bomber.

No. 72 Squadron, too, was in action. It destroyed a 109 and damaged another. Flying Officer Eldson was shot down. He was wounded in the knee by an incendiary bullet.

A complete wing of 12 Group took off from Duxford. The Hurricanes of 22 Squadron scored several victories, but the rest arrived too late.

Over Sevenoaks, two-thirds of the way to their target, the

close escort turned about; they had reached the limit of their radius of action. The others flew on.

The skies of London at last. There were the barrage balloons and the smoke . . . Under their wings the German crews could see the tightly packed houses, the splashes of green that were the parks, the squares, the crossroads, the broad streets and the famous U of the Thames between Blackwall Tunnel and Rotherhithe Tunnel where the London docks lay. How many times had they not looked at this city on their charts! Before they had started and during flight; again and again they had peered at it, and now – there it was! Splendid too, as the setting sun gave it a crown of golden dust.

Members of the Observer Corps in their post on top of the Senate building of London University were the first to spot the aircraft. They immediately passed on all the information they could.

Then the bombs began to rain down.

The Royal Arsenal at Woolwich was the first target to be hit.

Fink was over the Victoria Docks while Weitkus, over the very centre of the U of the Thames, looked down on the West India Docks. He took his Leica and photographed the scene.

An area a mile and a half square between North Woolwich Road and the Thames was razed to the ground, burnt out, obliterated. Everything went: the Arsenal, railway stations, factories, docks, power stations. Anti-aircraft shells were exploding all over the sky and from the ground rose the debris of the bomb bursts. 'Impossible to tell a Spitfire from a 109,' wrote Weitkus; 'aircraft were diving in all directions and flak bursting everywhere. The winner was the pilot who saw the other first.'

When one wave had passed another arrived. At Silvertown, which was in the area that received the worst blasting, the people who lived or worked there, the dockers, were encircled by a wall of fire. It was so hot that the wooden blocks with which the roads were surfaced caught fire. Everywhere the unfortunate inhabitants could be seen, wandering about. They left the wreckage of their houses, dragging their children, clutching bundles of their possessions, and went away. In the East End whole rows of old Victorian houses collapsed in flames. The Thames fire floats were sent to the docks and pumped tons and tons of water on to the fires, but it was so hot that the paint on the ships' hulls was blistered. The scene at the warehouses, which were stuffed with sugar and spices, grain and spirits, was enough to turn anyone's head. Along with the smoke, there was a smell of rum. Thousands of gallons of it had spilled, forming a gigantic punch. Little rivers of fire ran along the pavements. The homeless were evacuated by water. Three hundred tons of high explosives fell and thousands of incendiary bombs set alight the houses of Poplar, Limehouse and Tottenham. The fires spread from West Ham to Tower Bridge.

St. Paul's Cathedral stood out against a sky of deep khaki. All around was the roar and clatter of fire engines and ambulances. London's burning . . .

At 8 Kensington Palace Gardens, in an old house covered with Virginia creeper and surrounded by trees, a most curious scene took place. The blackout curtains were drawn and the lights were out. From time to time a bomb would make the windows rattle. Two men sat facing each other. One of them, a heavily decorated Royal Air Force Wing Commander with thinning black hair, was seated behind a mahogany table. The other was Franz von Werra, the German ace who had been shot down two days before not far from Maidstone. He had been brought to the house in Kensington Palace Gardens for interrogation. The house was known as the 'cage' among the prisoners, but they had no nickname for the British officer, who had an artificial leg and who walked with the aid of a gold-handled stick. They did not even know his real name. All they knew was that you had to be very careful of him.

Von Werra was in a hole. He had burnt his papers, but the tail of his aircraft had remained intact and it was because of this that he was receiving the Wing Commander's special attention. The thirteen ill-starred symbols painted on the fin had picked him out. This was the von 'Werrer' who had boasted over the Berlin radio that on a single sortie on August 30th he had destroyed three and perhaps four Hurricanes in flight and five on the ground. This had attracted a lot of attention, both in Germany where the press had recorded it with pride, and in England where an inquiry had been ordered. Now, it was established that no squadron, whether of Hurricanes or Spitfires, had lost aircraft in the way von 'Werrer' described. Furthermore, to achieve his nine victories in the manner he claimed, he would have had to remain airborne for over three hours. The endurance of a 109 was not greater than one hundred and five minutes. Finally, there had been no low-level attack that day by a lone enemy fighter. What then remained of the 'greatest fighter exploit of the war', as it was referred to in Berlin?

That von Werra was von 'Werrer' seemed beyond doubt. Everything fitted. The Luftwaffe table of battle honours for August 28th showed von Werra in seventh place with eight bombers destroyed.[1] The five arrows painted with British roundels on his fin represented five fighters. Therefore, for five of the eight or nine Hurricanes that von Werra had claimed to have destroyed, he had received confirmation. In fact on August 30th he had not shot down any.

The British Wing Commander knew what he wanted. He was trying to get von Werra to admit that he was von 'Werrer'. Once he had achieved this he would prove to him that he had lied to his superiors and then all that remained to be done was to explain that unless he were prepared to cooperate, his false claims would be disclosed to his fellow prisoners. For the 'red devil', for 'Baron' von Werra whose photograph was in all the papers with his mascot, a lion cub, this would be the end; he would sink beneath the waves of ridicule.

Von Werra saw the trap very clearly. He had not realized that the British would be so well informed. But then, he was one of the very last German pilots to fall into enemy hands and in a few days, perhaps in a few hours, the invasion would be launched. The explosions now shaking the house were a prelude to it. *Then* who would be believed; the enemy Wing Commander or the shot-down hero? A week earlier von Werra had made a recording about his pretended exploits. In his camouflaged quarters on the airfield in the Pas de Calais he had sat stroking his lion cub, embroidering and inventing for all he was worth. And what did he risk, even now? He knew the fellows he would be imprisoned with. They had all laughed together in the mess. How they had laughed that time when one of their pilots had been called on to fly at the last minute and had been captured by the Home Guard wearing his evening dress! Or the other time when one of them

1. Behind Mölders 29, Galland 24, Schopfel 19, Joppien 13, Schneel and Bohr, 9.

had gone into 'the cage' carrying a suitcase full of Normandy butter and liqueurs that he was hoping to go off on leave with. They would all say, 'The English are lying. They just don't want to admit that one of our fighters, all by itself, could have wrought such havoc among their Hurricanes.'

Von Werra put a bold face on it. The whole thing was out of proportion. An accusation of making false claims couldn't be compared with betrayal of military secrets. He regarded the 'conversation' as over and rose from the table. Even if the war lasted a long time he wouldn't be spending much of it in Great Britain. He said in English:

'I bet you a magnum of champagne to a packet of ten cigarettes that I shall escape within six months.'

He kept his word.[1]

He was led from the room.

Outside in the docks down the Thames, the flames burnt on.

An exultant Goering was following the battle minute by minute. How he would love to be there instead of Fink, his nose glued to his cockpit window, sniffing the cooking smells of the London docks – the great grocer's store stuffed with all the produce of the colonies and now thrust into the Luftwaffe's oven!

Christa Gormanns called him. Frau Goering on the telephone.

The bloated and bejewelled fingers grasp the receiver:

'Hello ... Yes, this time we've done it ...! London is in flames ... My pilots have struck a blow straight at the heart of the enemy ... This is an historic day!'

A little after 6 p.m., 609 Squadron, which was one of the squadrons that had been allocated to Keith Park as a reinforcement for the protection of the aircraft factories on the line Brooklands–Windsor, sighted the German bombers over London. They rushed to the attack. The German fighters were there; lots of them, pugnacious and as persistent as flies on a thundery day in summer. Even so the leader of Blue

1. After some extraordinary adventures he got back to Germany. There he died in a flying accident in a Messerschmitt 109 on October 23rd, 1941. See *The One That Got Away*, by Kendal Burst and James Leasor.

Section got himself a Dornier which plunged into the Thames.

Elsewhere, the Polish pilot Daszewski of 303 Squadron was forced to take to his parachute. He was severely wounded in the arm and leg. 'I was returning with a heavy heart in spite of my victories, for the whole eastern suburb of London seemed to be burning. It was a very sorrowful sight, reminding me of a flight a year ago over Poland, near Lublin; it was the same spectacle.'

At 8 p.m. the code word 'Cromwell' was issued.

It indicated that the invasion was imminent.

In the villages church bells were rung. Bridges were destroyed and tank traps set up in the streets. The Home Guard patrolled the countryside. In Lincolnshire three of its officers were blown up by a mine and killed. In the Supermarine factory at Southampton there was a rumour that the landings had started. The workers expected to have to defend their factory buildings yard by yard.

He's coming!

It was the old cry and it had been almost forgotten. But now it was heard again and nobody smiled any more. Why this sudden invasion-consciousness? First, of course, there was the raid of the previous day, then the thousand and one rumours. The four spies who had been arrested near the coast and of whom three had been hanged, had talked. They revealed that their task was 'to inform the German High Command of the movements of those divisions which were brought up to strengthen the defences around the disembarkation zones.' The famous story of the 'sea on fire' was resurrected, as well. But that was not all. There were the concentrations of invasion barges, and the instruction issued on the night of the 6th–7th, ordering all cruisers, destroyers and smaller vessels to be brought to state of alert No. 1, with steam up ready for sea. This state of alert meant 'invasion imminent and expected within twelve hours'.

London got little sleep that night. It is always the first blow, the one you get while you are still calm, that hurts the most.

At Cap Blanc Nez, Goering had some staggering news for his radio broadcast. He told the reporter who interviewed him:

'I have taken over personally the command of the Luftwaffe in its battle against Great Britain.'

And added:

'For the first time London has been bombed by day. This is an historic hour. Our bomber crews, accompanied by their gallant comrades, the fighter pilots, will continue to carry out their orders until our aims are completely fulfilled.'

Back in his special train, exhausted by the fresh air, the nervous tension and the excitement of victory, Goering fell on his bed. He was happy, he felt sleepy. He only hoped he didn't start to sweat, as he did sometimes. That would spoil all the pleasure.

Overhead he could hear a rumbling.

Two hundred and forty-seven aircraft were on their way to bomb London. This time it would be by night and they would be guided by the light of the fires.

In London they were still collecting the dead – nearly a thousand of them – when the sirens sounded again.

When the night's raid was over a communiqué was published. It was extremely sober in tone:

'Fires were caused among industrial targets. Damage was done to lighting and other public services, and some dislocation to communications was caused. Attacks have already been directed against the docks. Information as to casualties is not yet available.'

Returning from a sortie, Deacon Elliott of 72 Squadron noted in his diary:

'London experienced its heaviest raid to date ... How long could the people endure?'

September 8th found Goering bent over a map of London, studying the effects of the previous day's bombing. He too was designating things by a system of letters; not, as Dowding was doing, squadrons, but targets. The eastern part of the British capital which contained the docks became sector A, while the west was named sector B. It is a curious fact that on exactly the same day the supreme commanders of the forces engaged in the battle on both sides should be playing the same game.

On that day, a day which by the King's command had

been declared a day of national prayer, there was somewhat reduced activity. But still the fighters were kept constantly in the air: 'Routine patrols continued,' wrote Deacon Elliott, 'interceptions being made almost without fail. Averaging three missions a day and on occasions we flew as many as five.'

By the evening the account was favourable. Great Britain beat Germany 15 to 2. But that night London again felt the weight of the German attack; this time by two hundred and seven bombers.

'The systematic bombing of London has begun,' wrote René Mouchotte. 'Four hundred killed yesterday,[1] two hundred and eighty today. What will it be tomorrow? Is this the beginning of the great offensive Hitler promised? He announced the invasion of Britain for the end of August or the beginning of September. The English have been bombing Berlin since yesterday.'

This was true. From now on the bomb became the only form of contact between England and Germany. In July there still remained some diplomatic effervescence and a speech would be echoed by a replying speech from the other side. In August there were rumours of invasion, attacks on convoys, the odd parachutist incident and the swaying power of the broadcast word. But in September the iron fist of total war beat on the door.

The bombing on the 7th hit England like a cold shower. The damage was on an impressive scale. The working-class areas had taken especially hard knocks and as the fires burnt on into the night, the people who lived in dockland had really believed that they would never live to see the light of day. During the days which followed, days of constant bombing, recriminations were heard, mixed with the cries of anger against the Hun. To be poor had suddenly a new meaning. There was talk of 'kicking up a row outside the Savoy'. But then, slowly at first, people became accustomed to danger. Death was a neighbour to be lived with. How to keep the

1. The Sunday papers which went to press that night carried this figure. On Monday the 9th, *The Times* devoted a long article to the story of the great raid. In this article it was stated that one hundred and seven German aircraft had been shot down. In fact forty-one were.

shelter warm when winter came: that was the question. People would look up at the sky to see if there was a 'bombers' moon'. And, of course, people went out for the evening. At the Garrick Theatre there was a play by Sacha Guitry; profits for the Red Cross. On the screen *My Favourite Wife* was all the rage. There was a slightly *risqué* version of 'A Nightingale sang in Berkley Square' going the rounds now; it ran:

> There were six miscarriages,
> Under Claridges,
> When a screaming bomb fell in Berkeley Square.

The song itself had been displaced by another 'hit', 'Begin the Beguine'. Mr. Neville Chamberlain, who had just undergone an operation, was back at work in Downing Street after a holiday in the country. Mr. Ernest Bevin, the Minister of Labour, was at his desk again after a short absence for an ear, nose and throat operation. At the War Office, the Under-Secretary of State for War, Lord Croft, received a delegation of the Standing Conference, headed by Lord Horder, which had been discussing the question of sex education for the Army. There was an official denial of a statement, from a German source, according to which the Diplomatic Corps was on the point of abandoning the British capital.

The worlds of commerce and fashion went on as usual. One favourite of the autumn collections was a suit called 'battle dress' in washable velvet. A member of the Royal Academy offered life-size portraits executed 'very quickly and for five guineas' as an insurance against being 'altogether dead'. The statisticians took a hand. Did the casualties of the first raid seem heavy? The statisticians calculated that to kill one person in ten in the British Isles, the Germans would have to kill one thousand people a day for thirteen and a half years . . .

On September 10th the weather turned sour. The N.B.B.S., the radio station in the pay of the Germans, issued an appeal: 'We ask our compatriots to join us in a last effort to secure peace.'

The day was fairly quiet but that night one hundred and forty-eight bombers attacked London.

By the 11th it was time to face facts: the R.A.F. was not

defeated. Hitler had fixed Operation *Seelöwe* for September 24th. The 14th, therefore, was the last day for passing the signal to Raeder who had demanded ten clear days to put the Navy on an invasion footing.

The weather grew fine again except for a few autumnal showers that fell unexpectedly, short and sharp, but warm. At Uxbridge, Keith Park was preparing an analysis of the results of the previous days' raids. He stated that the German raids had increased from two a day to three, and that they were carried out by 'Valhallas' of three to four hundred aircraft divided in two waves. For a period of between forty-five minutes and one hour these formations would cause 'total saturation' in all areas. Faced with this hard fact, the leader of 11 Group was obliged to tighten up his defence system. He arranged his squadrons, still in pairs, in the following order: squadrons in readiness for the first wave of attackers, squadrons at fifteen-minute availability to meet the second wave, and squadrons available at thirty-minute notice for reinforcement and patrolling airfields and factories. What if there should be a third wave? The final reserve squadrons would be sent up in pairs. These final reserve squadrons were now looking more and more makeshift. Deacon Elliott wrote: 'New pilots arrived to replace the losses – all of them very young and inexperienced. The first few replacements had only an average of nine hours' flying on Spitfires before being subjected to daily combats with the enemy. Some lasted longer than others – some even survived.'

That day the Luftwaffe made a surprise attack on the Supermarine factory at Southampton. There was no time to sound the sirens. Considerable damage. Nearly seventy dead.

In the air, Corporal Wojtowicz was shot down and killed after himsclf having shot down yet another Messerschmitt 109.

Over the B.B.C., Winston Churchill, sounding more grave than ever, announced:

'Several hundreds of self-propelled barges are moving down the coasts of Europe. From the German and Dutch harbours to the ports of Northern France; from Dunkirk to Brest; and beyond Brest to the French harbours in the Bay of Biscay . . .'

He went on:

'This effort of the Germans to secure daylight mastery of the air over England is, of course, the crux of the whole war. So far it has failed conspicuously.'

And then concluded:

'If this invasion is going to be tried at all, it does not seem that it can be long delayed . . . Therefore, we must regard the next week or so as a very important period in our history. It ranks with the days when the Spanish Armada was approaching the Channel . . . or when Nelson stood between us and Napoleon's Grand Army at Boulogne.'

That night one hundred and eighty bombers were hammering at London.

'On September 12th,' wrote Deacon Elliott, 'we moved back to Biggin Hill, just across the way. I had the day off and spent it visiting the hospitals. Hiram, Happy and Desmond were at Queen Mary's Hospital, Sidcup. Happy and Desmond were now almost recovered and were to be released on sick leave, but Hiram must stay longer. Dutch and I later called on Jimmy at Farnborough – may have to have his leg amputated – fortunately, this was avoided.'

The Times printed Winston Churchill's appeal to the nation. It also recorded the indignant Nazi protests about the R.A.F. bombing attacks. The Reichstag building, the victory column in the middle of the Tiergarten and the famous House of German Engineers, where so many representatives from all corners of the world had been received, had all been damaged: 'The assassin Churchill has given the order to the Royal Air Force to avoid all targets of military importance and to destroy as many monuments as possible. There can be only one answer to these cowardly crimes – the answer of the German Air Force.' As a further barbarity British aircraft had been dropping sacks of weevils on the fields of Germany, Belgium and Luxembourg to ruin the harvest: 'At a meeting in London last night,' wrote the newspaper, 'it was established that this accusation is entirely unfounded.'

British doctors were asking for steel helmets so that they could move about the streets while alerts were still on, helping the wounded.

London was bombed.

A delayed-action bomb fell a few yards from St. Paul's

Cathedral. An officer of the Royal Engineers, Lieutenant Davies, together with his assistant, Sapper Wylie, worked for three days to pull it out of a crater twenty-five feet deep where it was stuck. They both received the George Cross.

Another bomb exploded near Buckingham Palace. All the windows on the north side, where the apartments of the King and Queen looked out, were shattered. Doors were blown in and plaster fell from the ceilings. Fortunately the King and Queen were away.

On September 13th the weather was poor at first, and then plain bad. 'What a day for flying!' Deacon Elliott exclaimed. A few isolated bombers managed to slip through to London in the course of the morning, using the clouds for cover. Their bombs struck a selection of the finest targets: Downing Street, Whitehall, Trafalgar Square and, once again, Buckingham Palace. This time the Royal Chapel was badly damaged.

At Kenley, an airfield buzzing with swarms of gorgeous W.A.A.F.s – if we are to believe 'Ginger' Lacey – a volunteer was called for. The red-headed man from Yorkshire stepped forward; that's how it was with 501 Squadron. What had he volunteered for? It was a question of shooting down a Heinkel 111, but this time it was a job for the professional killer. You will be led blindfold through the clouds by the ground controller. He will be your white stick and you will be blind. He'll call your headings – east – south-east – east – south – south-east again.

At the controls of his Hurricane, Lacey felt fine. He had only one regret: he was going to have to kill his old war-horse and then leave it. There would be no question of attempting a landing. All the airfields were closed in. He would have to jump.

'Lacey said he had always wondered what it would be like to bale out ...' and now here he was up in his faithful old Hurricane.

'South,' said the voice from the ground.

The pilot eased the stick over and gave a gentle touch of rudder. I'm under his helmet with its earphones, his eyes watched the compass. He waited. He had a rendezvous with a man he had to kill. He had no idea where he was, he just let himself be led.

'South-east.'

What could the German be doing, changing course so often? It was as though he knew he was being followed and was trying to throw off the pursuit. The Hurricane was flying in a thick milky ghost-world as the chase went on and on. It lasted more than an hour.

There he was at last, half in and half out of cloud, semi-hidden; but there, with his two engines, glasshouse nose, his black crosses and his swastika on the tail. Lacey didn't wait. He opened fire ... A long burst, which smashed the rear turret, killing the gunner. Lacey saw him slip until he was 'lying over the edge of the rear cockpit'.

The bomber dived at once.

Lacey followed him down into the thick greyish cotton-wool clouds. The Heinkel changed course again two or three times but Lacey, not to be shaken off, followed suit.

'I'm quite certain he thought he had lost me ...' wrote Lacey.

He hung back slightly below and to one side in the blind spot. He wouldn't let go. The front windscreen of a Hurricane did not give very good visibility, especially in cloud, so Lacey kept him in sight through the side quarter panel. He never left the man he was going to kill; if the German climbed, he climbed; if he turned, Lacey stayed with him. Together they were progressing south.

Lacey was waiting for the first gap in the clouds. Even a little one and he would be able to get in a shot. Never can an enemy have been watched so long and so hard before the fatal moment. An enemy, but a brother too; there beside you, walking almost shoulder to shoulder, but never seeing you.

There! He was out of cloud and Lacey dropped back to fire. But the German had seen him. The two aircraft were so close that Lacey could see what was happening as well as if he had been in the Heinkel. Someone pulled away the dead gunner and took his place, opening fire at once on Lacey. 'I remember a gaping hole appearing in the bottom of the cockpit. The entire radiator had been shot away.' It was a question of seconds before the motor would catch fire. Pull out, Lacey! He pressed the gun button and kept it pressed till he had fired off all his rounds. Both the Heinkel's engines were now blazing. But Lacey was on fire too; a glycol fire, he thought, judging from the colour – not that it mattered which. Before baling out he had time to see the Heinkel going down like a torch. Then he went over the side. Goodbye, old Hurricane!

As he came out of cloud, hanging from his parachute, he saw his own aircraft dive into the ground and explode. People were running across the fields towards it. He watched them and noticed a few hundred feet below him a member of the Home Guard. He called out:

'Right above you . . .'

The man heard him and looked up, then raised a double-barrelled shotgun to his shoulder. To Lacey, who was looking straight down them, the barrels looked like 'twin railway tunnels'. Lacey shouted all the swear words that he knew; and there were a lot. They saved his life. The Home Guard said to him a moment later, 'Anyone who can swear like that couldn't possibly be a German!'

Lacey landed on the grass. He had qualified for membership of the Caterpillar Club.

It was only later that he learnt what he had been sent to do; the Heinkel he had shot down was the one that had bombed Buckingham Palace.

While 'Ginger' Lacey was shooting down his Heinkel 111 over England, Hitler was lunching with his generals in Berlin. Goering was there. He had come specially from his look-out post at Cap Blanc Nez. Hitler insisted on the prime necessity of securing absolute command of the air. When the meeting broke up, some of those who had attended it wondered whether Hitler did not favour bombing England into capitulation rather than relying on the always hazardous course of invasion. One fact seems to confirm this. That very evening the N.B.B.S. announced:

'Even if there should be no invasion in the immediate future, air-raids will make life impossible.'

In Kent the weather was dreadful.

Deacon Elliott wrote: 'Did two trips with Robby – apart from running into some Me 109s, both were uneventful.'

That night one hundred and five bombers hammered London.

Squadron Leader Oxley, leading a formation of Hampdens, was over Ostend bombing the invasion barges. 'We felt', he wrote, 'that there was not enough night to do as many trips as we wanted – that was the sense of urgency we had.'

The 'Sea Lion' had never received so much attention.

On September 14th, Hitler called another staff conference. He was in a reasonably optimistic mood. According to him, the naval preparations for the invasion were complete. He seemed to take no account of the situation report received the previous day from German Naval Headquarters in Paris and dated September 12th.

'The activities of British bombers, high-speed surface vessels and long-range coastal artillery have been, for the first time, seriously increasing. The moorings at Calais, Dunkirk, Boulogne and Ostend can no longer be used in the face of bombing raids and coastal artillery fire. British naval units are able to operate in the Channel practically without interference. For these reasons, delay must be expected in the concentration of the invasion fleet.'

Hitler turned to the Luftwaffe. Goering listened. He had his own ideas about this.

Operation *Seelöwe* was beginning to get on his nerves. From the very start he had been convinced that the Luftwaffe alone could make the thing a success. All that would be left for the soldiers and sailors to do would be to exploit the victory of the airmen. Hitler regarded the Luftwaffe's accomplishments as 'beyond praise'. He deplored the fact that the bad weather had made it impossible to bring matters to a conclusion more swiftly and summed up: 'Victory will be obtained by a successful invasion, but for such an operation to be undertaken at all, complete air superiority is essential.'

Perhaps Hitler had already seen Raeder's memorandum of the same day. Its first paragraph was definite enough:

'The situation in the air does not at present permit the operation to be staged when account is taken of the grave risks involved.'

In any case, the Führer decided to postpone the date for the mounting of Operation *Seelöwe* until September 17th. He was giving himself a breathing space. Goering was, no doubt, chewing over what he would say to his generals when he met them in two days' time. 'Keep after the enemy and in four or five days his fighters will be liquidated! Then for the destruction of the aircraft factories. "Sea Lion" must not be allowed to interfere with the Luftwaffe nor to tie it down!'

The conference drew to its close. Von Brauchitsch was pleased with himself. He had dropped a word in Halder's ear that if the Luftwaffe found it impossible to destroy the R.A.F., it might still be possible to make the landings under cover of huge smoke-screens. What better way to point out that the Luftwaffe looked like failing to fulfil its part of the bargain? Raeder had covered himself beautifully in the third paragraph of his memorandum:

'Air attacks against England and particularly against the London area must continue without interruption. If the weather is favourable, we should be prepared to intensify our raids...'

Everyone had made sure that he was in the clear. The machine had been set in motion. It had been moving, in fact, for ten days – in the wrong direction. But by now no one could see this any longer; or, if they could see it, no one was prepared to say so. The Luftwaffe was relentless in its attacks on bricks and mortar when it should have been destroying pilots and aluminium.

The atmosphere had changed on the British airfields. Gone were the days when the pilots could relax after a hard day and watch a show laid on specially for them. Gone was the soft feminine voice announcing over the loud-speaker in the corridors, 'Twenty-two hours. Good night everyone, good night.' Gone, too, the evenings when the station commander and his wife were 'at home' to his officers. 'That evening,' wrote Deacon Elliott, 'he and his wife gave a farewell party to all available officers – some were at night readiness. A wonderful evening terminating at the "Schooner" in Alnmouth, where the C.O. – strong as he was – failed to prevent the not unusual ceremony of being de-bagged.' A few weeks earlier there had been time for all this. Nobody had thought there was time, but there was. Now everyone realized that there was time no longer. On the walls of the mess at Acklington, John Parker, an artist of great talent, sketched portraits of the pilots of 72 and 79 Squadrons. Now the squadrons, worn out, were moved from sector to sector and sent north to lick their wounds.

In one of the Air Ministry publications there was a picture of a mound with a cross standing in wild grass blown by the wind. The caption said 'What did he die of' and there followed a long list:

He forgot to set his altimeter before take-off.

He thought everything would be all right.

He said that the chances of needing his parachute were one in a million.

He thought the bombers were unescorted.

He enjoyed low flying.

He *thought* he had set his compass correctly.

He couldn't see the point in learning how to use his dinghy.

To keep things in their right perspective, the enemy was mentioned in only one of the seven ways of getting killed; sad reflection.

Eventually doubts began to creep in. The weather was bad. There was less flying and therefore tired nerves relaxed. Too many friends were gone. There were too many in the hospitals and some of them had been turned into monsters. A special atmosphere hung around the airfields as a smell of ether hangs around a hospital. 'Feeling very tired these days,' wrote Deacon Elliott, 'cannot think why.' And he went on: 'I think most of us at that time felt very much the same.' The air-raids were beginning to get the pilots down. They had preferred it when *they* were the ones who were catching it. At least it simplified things. When you met up in the evening to discuss the day's score and found you still had both arms and legs, there was nothing much to worry about. The war was strictly confined to the four walls of the dispersal hut; there were no nasty surprises waiting outside. You really had the feeling that you were fighting. It was hard, but it was good. But now, as you wandered about in the grey sky, you would occasionally come across vast stupid flocks of Dorniers dropping their bombs on old women and schoolchildren. It made you worry about those you loved. You felt helpless; your magic powers had evaporated.

'The orthodox minds of the Air Staff ... did not appear to show adequate interest in the great defensive battle which was raging,' wrote Air Marshal Sir Gerald Gibbs. 'It is, of course, true that the defensive will not of itself win a war, particularly in the air ... Whether our feeling of a lack of appreciation was justified or whether it was just undue sensitiveness under a heavy strain it is hard to say.'

Repair work was going ahead on the airfields and great piles of rubble were collected ready for use to fill bomb craters. The dramatic yellow flags that marked unexploded bombs had not been used for some time now. As Gerald Gibbs observed: 'Naturally this [the use of flags] often stopped an airfield being used – until it occurred to us that the bomb was only going to be active for some unknown split second of time and that it was a legitimate war risk to take off and land close to it.'

There was trouble with some of the workers repairing the airfields. Gibbs wrote: 'Victor Beamish ... tried everything with them – blandishments, exhortation, rewards, insults, all to no avail. They said this was a free country and they weren't going to work if they thought it was dangerous and didn't want to work. Victor pointed out that it wouldn't be a free country much longer if we didn't get the airfield going, but no good.' Finally it was decided to entrust the task of airfield repair to parties of airmen.

In the same way everyone had quickly got used to the presence of the W.A.A.F.s – which was agreeable anyway – and especially to their efficiency. As Gibbs said: 'We had long passed the age when some grey-beard of the past refused to employ women ... "*No* women, they quarrel incessantly and their shrill voices would frighten the dogs." '

Gerald Gibbs had lost nearly three stone. One can understand why. He spent his whole time watching the map in the Ops Room and every raid placed a strain on his mind and his emotions. He knew all the tracks the raiders took and as the counters moved from one square to another he would say to himself 'Ah, they're heading for Duxford,' or 'The bastards, they're over Chelsea!' And, of course, he knew the place on the map where his house was with his wife and children. It was not marked, but it might as well have had a flashing red warning lamp.

'I must admit to having spared a few seconds occasionally to warn them on my direct line to duck down when an attack was closely approaching them. That direct line could also talk back, of course, and I got seriously into domestic trouble on one occasion. My wife telephoned that incendiary bombs had fallen on the house and garden. I replied, 'Is the new car all right?' I have often tried since to explain quietly and logically that I knew already that she and the family and the house were all right – or she would have told me first – whereas the car was in a flimsy wooden shed; but no good, as men readers will understand.'

The American journalist Ralph Ingersoll was in London. In one of a series of articles he wrote for the *Daily Express* in November, he wrote:

'Between Saturday 7th and Sunday September 15th, Hitler took London and didn't know it.'

He painted a striking picture of the British capital:

The streets were full of rubble blown up from direct hits,

filled with glass[1] and brick and furniture and plaster, piping and what have you from houses blown down . . . during those eight terrible days in September the water mains were smashed right and left, all over the town . . . It is no wonder that Adolf Hitler stamps and raves at the psychopathic British. It must be difficult for such a coward to understand such courage. It is extremely difficult for anyone to understand it. But it happened.

The King and Queen set an example. Buckingham Palace was bombed on two more occasions, but they remained in residence; they wished to be Londoners like everyone else. A German note pointed out that it was not easy to avoid historic buildings. St. Paul's stands near a railway bridge and Buckingham Palace is near Wellington Barracks and Victoria Station. His Majesty instituted the George Cross and the George Medal as special awards in recognition of courage. It will be recalled that Lieutenant Davies, who had rendered harmless the unexploded bomb at St. Paul's, had been decorated with the George Cross. He was its first holder.

The weather grew fine again. The night of September 14th–15th was quiet.

There was dew on the lawns. For miles around the countryside was covered in mist, and only a few trees stood out as splashes of gold. You could feel it was going to be a lovely day – 'Hitler's weather'. Alan Wright got up and dressed. He took off on a spotting mission; a trip up and down the Channel filling in the details by radio, details that the radar stations could not supply, notably the type of enemy aircraft involved in any raid. This information made it possible to decide what sort of response was appropriate. He was too late. They were on their way! Heading for London!

No. 504 Squadron had a visit from some American generals who had come specially from the United States to study 'life in a fighter squadron'. There were the usual salutes, introductions, tours of inspection ... Then 'Scramble!' The pilots turned and ran for their Hurricanes. They were ordered to

1. Winston Churchill asked the Home Secretary to provide him with statistics of the damage inflicted, including the total surface area of broken glass. His view was that if the monthly production figures exceeded the monthly destruction, the damage inflicted was of relative importance only and did not give cause for alarm.

patrol overhead North Weald. One of the Americans took out a stop-watch and said quietly that between the warning and the time that the last of the twelve Hurricanes was airborne, no more than 4 minutes 50 seconds elapsed. This detail was noted in the report.

Above, the sky was blue again; a giant blue canvas streaked with the white lines of contrails. A war of geometrical composition – almost an abstract war for those on the ground. The participants only became visible after they had received the fatal blow. Then there would be a line of black smoke plummeting towards the ground and for a brief moment, before the explosion, the aeroplane could be seen. For the rest of the time it was a battle between the white lines.

Sergeant Holmes of West Kirby (Liverpool) was with 504 Squadron at 17,000 feet over Gravesend. Suddenly there they were: about thirty Dorniers!

'We were flying up the river which we could see between patches of cloud,' he said. '. . . I was in the last section of my squadron and the squadron leader led us into the attack.'

Tally-ho!

It was Holmes's first combat and he flung himself into it wholeheartedly. 'My Dornier took all that I had to give him. Bits flew off him, and I broke away, intending to turn round to attack him again. Black oil covered my windscreen. I did attack again, but I think it must have been a different machine. Anyway, as soon as I fired a big flame shot up. I must have got his petrol tank.'

Still not satisfied, the sergeant pilot leapt on his second Dornier in a head-on attack. He fired a burst straight into the cockpit. He thought he saw a piece of the Dornier break away, but then realized that it was a German baling out. He passed so close to him that he nearly caught his parachute.

By now the battle was extremely confused and suddenly Holmes felt a terrible shock in his right wing. His aeroplane fell away in a spin and there was no response form his controls.

"I spun towards the earth. I flung the hood back and struggled to get out . . . While I was spinning down I went through cloud. When I did get out the wind was so strong it was like a piece of an aeroplane hitting me. People on the ground later told me that my parachute opened at only 300 feet.'

Holmes had the impression that he had only been floating for ten seconds. That was enough to allow him to see a Dornier coming down in flames. No doubt it was his. His feet were by now touching a gutter and he slid down a roof and fell on his back in a garden. Some people say that he finished up in a dustbin.

'Two girls came to me and saw that I was an R.A.F. man. I was so glad to see them that I kissed them both.'

Below, the alert had taken London by surprise. The weather was beautiful. In the West End the sunlight shone in the empty squares. A fine late summer's day when the air is light and the parks, breathing again after the heat of August, smell of grass and the first dying flowers. In the *Sunday Times* the Grosvenor House Hotel advertised dancing in its new underground restaurant.

Colonel Passy, chief of the Free French Intelligence Service, was playing bridge at the moment when Holmes's Dornier crashed on Victoria Station. 'Nobody moved and there was no flicker of emotion on any face. I had to force myself to stay seated, sacrificing my tremendous curiosity to the overriding necessity of remaining imperturbably phlegmatic.'

Tin-hatted soldiers wearing packs and led by N.C.O.s climbed to the roof of Victoria Station. The bomber's fuselage had been shattered into tiny pieces and all that was found was a part of the tailplane and one of the twin fins bearing its swastika. A chimney-pot had been knocked down and bricks lay scattered about where a breach was made in a wall.

And the battle continued. One squadron leader remembers, in the middle of the fight, seeing the neat green dot of Kennington Oval Cricket Ground. He saw it for a second before he chased a Heinkel 111 as far as Essex and watched it crash among some trees outside a house. 'A tremendous sheet of flame went up,' he said, 'and I turned round to look for more raiders. I found one in a bad way being chased by three Hurricanes and two Spitfires. I joined in and we all saw him gliding down towards an R.A.F. aerodrome on which he landed quite nicely. His undercarriage collapsed and after skidding along for about fifty yards he stopped in a cloud of dust. All of us dived low and saw one of the Germans get out and help a second to leave the machine. They both staggered towards the hangars.'

Horst Zander, a Dornier wireless operator, looked out on both sides and behind. He had the immensely satisfying feeling of being part of a vast invincible fortress. To left and right his comrades of the sixth squadrons of KG 3 were spread out. With them flew the other squadrons of *Gruppe* 2. Ahead and in the rear and a little higher were other formations bringing the *Geschwader* to its full strength; not a gap in the ranks. It was just like a fly-past. So much metal in the air, even in its dull paintwork, gave an impression of invincible strength. During the course of the day the Luftwaffe flew 328 bomber and 769 fighter sorties. 'The whole German Air Force seemed to be airborne,' wrote Deacon Elliott. At Uxbridge, Keith Park received the information from the radar stations with a sigh: 'It's going to be quite a party!'

The objective was London; more precisely the famous U in the Thames. The 'Valhalla' flew steadfastly on.

The most vicious were enjoying themselves. 'Sitting up there, high in our aircraft, we were happy. It gave us a moment of unforgettable joy to think of the havoc our bombs would wreak on the city below.'

So give me your hand, your pretty white hand...

Others, veterans of night raids, had become blasé. Flying in the dark, they had fallen into the habit of tuning in to the B.B.C.

'It made the trip pass quicker, but at the same time it made us mad to hear music coming from the very place we were about to smash. How did they manage to sing as though there was no danger when we were there, right over their heads?'

There were some gentler spirits. Or perhaps they were just tired of sowing death. They rationalized their conduct.

'It wasn't so much to kill the English. It was just the best way to finish the war quickly.'

Zander looked at his watch:

'1300 hours. It was the afternoon of September 15th, 1940.'

At this moment the British appeared. Twenty-four squadrons were sent up, of which twenty-two made interceptions.

The battle started over Kent in the region of Canterbury. Oberleutnant Laube called out:

'Enemy fighters straight ahead!'

These were the Spitfires of 72 and 92 Squadrons. They didn't pause to find the most favourable position for attack; they came in firing with everything they had.

'Dozens of Spits', wrote Zander, 'spread out on an immense front. They never stopped shooting at us until their ammunition was exhausted. They were everywhere, above, below and all round. Fire was coming in from all sides and twice it got very close. I think British fighters collided with two of the Dornier 17s of our group. Aircraft were falling in flames and beneath us we could see parachutes opening. In our aircraft we looked at each other with big smiles and gave the thumbs up. "We've made it. They didn't get us this time!"'

Not so fast! Bader's Hurricanes were on the scene. The legless pilot had had things out with Leigh-Mallory, the commander of 12 Group. His position was that he, Leigh-Mallory, had chosen him to lead the wing and that he would lead it the way he thought best or not at all.

His point was conceded and he was authorized to fly big formation tactics. It was 'Valhalla' versus 'Balbo'. Bader called out to his sixty fighters:

'In we go – every man for himself!'

In for the kill – the pay-off! The Czechs of 310 Squadron and the Poles of 302 had old scores to settle with their countries' invaders. Satchell, leading 302 Squadron, shot down two Dorniers one after the other and then was hit himself. He broke off and landed back at base. Four of his aircraft did not return. Then 504 Squadron took off again to intercept an enemy formation between London and Hornchurch. They did not have the sky to themselves. A Spitfire pilot, emerging victorious from a dogfight with a 109, just managed to avoid flying straight into a burning Junkers 88. He broke off.

'Then suddenly,' he writes, 'the sky ahead was absolutely clear. Not an aircraft in sight.'

He scarcely had time to notice this before more Junkers 88s appeared. He set one of them on fire and was chasing it when his earphones came alive.

'They were calling me on the R/T and I turned towards

the rest of the squadron. Another Hun formation was coming in and we climbed to get altitude. Above the bombers I saw Me 109s and Me 110s. It was damned hot and my arms were tired.'

Zander's Dornier 17 had a rough time. The captain was hit and the aircraft was pitching like a ship in a rough sea.

'The cockpit is full of blood,' wrote Zander, 'we are lost. Then there was a voice, marvellously gentle. It seemed to come from somewhere above the instrument panel. It said "Laube, go home. Go home." '

They went home. On both sides of the Channel the aircraft were refuelled, the pilots had a cup of tea or coffee and a bite to eat. The armourers refilled the gun and bomb bays. A count was made of missing friends, and then they were off again.

On his way to spend Sunday at Chequers, Winston Churchill stopped at Uxbridge. He went to the nerve-centre of 11 Group, the underground Operations Room. It has been kept intact and can be visited today. It feels cool as you go down the steps leading to the room. It must have felt the same on September 15th, 1940. There are staircases, long submarine-like passages with yellow tubing – the bowels of the earth – and at the end the 'Ops Room'. In the centre there is the famous table with its gridded map of southern England and the Channel. On the walls are boards showing the state of each of the squadrons of the Group. Around three sides of the room stands a wooden platform with a row of desks. You have to climb up a narrow stairway to get to it and when you are up there you have to stoop. There the controllers sat, helmeted and with telephone at hand, giving orders to the operators and to the W.A.A.F.s working on the table with their clawed croupiers' sticks. 'The ceaseless orderly activity of this nerve centre,' wrote Gerald Pawle, 'with the plotters moving their discs to and fro on the table, the Army liaison officers passing information about the anti-aircraft units in action, and the winking of the red and white lights on the far wall, created an instant sense of drama. Mr. Churchill had paid one previous visit there.'

When the Prime Minister arrived 'everything was quiet'. It was only a pause. 'Not so many today,' somebody whispered.

With Keith Park was the duty controller, Group Captain Lord Willoughby de Broke. Park was expounding his theories and Churchill listened. An armchair was brought and Park had to leave from time to time to give his orders. Churchill did not move. He seemed unable to take his eyes away from the winking lights and the counters sliding on the table. It is said that he went to sit in the 'aquarium', a sort of cage of curved glass that looked down on the Ops Room from the right. From here he could see all that was going on. He must have smoked. His cigar ends are still there, carefully preserved.

Very soon the performance was resumed. The interval had lasted less than two hours. Gerald Pawle writes: 'As the attacks began that afternoon, Churchill sat hunched in his chair, silent and absorbed ... The German Air Force came over in wave after wave.'

To be precise, they came in three waves, and thirty-one squadrons rose to meet them. Galland was leading the first German formation. He encountered some Hurricanes and Spitfires and engaged them. The dogfight lasted ten minutes. 'It was terribly long,' wrote Galland. Terribly long for a pilot trying to conserve his fuel, knowing that in a previous raid, twelve aircraft of his group were lost when they had to ditch or make belly-landings on the beaches of Normandy.

Finally, the German ace got a Hurricane. Its flames were extinguished only when it plunged into the Thames. The 'Valhalla' continued on its way. 'It stretched for several miles,' said one Hurricane pilot. 'The bombers were flying in formations of nine; three sections of three like a sergeant's stripes. Each formation was accompanied by nine Messerscmitt 110s and the 109s were prowling about up above at 35,000 feet.' Once more the Poles of 303 Squadron were involved in one of the crucial stages of the battle. Satchell was leading them, furious, because he had the feeling that yet again, he had arrived too late. This was the price that had to be paid for the big formation tactics. Frequently, by the time they had formed up, the chance was gone. From all sides machine-guns were spitting fire. Five German aircraft went down streaming plumes of smoke, to crash on the ground far below. 'The battle was fought in a clear blue sky 4,000 feet above a thick cloud layer.' Group Captain Vincent, the commander of Northolt Sector, made a single-handed attack with his Hurricane on an enemy formation. He pressed it home with such determination that the Germans turned about and headed back for France.

In the Ops Room, where Churchill was watching, this action was represented by a yellow counter marked with a black H which was moved back across the coastline. But all the time there were others coming. The telephone never stopped ringing and each time a squadron returned to refuel and rearm, lights would flash.

Three sergeant pilots were flying in close formation. Their task was to intercept a formation of bombers that were attacking the London docks in the U of the Thames. They each picked out a German and went for them as hard as they could go. The first bomber ended its flight on an aerodrome in Surrey, the second just north of Dungeness and the third right on the south coast.

New formations appeared. 'There were Messerschmitts painted all different colours. Not just the yellow-nosed ones wc were used to seeing, but others; white noses, orange noses, red noses, dotted all over the sky.'

A new yellow counter with a black H appeared at the coast, not far from Portsmouth. This was *Kampfgeschwader 55* engaged on a diversionary raid. Up till now Churchill had said nothing. Was he thinking of what he had said at the start of this immense aerial conflict: 'We have learnt to fly. What a prodigious change that implies. Even old parliamentarians like myself are forced to acquire a high degree of mobility.' A little later he turned to Park, asking him in a rather terse voice:

'What other reserves have we?'

The commander of 11 Group turned round to face Churchill. He was preoccupied. He had just called Bentley Priory and asked Dowding to contact 12 Group and have them make ready three squadrons as reinforcements. His reply was respectful, but it had the effect of a whip cracking:

'There are none.'

'In an account which he wrote about it afterwards,' wrote Churchill, 'he said that at this I "looked grave". Well I might.'

A few moments later the last yellow counters had been

moved off the squares of the map table that marked the south of England. Park took a deep breath. Churchill left the room and started up the stairs. He climbed slowly and steadily; the staircase was long and narrow. When he reached the top and emerged on to the broad grass area, he had to pause for breath. The air was warm in the late afternoon. He said to Gerald Gibbs:

'I was much moved when in your Operations Room I saw the panorama of Nazi might flung against the forces of civilization . . .'

The visit was over. A last cigar and then, accompanied by Ismay, Winston Churchill got back into his car and was off towards Chequers.

He had contrived to be at Uxbridge at the precise moment when the Battle of Britain was won.

At six o'clock in the evening the Germans managed to mount another attack, this time with a score of Messerschmitt 110s, on the Supermarine factory at Woolston.

Bader, who had added to his score once again, was called to the telephone by Leigh-Mallory:

'Douglas, what a wonderful show today. It's absolutely clear your big formations are paying dividends.'

Deacon Elliott returned to base from his third sortie. He was exhausted.

'By the end of the day,' he wrote, 'I was tired, annoyed at being shot at so frequently and feeling rather sick. I was not alone in these feelings. Also my aircraft (P.9460) for some unaccountable reason was most difficult to fly. The total claims of enemy destroyed on all fronts today was, I believe, finally confirmed at 185 aircraft.'

This was the figure announced. Indeed, it was said that when the wrecked German aircraft had been counted, the figure would be higher still. Of the 185, seven had been shot down by anti-aircraft guns. The total score represented 450 German airmen put out of action, for more than 130 of the aircraft destroyed were bombers and not single-seaters. On the British side only twenty-five aircraft were admitted to be missing and twelve of the pilots had descended by parachute and were unhurt.

In fact, the German losses were no more than sixty, but on

the Monday morning, the newsvendors' boards at the corners of the bombed streets read:

'185 shot down and score not complete!'[1]

London licked its wounds and counted the dead. A large bomb had fallen on Buckingham Palace in the Queen's private apartments. Another had fallen on the Palace lawn. Beckenham, Westminster, Lambeth, Lewisham, Battersea, Camberwell, Crystal Palace, Clapham, Tooting, Wandsworth and Kensington, had all been severely hit. Everywhere there were columns of smoke and the light of fires.

On the airfield where the Hurricanes of the Poles of 303 Squadron were based, mechanics worked with shaded mobile lights. When the squadron commander had made his returns his whole squadron consisted of only four serviceable aircraft. The rest, to use a phrase of Deacon Elliott's, looked more like pepper-pots. The repair crews worked without pause and when dawn broke the Poles had sixteen aircraft ready for action.

September 15th was to become an historic date in the British calendar, equal to Trafalgar Day.

In his usual calm, balanced way, Dowding's only comment was:

'On September 15th, the Germans produced their maximum effort.'

The day ended. 'Fine night,' announced the Meteorological Office.

1. When the war was over, the British admitted, with a certain humour, that all in all, they had only exaggerated the number of their victories by 55 per cent; while the Germans, on the other hand, had done so by 224 per cent.

16: Death of the Sea Lion

In occupied France it was raining. The woods near Le Coudray were dripping and the two swimming pools deserted. It was raining in the Channel and Fink looked out over the waves that had suddenly become steel-grey. It was raining over the south of England . . .

Yesterday was September 15th and it had been fine, now everything was different. The loss of sixty German aircraft had made the difference. Looked at from this remove of time, sixty seems a small number. Between August 23rd and September 6th the Germans had lost 378. During good weather they would put up between three hundred and five hundred aircraft a day. On September 15th they had flown over one thousand sorties. So why should the loss of sixty aircraft suddenly change the whole picture? But the fact is that it did. On September 16th, Goering called the commanders of the Luftwaffe together to inform them that he had decided on a change of tactics. It is not known whether this meeting was held at Cap Blanc Nez or at Le Coudray. In Goering's biography it is stated that on September 17th he gave orders for his train to have steam up. It seems most probable, therefore, that the meeting was held on board 'Asia', wherever the train happened to be at the time.

Goering was both uneasy and angry. The German radio was crying victory. It reported that Hermann had flown over London in a Junkers 88. His aircrew, who had been in action, knew very well that it had been a day of particularly heavy losses. They also knew that their fat commander-in-chief couldn't get through the door of a Junkers. The Reichsmarschall was ill at ease. He did not like the raids on London. Not long before, he had said to his wife, Emmy:

'In Berlin the people shouted out after me, "What's going on, Hermann? Why aren't we bombing London?" I'm still holding off, and for a good reason. I believe that if we don't reply, the English will soon realize that it's stupid to drop bombs on cities. It's certainly no way to win the war!'

Though he had given in on September 3rd, he still continued to express his preference for the destruction of Fighter

Command. There is no doubt that during the meetings of September 13th and 14th in Berlin, he had been affected by von Brauchitsch's remarks and by Hitler's hesitation. He was afraid that the indecision over Operation *Seelöwe*, all the postponements, would compromise the Luftwaffe's chances of success. What did he really think? Those who wished him no good asserted that if one morning, with London in ruins, Britain had been brought to her knees and had sued for peace, Goering would have let it be known that he had always been in favour of hammering away at the capital city and that the victory was his work. Perhaps so, but what military commander would act in any other way? However, this was not the situation on September 16th. London was holding out and the Royal Air Force had not been defeated. The Reichsmarschall explained the situation with great clarity. He must have been forcing himself to keep calm, for one of the people who attended the meeting reported that his face was purple:

'The successes we won on September 7th and 12th have deceived us,' he said. 'There are serious lessons to be drawn from what happened yesterday.'

Goering was convinced that Park's forces had been reinforced. Yet another subject for controversy! It will be remembered, no doubt, that when, at Uxbridge, the commander of 11 Group had replied to Churchill: 'There are none', he had already called Bentley Priory to ask for three of 12 Group's squadrons to be held in reserve for him. Later, Dowding was to be criticized in British circles for not concentrating *all* his forces in the 11 Group area which was the one that suffered the most frequent and the most violent attacks.

Leigh-Mallory reminded Bader once more that any intervention on the part of 12 Group must follow a request from the Air Officer Commanding 11 Group. As long as he had not requested continuous reinforcement, 12 Group would always be in the position of a police flying squad which arrives on the scene only when the fight has started.

The Air Chief Marshal had disposed his forces with great care and in proportion to the risks that could be foreseen for each sector. How could he know in advance that the Germans would make no further use of *Luftflotte V* from Norway and would give up their attacks on the north? He preserved the basic structure of his disposition of forces but at the same time reinforced 11 Group with squadrons from 12 Group and 13 Group. He seems to have deceived the enemy.

Goering's words show that he was prepared to stick at nothing. Now that Hitler had made his fire-eating speech, it was political impossibility to leave London in peace. To do so would be to admit that the Luftwaffe had been beating its head against a brick wall. But even so, was it really necessary to throw so many crews into the furnace of 'the greatest target in the world'? What good would come of it? The Blitz – this word was an English abbreviation of the German *Blitzkrieg* – wasn't going to reduce the British to submission. Goering was to say as much, later, to Hitler; but everything indicates that he had believed it from September 16th on. The ending of the war required capitulation by the British, and this could only be brought about by an invasion, which in turn could only be embarked upon after the liquidation of Fighter Command. The Reichsmarschall decided on the use of smaller bomber formations. This would mean that with the same sized fighter escort, a greater degree of protection could be achieved. The Hurricanes and Spitfires would still take off, since they were obliged to attempt the destruction of the Heinkels, Junkers and Dorniers, but they would then find themselves confronted with a formation in which the proportion of Messerschmitt 109s was unlike anything they were used to. This, surely, was the key to the problem.

'We shall destroy as many fighters as possible,' said Goering.

He then repeated his favourite phrase, though its force must have been considerably reduced over the last five weeks:

'Four or five days! Four or five days of good weather and the R.A.F. will have lost all its fighters!'

If we consider the cards that Goering held and make allowance for his habitual bombast, we shall see that his reasoning was not bad. London was a task that he was forced to undertake. He might as well make as light work of it as possible. The recipe was fewer bombers and more fighters. The Reichsmarschall saw the bombers primarily as bait, in any case. Goering, as former leader of the Richthofen Circus, looked to the fighters. They were cast in the role of Napoleon's cavalry under Murat. It was up to them to capture territory. It was they who should dispose of Dowding's men. Anyway, he could not accept the death of any more German airmen simply for the sake of knocking down Victorian houses. On this sort of question Goering was always ready to show his teeth. On May 28th, 1940, he had announced in public that as a reprisal for the bad treatment German pilots were receiving in France, all the French aircrews held by the Germans would henceforth be chained.

'Come on!' he cried, 'my Luftwaffe never let me down yet! One more push! Remember Poland! Remember France! Remember the grand days of the happy warriors! In five days ... In four or five days from *now* it will be all over!'

Suddenly the leaders of the *Gruppen* dared to open their mouths. They spoke of their weary pilots, of the terrible nervous exhaustion. They spoke of the growing discouragement at seeing the goal retreat every time you thought you were getting near. Goering understood. His earlier anger seemed to have vanished.

'In five days', he repeated, 'we shall have won. Then we can forget our weariness ...'

Outside, the rain fell steadily.

Sergeant John Hannah was stretched out on a bed that he didn't recognize. He did not yet know that he had just been awarded the Victoria Cross.

The night before he had taken part in a raid by 83 Squadron on Antwerp. The Hampden in which he was wireless operator received a direct hit from an incendiary shell. The bomb bay was destroyed and the fuel tanks ruptured. The aircraft caught fire and, seizing an extinguisher, Hannah rushed forward and directed the jet at the source of the fire. Through the flames he could see that the rear turret was gaping open; the gunner had been blown out. Soon there was a long series of explosions as the ammunition belts went off. Hannah grabbed a second extinguisher. It felt as though he was inside an oven. His eyes were stinging. The aluminium was melting beneath his feet. Never mind! He emptied the second extinguisher and then beat out all the remaining flames with his log-book.

Only then did it occur to him that he was on fire himself. He dropped to his knees. His trousers were on fire. He tried to rise again – impossible. Very well then, crawl! He crawled, clinging to the metal that was now glowing red like an electric hot-plate. Up forward he realized that the navigator must have jumped, because the pilot was alone. Hannah climbed up to the cockpit. He was finished. He managed to pass up the navigator's maps to the pilot with an indication of the course for home. Then he collapsed.

And now, bandaged and plastered with tannic acid, he was alive in the white world of hospital.

At Cap Blanc Nez, Fink was looking up his tide tables. Only a few weeks ago he had used them to know when the next convoy would fall like a rat into his trap. Now they showed, in a way that brooked no argument, the last opportunity for Operation *Seelöwe*. If it was not set in motion the next day, September 17th, it could not be launched on the 27th. After that, the next favourable tides would not occur until October.

The matter was not left in doubt. On the 17th, Hitler made his decision; it was quite specific: 'Taking account of the meteorological situation as a whole, there are no grounds for expecting a period of calm, especially in the Channel. The Führer has therefore decided to postpone Operation *Seelöwe* until further notice.'

When Goering heard of Hitler's decision he had his train made ready. He was leaving. Eye-witnesses say that 'a visible change had come over him'. The previous day he had been keyed up with excitement, but Hitler's decision, even though he had been expecting it, had the effect of a cold shower. If only Professor Kahle had been there with his sleeping draught! But he was far away. Karinhall was at the other end of the world and too many dreams were fading away all at once. There had been too many music-hall jokes about 'fat old Goering' on the lines of the one that went 'If you want to cross the Channel, Herr Reichsmarschall, you had better use Moses' rod; then you will be able to part the waters and the divisions can march through.' 'Very well, send someone to fetch it for me. Where is it?' 'In the British Museum, Herr Reichsmarschall.'

Goering summoned his officers for the last time. He had learned that on the previous evening, in a bomber mess, a red flag had been raised in honour of the R.A.F. This was no revolutionary gesture, but the traditional Luftwaffe ceremony in honour of a brave opponent. To Goering it seemed that it had been done just to annoy him. The crews were now before him, belted, determined: his clear-eyed demons. Should he turn them into Spitfire fodder? No! Let them continue to attack at night while the darkness held the enemy fighters on the ground.

Outside the rain had given way to thunder. The sky, whose possession had been so fiercely disputed, was now growling with anger.

The Germans possessed a system of beam guidance to assist them in finding their targets at night. From the beginning of June the British had been taking an interest in this system and on the 6th the Prime Minister had presided over a meeting which Dr. R. V. Jones had attended. He was a physicist responsible for the study of enemy equipment. Jones was convinced of the existence of German beams. British Intelligence got to work. Prisoners who were sent to 'the cage' were questioned and on June 17th some of them more or less admitted to some knowledge of the system. A careful examination of documents found on board shot-down German aircraft allowed the British to discover its name. *Knickebein,* the word kept cropping up like a *leitmotiv* in the codes used in night operations. It was found that a beam was laid from a certain town in the west of Germany to a map reference point not far from an industrial centre in the Midlands. On June 18th the Air Ministry established an organization whose task it was to discover what signal was being used and on what frequency.

The detection of *Knickebein* was entrusted to Flight Lieutenant Black, a specialist in blind flying. He had an Anson, specially equipped for the purpose. He succeeded at his second attempt. The beam crossed the coast at the mouth of the Humber and led to Derby. If its line was projected in the direction of the Continent, it pointed towards Cleves. It was these two towns that were mentioned in the documents found on board German aircraft.

Dr. Jones was now positive. He reported that the Germans had a beam network that enabled them to position a formation of aircraft over any point in the United Kingdom with a margin of error no greater than four hundred yards. *Knickebein* allowed them to aim their bombs at night. In early July a unit was created and put under the command of Air Vice-Marshal Addison. It was christened No. 80 Wing and its purpose was to transmit signals on the same frequencies as those of the German beams and so jam them. Radio receivers were installed on the radar masts and in the darkness they listened. Soon the beams were detected, one after another. When a beam was detected it was usually possible to plot its intersection with another beam and thus to know where the enemy intended to strike. Fighter Command could then be alerted and at the same time the jamming crews would try to make the beam as confused as possible.

Over a period of some weeks the German crews found their beams leading them astray and had come to distrust them. And then, some of the most experienced British pilots, like Malan, had started to chance their arm at night. Johnny Johnson records how one morning, as he was having a discussion with a sergeant pilot, Wing Commander Bader came in. The two men stood to attention. Bader grumbled a bit, sucking at his pipe, but he seemed in the mood to talk: 'The Spit isn't as good as the Hurricane for night flying. Its undercarriage is narrow and plays tricks on landing. You feel more comfortable in the Hurricane and the visibility is better. I'm going to get hold of one and try this night-flying game ...'

Hemingway was selected for a night-flying test in a Hurricane.

During the night of September 17th–18th two hundred and sixty-eight bombers attacked London. Famous streets like Bond Street, Saville Row, and Oxford Street were set on fire.

The British bombers were airborne too.

R. S. Gilmour, a Blenheim pilot, pulled off a master stroke at Ostend. He arrived off 'Blackpool front', that part of the French coast from which the invasion fleet was supposed to sail.

'It was an amazing spectacle,' he reported. 'Calais docks were on fire. So was the waterfront of Boulogne, and glares extended for miles. The whole French coast seemed to be a barrier of flame broken only by intense white flashes of exploding bombs and vari-coloured incendiary tracers soaring and circling skywards.'

Gilmour's target was Ostend. He found it and started his dive. When he released his bombs, he had the feeling that his aircraft, now lightened, leapt upwards in the air. He pulled on the stick and with a kick on the rudder broke away in a climb. He looked down into the pool of darkness beneath his wings. He waited. Not for long. Suddenly there were three great flashes as his bombs went off like a firework display. The last one exploded in a fountain of fire, cutting a path of light through the darkness.

'I saw the outline of the jetties in vivid relief. Between them the water boiled with thin black shapes. They were barges flung up-end and fragments turning slowly over and over in the air.'

At that moment there was a tremendous explosion. The Blenheim was flying at less than four thousand feet. There was a colossal blast and the aircraft was enveloped in a white world's-end blaze. It was no longer in the sky, nor on the ground, but hanging in an impossible empty whiteness – a colourless non-space that was never meant to be seen by human eye. Gilmour had no idea what was happening. He clung on to the controls, fighting to hold his aeroplane. He was literally 'knocked on the head'. No reference for piloting in the void.

It was only when he saw the photographs of the raid the next day that he understood what had happened. He had dropped his 'eggs' on a dump of five hundred tons of mines that were waiting to be loaded on to the minelayers. Everything within a radius of a mile had been reduced to rubble.

The weather cleared up again. 'Every day there was activity and more activity,' wrote Deacon Elliott, 'and now it seemed much better to stay with it rather than take your allotted days off. I found, like many others I am sure, that it was far less disturbing to fly on most days and on as many missions as possible than to take a break and be faced with the unsettling problem of getting re-acclimatized . . .'

On September 18th, Bader, leading thirty-six fighters from Duxford, dived on two German bomber formations. There ensued a great turning combat on level terms. Satchell and his Poles again distinguished themselves and Bader's men won decisively, claiming thirty victories without losing a single aircraft. Bader himself claimed two: a Junkers and a Dornier. In fact, nineteen aircraft were destroyed during the whole day, but this was of little importance; it had been established that big formations were very efficient when they arrived in time. It was a fortunate encounter but one which happened only too rarely.

Alan Deere wrote: 'From a fighter pilot's point of view, I hold that Bader's wing concept was wrong, and I consider that the German fighter tactics against the American daylight bombers prove my point . . . I know that most wing leaders agree with me, and certainly those who had the benefit of later experience. Johnny Johnson was one and in his book *Wing Leader* he supports this view. Douglas Bader, I know, won't agree.'

During the night of September 19th–20th, London was very heavily bombed. Huge cranes were used to clear the ruins around Marble Arch. Down by the Thames everyone went to ground in the shelters underneath the warehouses.

'Over two hundred people lay in groups on the cold stone floor,' wrote Drew Middleton. 'There had been some trouble on the first night. Lascars from the docks had raped a fourteen-year-old girl. Now the older men had formed a vigilante society. The Lascars were forbidden the place. The stink of sweat, dirty clothing, urine and excrement caught at your nose and throat.'

René Mouchotte noted in his book:

'I spent the night in London, in an hotel near the station. At about eleven o'clock the building was shaken so much that for a few seconds I thought it was going to collapse. Incessant bombing shook the city from nine o'clock on; the sky was reddened by the light of fires. The place being no longer tenable, we went out and visited the shelters to occupy ourselves. It really would have been too stupid to get oneself killed in that hotel on the eve of realizing what I have been waiting for for a year.'

On September 20th, the American mission which had been visiting the airfields of Fighter Command returned to the United States. Its leader, General Strong, reported: 'The German Air Force has not seriously impaired the strength of the R.A.F. and military objectives have suffered only superficial damage.'

Deacon Elliott and two other pilots from Hawkinge were detailed to escort an Anson on a mission to record the point of impact of the shells fired by the heavy batteries at Dover as they bombarded Calais. On their second sortie, the Anson pilot, who was fearful of enemy fighter intervention, cut short the mission. When Deacon Elliott landed that evening at Biggin Hill, he learnt that his best friend, Dutch Holland, had not returned. Apparently he had been hit by British anti-aircraft fire over the Thames and had baled out. His legs were crushed and he was taken to Chatham hospital, where he died.

On the night of September 21st–22nd London was bombed.

On September 22nd, after a fairly quiet day, the atmosphere in the mess at Biggin Hill was gay. The nurses from a nearby hospital had come over for a party. The little bar was decorated with caricatures and there was dancing in the dining-room and entrance hall. A few couples had wandered out on to the stone-flagged terrace from which a flight of steps, bordered with privet hedges, led down to the Kentish countryside. It was a beautiful evening. 'An excellent diversion ...' wrote Deacon Elliott.

That night London was bombed. Doubtless the pilots could hear the noise of the one hundred and twenty-three bombers grinding their way overhead towards the capital. Some Blenheims and Defiants, about a dozen in all, tried to intercept them; without success. The whole weight of the attack showered down on London. 'The approach to London looked like approaching Dante's Inferno,' wrote Lord Alanbrooke.

No. 72 Squadron was airborne early. The radar stations had picked up six waves of enemy aircraft, four large and two small, heading for Dover. Deacon Elliott wrote: 'Me 109s everywhere. I was just closing in on an Me 109 when unbeknown an Me 109 was doing precisely the same thing to me.' The second 109 fired first, using his cannon. Pieces started breaking off the Spitfire's port wing and glycol spurted from the engine cowling. Elliott saw another aircraft close in; this time it had roundels on its wings. Sergeant Norfolk had come to the rescue. He followed the damaged Spitfire down as it lost height and made a crash landing. The pilot got out unhurt. 'Yet another lucky break,' wrote Deacon Elliott.

Galland had taken part in the engagement. North of Rochester he had attacked a Hurricane. 'My first burst', he wrote, 'blew the aircraft to pieces and I nearly got swallowed up in the wreckage ... Taking advantage of the general confusion I broke off with a violent side-slip and as I did so I could see, 3,000 feet below, the canopies of two parachutes ...' But Galland's day was not finished yet. On his way home he came upon a lone Hurricane. He made a diving head-on attack and set it on fire. 'And then', he wrote, 'I saw its cockpit gaping open and the dead pilot clutching the stick. The aircraft lost height gently, gliding down towards the misty fields below. I hadn't the heart to finish it off.'

The day's score read Great Britain 16, Germany 11.

When the pilots landed back at Biggin Hill in the evening a wonderful surprise awaited them: thirty-six brand new fighters. Enough to equip a whole wing! 'The worst is over,' wrote Deacon Elliott.

This was true. In the last few weeks the situation had changed a great deal. Two days earlier Hitler had ordered Raeder to disperse the invasion fleet around the various Channel ports 'in order to minimize the damage suffered in the course of enemy air attacks'. British reconnaissance aircraft brought back photographs which confirmed a much lower level of activity in the invasion ports. Destroyers were no longer found manoeuvring around Brest and all along the coast the number of barges had been reduced by a third.

Churchill decided to turn this breathing space to advantage and to use the Hampdens, Wellingtons and Whitleys to attack Berlin. He met spirited opposition from the Chief of Air Staff. Churchill insisted. So did the Chiefs of Staff. Finally it was decided that the raids would take place, but that they would be directed at military targets.

On the night of September 23rd, two formations crossed in a clear sky but without seeing each other. They consisted of two hundred and sixty Germans bringing fire to London and one hundred and nineteen British aircraft on course for Berlin.

At the same time Galland, too, was en route towards the German capital. His fortieth victory had earned him an oakleaf cluster for his Knight's Cross. Following Dietl and

Mölders, he became the third soldier of the Reich to receive them. But at the same time he was forbidden to fly any more. It was the rule. Warriors weighed down with their laurels were not allowed to take risks. Their death would be a national defeat. 'I was sure I would be able to arrange things,' wrote Galland, 'for I was to receive the oak leaves from Hitler himself.'

The only account we possess of this meeting is Galland's. He was received by Hitler at the new Chancellery. Berlin had been bombed during the night but Hitler did not talk about it; or if he did, Galland breathes no word of it. This was the second occasion on which he was received by Hitler. The first was when a reception was given for the members of the Condor Legion. He was surprised to find that the Führer 'did not play the overworked leader'. Galland had to give a detailed account of the progress of the battle and began to feel confident. He even expressed his admiration for the R.A.F. and complained about the untruthful nature of the official communiqués. 'I was staggered to find that Hitler, instead of defending his propaganda service, agreed completely with what I said.' All this was written years later when the war was over and the Führer dead. Perhaps Galland is trying to steal a little limelight. He told Hitler what was what and Hitler agreed with him. At any rate he found his leader reasonable and understanding. 'He too had the greatest respect for the English. This made him even more sorry that he was obliged to make war on them – a war that could only end in the destruction of one side or the other.'

According to Galland, Hitler ended by saying:

'Even if Germany emerges victorious, the defeat of Great Britain will leave a vacuum that no other country can fill.'

In the streets of Berlin there were piles of ruins to mark where the British bombers had passed.

Hitler's words had impressed Galland. 'He had managed to take the wind out of my sails. I no longer felt bitter.' So it was with a light heart that Galland set off for Karinhall. Goering had invited his pilot to hunt the stag. He was to meet the Reichsmarschall at his hunting cabin the *Reichsjägerhof*. What he found was a huntsman straight from light opera. 'Goering came out of the house to meet me, wearing a green suede hunting jacket over a silk blouse with long, puffed sleeves, high hunting boots and in his belt a hunting knife in the shape of an old Germanic sword.' The forest was magnificent, its golden tones blending with the colours of the marshes and heathland. 'We could hear the stags out on the heath,' wrote Galland; 'it was rutting time. Every evening, beaters would go out and sound the horn along the route we were to take the next day.' Goering congratulated his guest on his promotion. Oak leaves indeed! The day was to come when Galland was awarded his diamonds. It happened in 1942 and Galland, 'the Führer's champion', made the most of it. Wearing his diamond-crusted cross he presented himself to Goering. The Reichsmarschall took hold of the decoration to examine it closely. It was fastened under Galland's tunic collar in the traditional way, by a woman's garter. This provoked laughter all round. The diamonds were not real. Goering kept the cross. A few days later he returned it to Galland. This time they were.

'These', said Goering, 'are the Führer's diamonds; and these are the Reichsmarschall's. Which of us knows more about diamonds?'

One went to Karinhall to hunt. For three days the horns led the party into the enchanted forest. 'Goering had a special treat for me: permission to hunt one of the royal stags which were usually reserved for him, a so-called "Reichsjagermeister stag". He knew them all and each one had a name; he watched over them and was loth to part with one of them.' Galland was a good shot. He had lost one eye in a crash, but the other was acute enough. He was accustomed to say that the four qualities necessary for a fighter pilot were: excellent sight, very quick reactions, a good eye and lots of self-confidence. Galland had them all. He shot his stag. 'It was really a royal beast, the stag of a lifetime.' It had a magnificent set of horns. Goering offered them to Galland.

Galland supposed that that brought his visit to an end. He looked at Goering. It would be more true to say he *saw* Goering. If you want to know a snail you must know his shell. The same thing holds good for the great and powerful of this world. The private world they have built for themselves as they have risen is what gives them away. It is just where they think they are best protected that they are at their most naked. At Karinhall Siegfried was to be *seen;* Siegfried played by a worn-out old actor.

There was a magnificent luncheon and then, in Galland's words: 'There was no further reason to prolong my stay at the *Reichsjägerhof*. Yet Goering kept his promise to Mölders and did not let me go.' Goering was about to receive the front-line reports from *Luftflotten II* and *III*. He wanted to look through them with Galland.

The three days September 24th, 25th and 26th weren't exactly great for the Luftwaffe. On the 24th the British military leaders, who knew nothing of Hitler's decision about *Seelöwe,* were still expecting the invasion. For three days the Germans attacked British aircraft factories. They caused a lot of damage and, above all, severe casualties. At Supermarine's factory at Woolston about a hundred employees were killed; at the Bristol Works at Filton, seventy-two, and at Supermarine's Southampton factory, thirty. Whole industrial installations were wiped out and production stopped for several days.

And every night London received its hammering.

But the attackers suffered heavy losses. The Poles of 303 Squadron had just been inspected by King George VI. They were fighting like game-cocks. It was an expensive fortnight. The Germans had two hundred and sixty-two aircraft shot down while the British lost one hundred and forty-four. The proportion which had been seven to five now rose to nine to five.

'Instead of the man who had been joking freely over lunch,' wrote Galland, 'I found a broken man. With a limp hand he pointed to the reports he had just received.'

The two men were alone in the Reichsmarschall's office. Goering was 'staggered'. He wondered whether the reports were lies, meant to deceive him. What he wanted was to win, to be given favourable reports. That, after all, was how he had always acted. The Führer wanted London reduced to ruins. Very well, his faithful Hermann bombed London, although he knew perfectly well that it was Fighter Command that he had to destroy. The people who want to be always right lose the right to be told the truth.

Goering turned to Galland, who had a piratical look as he sat there chewing his cigar and nibbling the ends of his moustache. Karinhall seemed to bring out the piratical side of his nature. The Reichsmarschall asked him to tell the truth without beating about the bush. The Luftwaffe losses were the heaviest since the start of the offensive. What could it mean? 'I repeated to him what I had said to Hitler,' wrote Galland. 'Although a considerable number of enemy fighters had been shot down, we could not detect any serious reduction in the enemy's strength, nor even the slightest drop in his morale. Rather the reverse; the R.A.F. was giving as good as it got.' Usually the Reichsmarschall did not like to be told that the moon was too far away when he had expressed his intention of reaching for it. But on this occasion he listend gravely to what Galland had to say. He said nothing. Inside he must have felt Siegfried starting to die.

'When, after this conversation,' wrote Galland, 'I asked Goering to allow me to rejoin my group, he had no objection. I flew back to the Channel. I had to make a forced landing over Pomerania, and in the train, as I continued my journey, the stag caused more of a sensation than the oak leaves to my Knight's Cross. My fellow passengers insisted that the stag's head stank to high heaven, or that it was dangerous to travel with the "horns" unprotected. A few hunters opened their eyes in astonishment. All of them were right.'

September 27th was a day of rain showers with intervals of sunshine and some patches of mist over the Channel.

It was also the day of the last 'Valhalla'; the Luftwaffe's farewell to the British capital.

So give me your hand, your pretty white hand,
For tonight we march against England . . .

Since early morning the squadrons had been airborne and formed up in packs. The Poles of 303 Squadron and the Canadians of 229 were among the leaders. Deacon Elliott's squadron, No. 72, had been incorporated in a wing formation and had been practising wing manoeuvres. The Bader style now held sway at Biggin Hill.

The first results were not bad; seven enemy aircraft confirmed, four probable and three damaged. The Biggin wing lost two pilots killed – one when he force-landed in the Thames.

In the afternoon the battle started again.

'The German bombers were literally massacred,' wrote Deacon Elliott. 'Their escort would not come down and fight. I doubt if a single one reached home.'

The 'Valhalla' was broken up. Attacked from all sides over Kent and more or less abandoned by its escort, it split up with aircraft flying in all directions. Some of the bombers dropped their loads in the open countryside and others turned tail and flew for the coast, pursued by the British machine-gun fire. There were combats all over the sky. The British pilots seemed to be fighting with a new fury. Perhaps they sensed that they were on the point of winning and were giving that extra effort to tip the balance definitely in their favour. They sat with their feet tucked into the toe straps of their rudder pedals, fingers resting on the gun button, and as they shouted into their mask microphones, their cries of 'Tally-ho!' rang out over the air.

The red, white and blue roundels were now really getting after the bombers. Firing burst after burst, diving, climbing back up, pulling tighter and tighter in the turns right to the blackout threshold, they hounded the enemy to destruction. Forty-five Germans were shot down, mostly in the sea, while the British lost twenty-eight, almost all over dry land.

'Personally,' wrote Deacon Elliott, 'I think this was the turning point of the battles in the south.'

By the evening, the Channel was covered with floating wreckage.

That night London was bombed.

September 28th was a sunny day. The new wheat crop was being sown. A message from the Prime Minister was received at Bentley Priory: 'Pray congratulate Fighter Command on the results of yesterday. The scale and intensity of the fighting and the heavy losses of the enemy, make September 27th rank with September 15th and August 15th, as the third great and victorious day of Fighter Command during the course of the Battle of Britain.'

By the end of September, Fighter command had six hundred and sixty-five fighters. On July 10th it had had six hundred and fifty-six. Thus the production of aircraft had almost exactly counter-balanced the effect of the losses. Lord Beaverbrook and Sir Hugh Dowding had both done their work well.

The King honoured Dowding with the title of Grand

Commander of the Order of the Bath. As Dowding was to write later:

'If the Fighter defence had failed in the autumn of 1940, England would have been invaded.'

Richard Hillary was allowed out for the first time since he had entered hospital. He wrote: 'London in the morning was still the best place in the world. The smell of wet streets, of sawdust in the butchers' shops, of tar melted on the blocks, was exhilarating.'

But the burnt pilot was a terrifying sight. He had many operations to undergo before he was to look human again. He was sent off to McIndoe at Queen Victoria's Hospital, East Grinstead. This was the home of the 'Guinea Pigs'. Their signature tune ran:

> We've had some mad Australians,
> Some French, some Czechs, some Poles.
> We've even had some Yankees,
> God bless their precious souls,
> While as for the Canadians –
> Ah! that's a different thing,
> They couldn't stand the accent
> And built a separate Wing.[1]

McIndoe's collection of waifs and strays lived in 'the huts'. 'Ward Three,' wrote Hillary, 'housing some of the worst cases, stood about fifty yards away from the hospital. It was a long, low hut, with a door at one end and twenty beds down each side. The beds were separated from each other only by lockers, and it was possible without much exertion to reach out and touch the man in the next bed.' In the middle of the ward there was a table with a radio, a stove and a piano. Immediately to the left of the entrance passage was the saline bath. The patients looked like monsters and the nurses, most of whom were Irish, had a hard time keeping order.

Behind his horn-rimmed spectacles, McIndoe looked like an American university professor. By his own energy he had brought about a revolution in the surgery of burns. He had

1 They did have a separate wing. It was built by the Canadian Government because there were so many members of the Royal Canadian Air Force at East Grinstead. The Canadian wing was bigger than the little hospital to which it was an addition.

realized that there was a psychological problem; he was dealing with overgrown lost schoolboys. He went off collecting burnt pilots from hospitals all round the country. Gathered together at East Grinstead, grumbling and unhappy at first, they soon found that they shared each other's interests and talked the same language. They were able to enjoy a secret stock of beer: a pleasure heightened for being against the rules. As long as things didn't go too far, the nurses would put up with a lot; they didn't resent being ribbed about being Irish. The patients were allowed to smoke and to go off to London to the cinema. As long as they were back for breakfast the next morning, the only trouble they had to face was the Matron's pretended disapproval. The approach to his patients was revolutionary too. McIndoe went in for the hard truth. He would explain to each patient the different stages of reconstruction work he intended to perform on him, tell him how many operations he would have to have and make no secret of how long he would have to stay in hospital.

Richard Hillary asked him when he could fly again:

'Next war for you . . .' he replied.

His treatment was equally new, although it was based on the method of a bombastic sixteenth-century surgeon named Fiorovanti. Fiorovanti declared that he was witness to a duel between two Italian gentlemen in Africa in 1551. One of the duellists had his nose cut off. Fiorovanti picked it up out of the sand and, having urinated on it to clean it, stuck it back in place on its unfortunate owner's face. A week later he took the bandage off and was astonished to find that, instead of a gangrenous mass, he was looking at a nose 'well attached in its correct place' and that the owner was 'in good health'. McIndoe had been impressed by this anecdote. Whether true or false, it aroused his interest. At the start of the war he had examined many soldiers and sailors who had been burnt and had then spent many hours in the sea. His examinations enabled him to affirm that flesh that was soaked in salty water responded to treatment better than flesh that had dried and suppurated. He decided to experiment with saline baths. That was the function of the tub behind the curtain in Ward Three. It just stood there on the floor with its taps still in position although it was fed with a complicated arrangement of pipes. 'I remember the first time we put somebody in the bath,' recalled Taffy, McIndoe's orderly. 'The boy was terribly burnt;

a real mess. The *maestro* (that was what all McIndoe's patients called him) had already stitched a strip of skin back in place and he told us to put the poor chap in the bath to refresh him a bit. It was horrible. He must have thought he was going into boiling water. He struggled to get away from us and you could hear his stitches tearing as clearly as anything.'

Little by little terror would give way to a feeling of relief. It is always difficult getting into the water though it is nice when you are in. Best of all it made your flesh more responsive to McIndoe's magic scalpel as he worked in stages, literally sculpting you a new face.

'A couple of real horse blinkers you've got there,' he exclaimed when he uncovered the eyelids he had grafted on Hillary.

There were endless days of terrible pain and frequent visits to the operating theatre as the slow work of darning and patching went on. Frequently you would emerge from the theatre covered in bandages and temporarily blind. You had the horrible impression that you stank.

'On the third day in our new quarters', wrote Hillary, 'the smell of the bandage under my nose became so powerful that I took to dosing it liberally with eau-de-cologne. I have since been unable to repress a feeling of nausea whenever at a party or in company I have caught a whiff of this scent.'

The long hard road to recovery was beset with many a relapse and many a day of despair, but when you have lost so much, when you no longer look like a human being, what are you not ready to undergo? Only yesterday you were a young man proud to be a pilot, proud to wear your blue uniform and your decorations. The sky was yours and if there was fear, there were girls too. You accepted the idea of death. It was all part of the game. What you did not accept, never for a moment, was that *this* could happen, that you could become a . . .

When Tom Gleave's[1] wife came to see him for the first time in Ward Three, she couldn't help flushing.

'What on earth have you been doing with yourself, darling?'

'Had a row with a German.'

1. Gleave, who became 'chief guinea pig', referred to his injuries as 'standard Hurricane burns'.

She forced a smile and sat down at his side. Only some weeks later, when he looked in a mirror, did Gleave realize how much courage his wife had needed to stop herself from breaking down. Hillary's description of Gleave's sufferings makes terrifying reading.

'Opposite me was Squadron Leader Gleave with a flap graft on his nose and an exposed nerve on his forehead: in Ward Three he had been unable to sleep, nor could the night nurse drug him enough to stop the pain.'

All the hospitals in southern England packed off their nightmarish mummies, plastered with tannic acid, to McIndoe. They looked grotesque, like strange monsters. Geoffrey Page[1] was one of them.

Colonel Phillipi telephoned McIndoe on behalf of his friend Smith-Barry, a veteran of the 1914–18 war:

'Mr. McIndoe? Good. Now look here, I want you to provide a private room, a beautiful nurse, a Vi-spring mattress and your personal attention four times a day for a friend called Smith-Barry. He's already been in two hospitals and had himself removed because he doesn't like being messed about. Now he wants to come to East Grinstead.'

McIndoe was furious but complied with the request. The veteran was wonderfully cared for. Some weeks later he sought out McIndoe and said that his ancient carcass could be of little use to the Air Force and could he (McIndoe) use it as a source of skin for the young men in his care.

McIndoe had the greatest difficulty in the world trying to explain that there was only one Smith-Barry in the world and his skin was of no use for grafting on other people. The volunteer veteran resolved that he would become the liaison officer between East Grinstead and the Air Ministry.

'Had he [McIndoe] known the future benefit a developing friendship with this resourceful veteran airman was to bring the club, he would – with his usual opportunism – have assured Smith-Barry not only of a bed but of a red carpet all the way from the ambulance.'[2]

In early October the German raids went on with terrible regularity. It became the fashion never to refer to them. The

1. It was Page who drew up the rules of the Guinea Pig Club in 1941 while sitting round a bottle of sherry with some others of the Few.

2. Edward Bishop, *The Guinea Pig Club*.

majority of Englishmen had finally become convinced that the raids would somehow have less of a hold on them if they simply ignored that they were happening. Fences were put up in front of ruined buildings. The dead were buried, the wounded cared for. But it was bad form always to be talking about such things. Richard Hillary, on leave in London, wrote:

'With the break of day London shook herself and went back to work . . . The Home Guards and air-raid wardens of the previous night would return home, take a bath, and go off to their respective offices. The soldier was back with his regiment, the airman with his squadron; the charming frivolous creatures with whom they had dined were themselves in uniform, effective in their jobs of driving, typing or nursing.'

The pilot replacements, so long awaited, began to arrive in the squadrons. 'Thank goodness they had missed the worst of it,' wrote Deacon Elliott.

But the nights were dreadful. The Germans had fitted some of their bombs with a terrifying whistle which produced a tremendous strain on the nerves. 'It felt as if every "screamer" would definitely fall on or very near to just where you were – most disturbing,' wrote Deacon Elliott.

On October 4th, Hitler and Mussolini met at the Brenner Pass. Count Ciano, who was present at the talks, noted in his diary:

'The question of a landing on the British Isles did not come up in the conversation.'

Two days later, Goering in Berlin, issued a five-point plan – a guide to the Battle of Britain. What he expected of the Luftwaffe was:

1) Complete control of the Channel and the British coastal areas.
2) The progressive and total destruction of London together with all its military and industrial targets.
3) The paralysis of civilian life and all technical, commercial and industrial activity in Great Britain.
4) The breaking of civilian morale in London and the provinces.
5) The progressive weakening of the British air forces.

A far cry from the days when the Reichsmarschall had announced: 'Give me five days, just five days of good weather!'

It was clear that his heart was no longer in it. The paths he had followed had not been of his choosing and now he was sinking in the quicksands.

On October 12th, Hitler confirmed his decision postponing the invasion of England. A memorandum from the High Command, marked 'top secret', was issued:

'The Führer has decided that from now until Spring, the preparation for *Seelöwe* will go ahead with the sole object of keeping up the military and political pressure on England. If, in the Spring or early Summer, it is decided to embark on the operation, orders will be given for fresh preparations. In the meanwhile all efforts will be made to ensure the best possible military disposition for a possible invasion.'

Signed: KEITEL

'Our squadron,' wrote René Mouchotte, 'has just had the honour of a visit, between two spells in the air, from Air Vice-Marshal Park. He shook hands with all the pilots. When he came to me he asked me about my escape and, after wishing me luck, congratulated me on my English. He must be deaf.'

Deacon Elliott drew some conclusions from the weeks of fighting:

'The first being one of exhilaration; the intense excitement of mixing with the enemy and the determination to shoot something down.

Then oneself having been shot down a time or two, and shot at on countless occasions, became a little more wary with more emphasis on trying to keep alive – or maybe it was the application of the adage 'discretion is the better part of valour' – perhaps this was wrong.

Finally, towards the end and during the days before we moved north again, every mission was the same to me. I did not really mind or care whether or not I survived. Perhaps in this I was not alone. I am not being smug in thinking these reactions were unique – I am sure they were not.'

London was bending under the weight of bombs. One of them hit Tower Bridge.

In his entry for October 13th, 1940, Deacon Elliott writes:

'Three important events.

Firstly, it was my Mother's birthday. She still wrote to me every week without fail – and the little tit-bit in her last letter said: "May each day find your heart content about the way the last was spent" and to my five brothers and sister all of whom were in the Services.

Next, F/O Desmond Sheen completely recovered from his wounds, rejoined the squadron for the third time since war began and for the second time during the year.

Finally, the squadron moved north to Leconfield for a well-earned rest. For us the Battle of Britain was over.'[1]

On the morning of October 14th, the cliffs on both sides of the Channel were hidden by drizzle; but from both sides, as on all the previous days, aircraft were taking off . . .

1. Officially it ended on November 30th, but it was already decided. The Blitz now began to take its place.

TOD DURCH DEN STRANG . . . Death by Hanging

There were tears in Goering's eyes. Nuremberg, October 1st, 1946. The next day the Reichsmarschall asked 'to be allowed to die like a soldier; before a firing squad.' The request was refused. He was thin, lost in the folds of his tunic, wearing neither belt nor decorations, swallowing pill after pill, a hundred a day. A shadow Goering. The bone structure of his head could be made out once more: the determined chin, the great forehead, the flats and curves of the face. Too late! Beneath the skin Siegfried was dead.

The Battle of Britain had been his last chance and it had been snatched from his grasp for the sake of destroying London. He had tried to save the situation. 'I argued that it was no use for us to have another hundred houses go up in flames . . . I told the Führer again and again that in as much as I knew the British people as well as I did my own, we should never force them to their knees by bombing London.' Again, too late!

Siegfried was wearing one of the three famous rings he had been allowed to keep. The stones measured a square inch. Every morning he would select one. Which should it be today, the ruby, the emerald or the blue diamond? He reached out for his poison . . .

> So give me your hand, your pretty white hand,
> For tonight we march against England . . .

Lord Dowding of Bentley Priory: such was the title the King was pleased to give Dowding after his fall from favour. Like all victorious military leaders, Dowding was replaced. Park was sent to a peripheral command. Dowding, when he received the highest order he was awarded,[1] wrote to Lord Balfour: 'If I could, I should like to cut the Decoration up into a thousand pieces and distribute it to the Fighter Boys who are the ones who have really earned it.'

1. Translator's note: Order of the Bath (Knight Grand Cross).

Now, considerably aged, a gruff, withdrawn man, he lives in retirement in the country. It is said that he sees nobody. This is not true, for he lives with the dead. They live in his house and he gets on well with them. Dowding has written several works on survival after death[1] and recounts some strange experiences.

'Yes, I was shot down and killed,' says a Polish pilot who had stayed with Mrs. Gascoigne and her daughter. 'I have survived many fights, but not this one.'

He had been brought down in France and had escaped from his shattered aircraft without difficulty. There were peasants and he called to them. They did not hear him. 'I am neither hungry nor thirsty nor particularly tired,' he tells us. Around him the world begins to change. Everything is flooded with colour. It is like a dawn or a sunset reflected in thousands of mirrors. The earth and the sky are caught in a delirium of colour. 'I do not know where I am. I ask, I pray, I forget that I have no faith in religion, I pray for help and it comes to me.' Someone, apparently a real being of flesh and blood, comes to reassure the pilot. He tells him that the change is good for him and that he must sleep. He touches him on the eyes.

When the pilot awakes he is back in his own body. He finds he is unable to leave it. The mysterious friend is there. 'Think very hard of something that has nothing to do with the war!' The Pole tries hard. He is back in Mrs. Gascoigne's house. 'I have strange feelings when you sit in the same chair in which I sit,' he says. 'I am close and yet not close at all ... I am between the worlds ...'

Dowding will never be alone.

In the chapel at Biggin Hill there is a golden book in a glass case. Every day for twenty-five years a page has been turned. On each page one can read the names of those who took off on that day and never returned. Their names and their ranks. Sometimes the page is filled to the last line.

They are all Dowding's 'boys'.

1. The best known is *Many Mansions.*

Select Bibliography

Bekker, Cajus, *Angriffshöhe 4 000* (Stalling, Oldenburg, 1964)

Bickers, Richard Townsend, *Ginger Lacey, Fighter Pilot* (Robert Hale, 1962)

Bishop, Edward, *The Battle of Britain* (Allan & Unwin, 1960)

Bishop, Edward, *Guinea Pig Club* (Macmillan, 1963)

Bowman, Gerald, *War in the Air* (Evans Bros, 1956)

Brickhill, Paul, *Reach for the Sky* (Collins, 1954)

Burst, Kendal, and Leasor, James, *The One that Got Away* (Wm. Collins and Michael Joseph, 1956)

Carter, Ernest F., *Railways in Wartime* (F. Muller, 1964)

Cartier, Raymond, *Hitler et sès Généraux* (Fayari, 1962)

Chesnaie, Philippe (de la), *Daphné 17* (Flammarion, 1946–8)

Churchill, W. S., *The Second World War* (Cassell, 1948–54)

Collier, Basil, *The Defence of the United Kingdom* (H.M.S.O., 1957)

Collier, Basil, *Leader of the Few* (Jarrolds, 1957)

Deere, Alan, *Nine Lives* (Hodder & Stoughton, 1957)

Dowding, Air Chief Marshal Lord, *Many Mansions* (Rider & Co., 1943)

Fellowes, Air Commodore P.F.M., *Britain's Wonderful Air Force* (Odhams, 1942)

Fleming, Peter, *Invasion 1940* (Rupert Hart-Davis, 1957)

Galland, General, *The First and the Last* (Methuen, 1955)

Gaulle, General de, *War Memoirs* (Collins, 1952)

Gibbs, Air Marshal Sir Gerald, *Survivor's Story* (Hutchinson, 1956)

Giraudoux, Jean, *Armistice à Bordeaux* (Ides et Calandes, 1945)

Görlitz and Quint, *Adolf Hitler* (Steingrüben Verlag, Stuttgart, 1952)

Gosset, Pierre and Renée, *La deuxième Guerre. Les Secrets de la paix manquée* (de Flore, 1949–50)

Hébrard, Général J., *Vingt-cinq Années d' Aviation Militaire (1920–1945)*, 2 vols. (Albin Michel, 1946–7)

Hegner, H. S., *Ascension et Chute du 111e Reich* (Presses de la Cité, 1960)
Hillary, Richard, *The Last Enemy* (Macmillan, 1942)
Johnson, Johnny, *Wing Leader* (Chatto & Windus, 1956)
L'Herbier-Montagnon, Germaine, *Cap sans Retour* (Solar, 1948, 1949–50)
McKee, Alexander, *Strike from the Sky* (Souvenir Press, 1960)
Manvell, Roger, and Fraenkel, Heinrich, *Hermann Goering* (Heinemann, 1962)
Middleton, Drew, *The Sky Suspended* (Secker & Warburg, 1960)
Mosley, Leonard, *Faces from the Fire* (Weidenfeld & Nicholson, 1962)
Mouchotte René, *Carnets de 1940–1943* (Flammarion, 1945–50)
Passy (Colonel), *Souvenirs – 11e* (*Bureau Londres* Solar, 1948)
Pawle, Gerald, *The War & Colonel Warden* (Harrap, 1963)
Rémy (Colonel), *Mémoires d'un agent secret de la France Libre* (Aux Trois Couleurs, Solar, 1946)
Rommel, Marshal, *Der Krieg ohne Hass* (Heidenheimerverlag, Heidenheim, 1950)
Spaight, J. M., *The Battle of Britain 1940* (Geoffrey Bles, 1941)
Taylor, John W. R., and Allward, Maurice F., *Spitfire* (Drysdale Press, 1946)
Weber, Dr. Theo, *Die Luftschlacht um England* (Flugwelt Verlag, Wiesbaden, 1956)
Wilmot, Chester, *The Struggle for Europe* (Collins, 1952)
Wood, Derek, and Dempster, D., *The Narrow Margin* (Hutchinson, 1961)
Wykeham, Peter, *Fighter Command* (Putnam, 1960)

Miscellaneous

Headquarters Fighter Command, Royal Air Force: *Fighter Victory*

Supplement to the *London Gazette* (September 11th, 1946)

The History of Fighter-Command

History of R.A.F. stations

Imperial War Museum: *Combat Reports*

The *Annual Register 1940* (Vol. 182)

The Times, Signal, The R.A.F. Flying Review, The Fighting Forces, Forces Aériennes Françaises

Index

ACKLINGTON, 31, 32, 106, 152, 154, 161, 164, 173, 207
Addison, Air Vice-Marshal, 225
Adelaide, Queen, 17
Adlertag, 80, 82, 92, 95
Aircraft, and pilots, comparative numbers of, 40, 43, 44, 76, 81, 96, 120, 187, 230, 235; losses, 18, 36, 60, 68, 72, 80, 81–2, 84, 89, 98, 107, 111, 120, 124, 136, 160, 170, 171, 174, 177, 194, 198, 218, 219, 220, 230, 233, 234
Air-raid warning system, 153
Alanbrook, Lord, 229
Alba, Duke of, 23
Allard, Pilot Officer, 165
Allen, Johnny, 68
Alnmouth, 207
Andres, Werner, 79
Arnold, H. H., 81

BADER, WING COMMANDER DOUGLAS, 37, 108, 146, 147, 148, 163, 214, 218, 221, 226, 228, 234
Balfour, Lord, 243
Barrage balloons, 57, 82, 163
Bazin, French pilot, 22
Beamish, Victor, 208
Beaverbrook, Lord, 50, 57, 77, 121, 151, 184, 235
Bechtle, Leutnant, 35, 36
Bekker, Cajus, 141
Bentley Priory, Stanmore, 17, 21, 24, 44, 46, 50, 70, 81, 83, 93, 96, 115, 149, 181, 187, 190, 235
Berlin, bombing of, 141–4, 230
Bevin, Ernest, 199
Biggin Hill, 23, 35, 122, 123, 154, 161–2, 173–4, 182, 201, 229, 230, 234, 244
Bircham Newton, 141
Black, Flight Lieutenant, 225
Blaize, French pilot, 22
Blake, Wing Commander, 118
Blenheims, 21, 98, 115, 187, 229
Blitz, 222, 242. *See also* London
Bodendiek, Leutnant Erich, 87
Bohr, *Luftwaffe* pilot, 194 n
Boreas, H.M.S., 71
Bouquillard, French pilot, 22
Bowman, Group Captain Gerald, 81 n
Box, Wiltshire, 48
Brand, Air Vice-Marshal Sir Christopher Joseph Quintin, 48, 108
Brenner Pass, 240
Bridlington, 108
Brilliant, H.M.S., 71
Brize Norton, 115
Brooklands, 176
Brown, Betty, 114
Burckhardt, Carl, 23
Burton, Billy, 113

CAMBER-ON-SEA, 180
Cap Blanc Nez, 29, 30, 34, 69, 79, 92, 120, 134, 135, 189, 196, 205, 220, 224
Cap Gris Nez, 134, 173
Cardiff, 31
Cardwell, Mrs Norman, 114
Carey, Pilot Officer, 33
Caswell, Wing Commander, 111
Caterpillar Club, 113, 145, 205
Catterick, 84, 164
Chamberlain, Neville, 45, 119, 199
Choran, French pilot, 22
Churchill, Sir Winston, 20, 21, 25, 39, 58, 78, 80, 82, 89, 103,

Churchill (*contd.*)
119, 136, 139, 148–9, 186, 210, 235; speeches *quoted*, 21, 39, 133, 200–201; against Hitler's peace overtures, 23; on Mersel-Kébir, 25; Hitler's hatred of, 45, 53–4, 178; and bombing of Berlin, 143, 230; at Dover, 153, 155; visit to Uxbridge, 215–16
Ciano, Count, 22, 60, 240
Clark, 'Nobby', 89
Coleman, Jack, 156–89
Collier, Basil, 161
Collins, Squadron Leader A. R., 106, 166, 175
Coltishall, 35, 146, 163
Condor Legion, 48, 231
Convoys, 87
Booty, 83, 84
C.W.8, 69–70, 71–2, 78
C.W.9, 78, 157
Coope, Wing Commander Bill, 47, 159
Coward, J. B., 164
Coward, Noël, 92
Croft, Lord, 199
Crossley, Squadron Leader Mike, 152
Croydon, 93, 110, 123, 153, 165, 172–3, 175, 182

DASZEWSKI, Polish pilot, 196
Davies, Lieutenant, 202, 210
Davies, Sergeant, 167
Debden, 123, 149, 163, 174
Deere, Alan, 67, 83, 109, 119, 127, 152, 155, 156, 157, 160, 170; *quoted*, 30, 43, 67, 72, 82, 85–6, 98, 105–6, 109, 111, 125, 127, 168, 176, 228; personal characteristics, 67; shot down, 116–18, 122, 156–9; bombed, 167–70
Defiants, 21, 154, 229
De Gaulle, General Charles, 21, 78, 115–16
De la Brière, Sous-lieutenant, 20, 22
De la Warr, Earl, 114
De Mozay, Sergeant, 20
'Dennis', 156–7
Detling, 162, 173
Dobbie, General, 151
Donat, Robert, 92
Dooley, Michael, 152
Dorniers, 35, 36, 82, 83, 85, 90, 93, 94, 104, 110, 122, 123, 139, 145, 154, 165, 173, 189, 191, 211–15, 227
Douglas, Air Vice-Marshal Sholto, 149
Dover, 29, 34, 58, 82, 85, 88, 153, 155, 228
Dowding, Air Chief Marshal Sir Hugh, 17, 18, 19, 20, 23, 30, 43, 48, 50, 76, 96, 101, 115, 120, 138, 178, 180, 187, 197, 217; requests retention of planes in England, 17, 43; *quoted*, 30, 49, 67, 127, 219, 236; on Alan Deere, 67; care for his 'boys', 81, 82, 89, 181, 244; and killing of parachuting airmen, 89, 112–13; decides on false 'angel' reports, 188 n; criticism of, 221; honoured with Order of the Bath, 235–6; falls from favour, 243; as Lord Dowding of Bentley Priory, 243; writings on life after death, 243
Dowding, Reverend Benjamin Charles, 181
Drem, 106
Driffield, 108
Dunkirk, 25, 39, 43, 58, 60, 72, 127, 184
Duxford, 145, 163, 191, 227

EASTCHURCH, 94, 145, 154, 164, 172, 174
East Grinstead, 117, 122, 186, 236–9

Edsall, Eric, 168
Eldson, Flying Officer, 191
Elizabeth, Queen Consort of George VI, 202, 210
Elliott, Deacon, forced down by lack of oxygen, 33; *quoted*, 107, 152, 163, 164–5, 166, 172–7, 181, 182, 185–6, 197, 200–202, 205, 207, 213, 218, 227–30, 234, 240, 242; shot down, 186
Exeter, 96

FAYOLLE, French pilot, 22
Felmy, General, 134
Fields, Gracie, 92
Filton, 233
Fink, Commodore Johannes, 29, 30, 34, 69, 70, 76, 79, 81, 82, 92, 93–6, 101, 105, 120, 134, 153, 166, 192, 220, 224
Finlay, Don, 152–3, 154, 159
Fiske, Pilot Officer W. M. L., 121 n
Fleming, Peter, 34, 75
Fuchs, Major, 94

GALLAND, *Luftwaffe* pilot, 48, 62, 67, 69, 71, 73, 79, 87, 102, 105, 109, 111, 119, 135, 136, 138, 153–4, 194n, 216, 230–34
Gardner, Charles, 40
Gascoigne, Mrs, 244
George Cross, 210
George Medal, 210
George VI, King, 56, 197–8, 202, 210, 233, 235–6, 243
Gibbs, Air Marshal Sir Gerald, 208–9, 218
Gilder, Sergeant, 185
Gilmour, R. S., 226
Giraudoux, Jean, 22
Glasser, 118
Gleave, Tom, 238
Goebbels, Joseph, 24
Goering, Emmy, 29, 195, 220
Goering, Hermann, 22, 27, 28, 54, 64, 78, 119, 132; early history, 27–9; personal characteristics, 28–9; and invasion of Britain, 61, 206, 224; at Karinhall, 68–9, 99–103, 129–31, 136, 231–2; receives Plesman, 68; launches *Adlertag*, 80–82, 84, 92, 96; on Channel shores, 134–6; and bombing of London, 140, 175, 179–80, 197, 220–23, 243; greatest error of, 177–8; at Cap Blanc Nez, 196–7, 198; five-point plan for battle, 240
Goering, Karin, 28, 99–100
Gormanns, Christa, 29, 189, 195
Graham, Flight Lieutenant Ted, 106, 175
Gravesend, 86
Gray, Colin, 67, 70–1, 84, 125, 155, 157, 169
Gray, Sergeant 'Mabel', 185
Gribble, George, 70, 84, 125, 157, 170
Grice, Group Captain, 165
Group *10*, 48, 93, 104, 108, 149, 182, 187
Group *11*, 30, 48, 93, 104, 109, 149, 151, 181, 187, 215, 221
Group *12*, 48, 105, 108, 150, 163, 187, 191, 214, 217, 221
Group *13*, 49, 104, 108, 154, 185, 222
Guérin, French pilot, 22
Guinea Pig Club, 186, 236
Gustav V, King of Sweden, 23, 60, 75

HALDER, GENERAL FRANZ, 23, 38, 61, 72, 101, 137, 206
Halifax, Lord, 64, 73
Hamilton, Lady Emma, 17, 20
Hannah, Sergeant John, 223
Harris, Air Marshal, 136

Hawkinge, 87, 92, 105, 123, 173, 175, 177, 182, 228
Heinkels, 66, 75, 83, 89, 104, 107, 123, 137, 139, 153, 159, 162, 172, 189, 202, 212
Hemingway, S. A., 18, 124, 145, 158, 165, 226
Henderson, Corporal Elspeth, 173
Henderson, Sir Nevile, 129
Hess, Rudolf, 44
Highlander, SS, 75
Hillary, Pilot Officer Richard, 105, 118, 132, 166–70, 236–7
Hillingdon, 34
Hintze, Oberleutnant Otto, 88
Hitler, Adolf, 21, 23, 53, 54, 61, 64, 184, 230, 231, 234; meetings with Mussolini, 22, 240; wish to make peace with England, 22, 23, 38, 45–6, 53, 81, 231; and invasion of England (Sea Lion), 24, 61–2, 74–5, 200, 205–6, 221, 224, 240; hatred of Churchill, 46, 53–4, 178; and destruction of British air force, 74, 179; at Karinhall, 100; and destruction of London, 178, 179–80, 222
Hohenlohe, Duke of, 23
Holland, Pilot Officer 'Dutch', 177, 185, 229
Holmes, Sergeant, 211
Home Guard, 56
Horder, Lord, 199
Hornchurch, 83, 84, 86, 93, 105, 109, 154, 160, 166, 170
Howarth, Sergeant, 80
Hurricanes, 18, 33, 43, 48, 50, 52, 58, 65, 71, 72, 79, 86, 94, 96, 106, 112, 115, 116, 123, 125, 137, 139, 145, 161, 165, 177, 187, 189, 191, 194, 202, 210–19, 226, 230
Huth, Joachim, 93

INGERSOLL, RALPH, 209
Invasion of Britain, 61–2. *See also* Sea Lion, Operation
Ismay, Major-General Sir Hasting, 218

JESCHONNEK, GENERAL, 42, 134
Jodl, General Alfred, 44, 72
Johnson, Johnny, 145, 226, 228
Jones, Dr R. V., 225
Joppien, *Luftwaffe* pilot, 194n
Junkers, 58, 70, 79, 101, 104, 106, 107, 115, 123, 137, 170, 176, 227

KAHLE, DR, 100, 224
Karinhall, 68, 99–103, 136, 231–2
Keitel, Marshal Wilhelm, 24, 241
Kellet, Squadron Leader, 191
Kenley, 93, 117, 123, 162, 165, 202
Kennedy, Mrs Joseph, 184
Kesselring, General, 47, 62, 73, 81, 95, 101, 134, 178–80, 189
Klein, *Luftwaffe* pilot, 106
Knickebein, 225
Knights Whittome, Squadron Leader, 47
Knobel, Major Josef, 141
Knoyes, Mrs, landlady, 56
Kropp, valet, 29, 100

LA BOISSIÈRE, 26, 80
Labouchère, French pilot, 22
Lacey, James (Ginger), 59, 65–6, 80, 86, 123, 202, 204
Lafont, French pilot, 22
Lamberty, Leutnant, 122
Laroche, M., Mayor, 25
Laube, Oberleutnant, 214
Leconfield, 242
Le Coudray, 25, 62, 64, 80, 220
Le Déluge, 26, 80

Lees, Wing Commander, 175
Leigh-Mallory, Air Vice-Marshal Sir Trafford, 48, 105, 137, 149–51, 163, 214, 218, 221
Lewes, 158
Liensberger, Hauptmann, 96, 97
Liverpool, 172, 175, 177, 180, 185
London, bombing of, 140, 143, 178, 193, 201–4, 209–12, 219, 226–9, 230, 233, 235, 240–1, 243
  Bond Street, 226
  Buckingham Palace, 202, 204, 210, 219
  Docks, 192, 195, 198, 217
  Downing Street, 202
  Kensington Palace Gardens, 193
  Marble Arch, 228
  Oxford Street, 226
  St Giles, Cripplegate, 140
  St Paul's Cathedral, 193, 201–2, 210
  Savile Row, 226
  Silvertown, 192
  Tower Bridge, 241
  Trafalgar Square, 202
  Victoria Station, 212
  Whitehall, 202
  Woolwich, 192
Lörzer, General, 134, 136
Lympne, 87, 105, 173–5

McIndoe, Sir Archibald, 117, 186, 236–9
McKee, Alexander, 161, 167, 174
MacKnight, pilot, 163
MacMullen, Flight Lieutenant, 33
MacNab, Squadron Leader, 110
Magisters, 115
Maidstone, 183
Malan, Group Captain A. G. (Sailor), 82, 159, 226
Manston, 82, 85, 89, 93, 98, 105, 109, 125, 139, 149, 156
Martini, General Wolfgang, 44, 88, 102
Martlesham, 82, 110
Masselin, Henri, 26, 62
Maugham, W. Somerset, 30
Maxwell, 91
Mers-el-Kébir, 25
Méru, 26, 27
Messerschmitts, 35–6, 43, 46, 52, 58, 65, 67, 70, 71, 83, 85–7, 93, 95, 104–6, 123–4, 136, 145–8, 157, 158, 160, 163, 165, 170–1, 174–6, 189, 191, 194, 200, 215, 216, 229
Middleton, Drew, 31, 228
Middle Wallop, 58, 65, 93, 187
Milch, General, 42, 44, 68
Mölders, *Luftwaffe* pilot, 128–9, 146, 194 n, 231, 233
Montbon, French pilot, 22
Morris, Teddy, 155, 162, 164
Mortimer, Jean, 121
Mosley, Sir Oswald and Lady, 30
Mouchotte, René, 22, 51, 73, 81, 115, 145, 198, 228, 241
Munich, 21
Mussolini, Benito, 21, 44, 77, 240

Neuville, 26, 62, 80
Newcastle-on-Tyne, 48, 107
Nicholson, Flight Lieutenant J. B., 111–12
Norfolk, Sergeant, 175, 229
Northolt, 93, 191, 217
North Weald, 93, 139, 157, 163, 174, 211
Norwich, 35

Observer Corps, 94, 153, 161, 166, 192
Odiham, 81, 115

Osman, Major W. H., 190
Ostend, 160, 205, 226
Oxley, Squadron Leader, 141

PAGE, FLYING OFFICER GEOFFREY, 36, 72, 90, 91, 186, 239
Parfondeval, 26, 80
Pargiter, Major General R. B., 107
Park, Air Vice-Marshal Sir Keith Rodney, 48, 104, 106, 109, 131, 136–7, 149–51, 160, 181, 188, 195, 200, 213, 215–18, 221, 241, 243
Parker, John, 207
Passy, Colonel, 212
Pawle, Gerald, 215
Peel, Squadron Leader, 79
Perrin, French pilot, 22, 73, 116, 118
Pétain, Marshal, 20
Pevensey, 88
Phillipi, Colonel, 239
Phillips, Conrad, 40
Phillips, Frank, 68
Pigg, Oswald, 31, 33, 172
Pile, Lieutenant-General Sir Frederick A., 23
Plesman, Dr Albert, 68, 73
Pocock, Sergeant, 173
Portsmouth, 87, 153
Prestwick, 154
Pringle, Wing Commander, 111

QUEDNAU, MAJOR HORST, 140–1
Quill, Jeffrey, 48

RADAR, 44, 49, 69, 78, 83, 88, 93, 96, 102, 115, 162
Raeder, Admiral, 38, 39, 161, 206, 230
Ramsgate, 35, 139
Red Ace, *see* Crossley, Squadron Leader Mike
Reitsch, Hanna, 57
Ribbentrop, Joachim von, 22, 25
Robertson, Sergeant F. N., 35, 36
Rochester, 110
Rochford, 33, 66, 90, 152, 154, 160, 174
Rommel, General Erwin, 25, 54
Roosevelt, President Franklin D., 77, 92, 138
Ross, Sergeant, 169
Rössinger, Oberleutnant, 88
Rubensdorffer, Hauptmann Walter, 88, 110
Russell, John, 76
Ryan, Frank, 76
Rye, 88

ST ATHAN, 51, 73
Sander, General, 77
Satchell, Squadron Leader W. A. J., 106, 214, 227
Saul, Air Vice-Marshal R. E., 48, 106, 107
Schirer, William, 53
Schmid, Major Josef, 42, 44, 45, 64, 78, 82, 89, 126, 146, 179
Schneel, *Luftwaffe* pilot, 194 n
Schopfel, *Luftwaffe* pilot, 194 n
Schuschner, German officer, 62
Scitivaux, French pilot, 22 n
Sea Lion, Operation, 62, 72, 74, 137, 161, 200, 205–7, 224, 233, 241
Shaw, George Bernard, 30, 55
Sheen, Flying Officer Desmond, 107, 166, 172, 183, 185, 201, 242
Shoreham, 162
Skuas, 89
Smith, Flight Lieutenant 'Hiram', 107, 166, 201
Smith-Barry, Colonel, 239
Southampton, 182, 200, 233
Sperrle, General, 47, 81, 100–3, 178

Spitfires, 21, 32, 43, 48, 50, 51, 67, 70, 83, 84, 87, 94, 96, 105–9, 119, 125, 130, 137, 145–6, 154, 164, 167, 181, 184, 186, 187, 212–16, 226
Squadrons:
14, 106
19, 145, 150, 164
32, 23, 152, 163
41, 84, 155
43, 23, 33
54, 30, 33, 67, 70, 72, 84, 85, 87, 105, 119, 125, 152, 166, 176
56, 35, 90, 157,
65, 84, 87, 89, 106, 118, 155
66, 35, 186
72, 31, 106, 111, 152, 163–4, 165, 166, 172, 173, 174, 183, 185, 191, 197, 207, 214, 229, 234
73, 108
74, 83, 85, 126
79, 23, 106, 156, 161, 166, 207
83, 223
85, 82, 123, 145
92, 159, 214
111, 110, 191
141, 154
145, 23, 79, 83, 147
151, 139
152, 83
213, 83
219, 108
229, 234
238, 83
242, 146, 150, 163, 191
249, 111
264, 108, 154
266, 126
287, 83
302, 108, 115, 214
303, 115, 191, 196, 233–4
310, 115, 150, 214
501, 58, 65, 80, 86, 106, 202
504, 210, 214
600 (City of London), 87
601, 23, 83
603, 105, 108, 169–70
604, 89
607, 106
609, 83, 195
610, 173
616, 108
Stanmore, *see* Bentley Priory
Steinhof, *Luftwaffe* pilot, 48
Stoney, Flight Lieutenant, 123
Strong, General, 228
Student, General, 60
Stukas, 31, 58, 70–2, 79, 83, 87, 101, 104, 106, 124, 156
Stumpff, General, 47, 81, 104, 107, 111
Sutton Bridge, 116

TANGMERE, 23, 33, 93, 96, 116, 162
Thompson, Squadron Leader, 83, 110
Thomson, Happy, 172, 201
Tilbrooke, Mr, hotel manager, 56
Tilbury, 172
Townsend, Flight Lieutenant Peter, 83, 123, 145, 158, 165
Tunbridge, 180
Turner, Sergeant Helen, 173

UDET, GENERAL, 42
Umberto, King of Italy, 77
Uxbridge, Middlesex, 48, 131, 149, 188, 200, 213, 215–18, 221

VENTNOR, ISLE OF WIGHT, 83, 88, 92, 115
Victoria Cross, 112, 223
Viek, Colonel, 138
Vincent, Group Captain 216–17,
Von Brauchitsch, General, 38, 61, 206, 221
Von Döring, Major General, 35

Von Eschwege, Hauptmann, 164
Von Falkenstein, Baron, 177
Von Kleist, Colonel-General, 23
Von Manstein, Marshal, 60
Von Richthofen, General, 136
Von Selle, *Luftwaffe* pilot, 182
Von Werra, Leutnant Franz, 182, 193

WARMWELL, 96
Watnall, Nottinghamshire, 48
Watson-Watt, Sir Robert, 49
Way, Squadron Leader 'Wonky', 70–1, 157
Webster, John Terence, 183
Weitkus, Oberleutnant Paul, 94, 101, 134, 190, 193
Wells, H. G., 30
Wendel, Else, 59
Westhampnett, 79
West Malling, 110, 123
Wilcox, Willie, 166
Wilkinson, Sergeant, 80
William IV, King, 17
Williams, Squadron Leader, 47
Willoughby de Broke, Group Captain Lord, 216
Windmill Girls, 83
Winter, Pilot Officer 'Snowy', 185
Wissant, 35
Wittering, 126
Wojtowicz, Corporal, 200
Woolston, 218, 233
Wright, Alan, 159, 210
Wromsky, *Luftwaffe* pilot, 153, 172
Wylie, Sapper, 202

ZANDER, HORST, 213–15
Zanuck, Darryl, 77